Solve IT!

Version 6.0

Management Problem Solving with Excel,
Access and the World Wide Web

Kenneth C. Laudon
New York University

Kenneth Rosenblatt
Azimuth Interactive, Inc.

Megan Miller
Azimuth Interactive, Inc.

Spreadsheet and Database Cases for Excel
and Access with Internet Web Cases

Download student files from the Web!
(see last page for details)

INTERACTIVE

New Directions in Learning

Visit us online: http://www.MySolveIT.com

Azimuth Interactive, Inc. ©2009

Azimuth License Agreement

Carefully read the licensing agreement before using the Student Data Files or case book. By using the data files and case book, you accept the terms of this agreement. This package contains valuable proprietary materials of Azimuth Interactive Inc. ("Azimuth"). Azimuth retains the title and ownership of the software, including all patent, copyright, trade name, trademark, and other proprietary rights related to the software. All written materials are copyrighted.

Permitted Uses

The data, programs, and case book included in this package are licensed only for individual use on one or several computer systems by the original purchaser. You may make a single backup copy of the files to support your use of the package.

Prohibited Uses

You may not make the software, or any parts of the package, available to other persons by copying, translating, lending, leasing, or selling. This package may not be re-sold as a "used book" and to do so is a violation of federal copyright and software protection laws. The Student Data Files may not be placed on a network of any kind without permission of Azimuth.

Limited Warranty

Azimuth warrants that the book and data files on which the software is distributed are free from defects in materials and workmanship for a period of 90 days following original purchase. If you experience a problem, return the case book and sales receipt to Azimuth through your local bookstore. You must have evidence of purchase. A replacement unit will be shipped promptly. Azimuth makes no other warranty express or implied.

Trademark Acknowledgement

IBM is a registered trademark of International Business Machines Corporation. Windows XP, Office 2003, Office XP, Microsoft Word, Access, Outlook, and Excel are registered trademarks of Microsoft Corporation.

Copyright 1992-2009 Azimuth Interactive Inc.
Printed in the United States of America
Azimuth Interactive Inc.
23 North Division Street
Peekskill, New York 10566

ISBN: 1-930581-95-5

2009

Table of Contents

Preface to Solve it! 6.0

Solve it! was created by the authors based on their experience teaching information systems and management courses in the United States and with the help of colleagues at other universities in Australia and Europe. Regardless of your major, as a business student you need to learn how information technology can be used to solve business problems and enhance management decision making. This is true of not only of finance majors, but also of majors in management, operations, marketing, accounting, and information systems.

In introductory courses students learn basic computer literacy and develop hands-on experience working with productivity software-spreadsheets, databases, project managers, and word processing. These are valuable skills, but obviously much more is needed in today's business marketplace. Employers are looking for potential employees who can solve problems, not run spreadsheets.

Solve it! builds on basic computer literacy skills. We focus on problem solving, and critical thinking skills rather than teaching key-stroking skills. Each of our cases requires students to build spreadsheets or databases and learn how to use these information tools to improve management decision making. We believe the most effective way to learn how to use productivity software like spreadsheets and databases results is by having students use the software to solve classic problems in business. Students need to solve problems by exercising their own judgments. Students learn problem solving skills by actually solving problems.

Solve it! began in its early versions as a collection of cases and a case service. We relied on business colleagues and friends to supply us with real-world cases, recast them for class use, and then tested them in university and industry software labs and training programs. Since then we began publishing new cases in a new edition every November. This way Fall semester students will have different problems than Spring semester students.

From working with business recruiters and interviewing corporate human resources personnel, we have learned that industry wants students to possess not only certain computer skills, but to be adept at solving some common, even classic, business problems. Problems like inventory management, accounts receivable and payable, payroll, financial analysis, sensitivity analysis, human resource tracking, and even some small applications development. *Solve it!* continues to reflect these concerns.

New Features and Web Exercises: Solve it! 6.0

Solve it! 6.0 is designed to support Office 2007. Version 6.0 reflects the growing business use of the World Wide Web and the Internet by including a chapter containing a brief introduction to the Web, and nine case studies. Other new features of *Solve it! 6.0* include the more frequent use of screen shots to guide students through the software. In addition to expanding the software base, we have added a number of unstructured exercises that usually require a written response, or enhancement to an existing data set. The Tutorial instructions have been expanded and refined considerably to assist learning, and more screen shots have been added.

Using Excel and Access Files: Compatibility

Solve it! is fully compatible with virtually all Windows-based software tools. The Student Data Files are delivered in Microsoft standard formats for Excel spreadsheets (.XLSX or .XLS) and Access databases (.ACCDB or .MBB). These files can also be imported to other packages such as Lotus SmartSuite and several open source spreadsheet programs including Google Docs and Open Office. Access database files are available at the Web site (see below) in Access 2007 and Access 2002-2003 formats, which are not compatible. *Solve it!* 6.0 files can also be used by Linux-based programs such as StarOffice.

Macintosh Compatibility

The files for both spreadsheet cases and database cases can be used on Macintosh computers. For instance, Microsoft Excel on the Mac reads the .XLS files distributed on our Web site (see below). You can download the Student Data Files from the *Solve it!* Website using any Macintosh compatible browser.

Where to Download Student Files

Download Student Data Files From www.MySolveIT.com/Student/.

In order to complete the cases in this book you must download the Student Data Files from the *Solve it!* Web site **www.MySolveIT.com/Student/**. See the last page of the book for instructions and for your personal access code printed in this book. If this book contains no student access code or last page with this information, return it at once to the bookstore for a new product. If you have questions about Solve it!, visit the Web site first for answers. If you need additional information or have suggestions for improving *Solve it!*, email us at **support@www.mysolveit.com**. The authors would very much like to hear from students and instructors in order to make this a more useful product.

We sincerely hope you find the new *Solve it!* both challenging and rewarding!

Ken Laudon

Ken Rosenblatt

Megan Miller

2009

1

Introduction to *Solve it!* 6.0

Welcome to the challenge of *Solve it*!

Solve it! For Windows 6.0 is a new learning system that teaches management problem-solving skills through the use of spreadsheet and database software. *Solve it!* is designed for use by college and university students in schools of business and management.

The management cases in this *Solve it!* package will help you learn how to address management problems using contemporary spreadsheet and database software. The cases are all derived from actual business applications.

When you successfully complete these cases, you will have mastered the basics of the software and learned how to apply this knowledge in realistic settings.

Learn Through Discovery

Solve it! uses real world case studies to present students with problems and challenges. The cases range from small businesses on Main Street to banks and brokerage firms on Wall Street to government agencies. It's up to you to discover the answers.

For each case there is a corresponding data file that you will download from the Web site. You will then be asked to enter new data, formulas, and data fields, and to create reports, queries, and lists in response to business problems posed in the cases.

In general, we have sought to keep the amount of elementary data entry to a bare minimum and to emphasize conceptual tasks. The cases do not require advanced financial analysis or accounting skills. Explanations are provided for all formulas and analytic tasks.

Industry Standard

Solve it! is widely used in Fortune 1000 training programs. It is designed to bring students and working professionals up to a common intermediate level of proficiency in Microsoft Excel and Access. Beyond this level, industry training programs and seminars are advised for more advanced training.

Many universities and businesses use one of several powerful alternatives to Excel and Access. *Solve it!* works well with Access work-alikes and Linux-based databases. *Solve it!* also works with most known spreadsheet programs including Lotus SmartSuite, Quattro, Linux-based programs like StarOffice, and other open source alternatives.

You may also use the data files included with *Solve it!* on Macintosh computers using software such as Microsoft Excel. You can use the *Solve it!* data files with any Macintosh software that can read .XLS, .DBF, and/or ASCII files. Ask your instructor for more information.

You may wish to keep both the book and the completed and graded exercises to show potential employers precisely what skills you have learned. You should also place this information on your resume.

Classic Business Problems

Solve it! uses cases that illustrate classic business problems typically encountered in the real world, such as net present value analysis, payroll accounting, inventory management, break-even analysis, accounts receivable aging reports, pro forma financial statements, quality assurance, production planning, marketing database management, sales management systems, and personnel tracking.

When you complete the cases in *Solve it!*, you will be well prepared to work effectively in a contemporary business environment.

Web Exercises and Cases

The World Wide Web is a major source of information and analysis for business professionals. It is very important that business students learn how to integrate this information into desktop spreadsheet and database programs, and how to analyze Web-based data for management purposes.

Solve it! now contains a new chapter of exercises and case studies that explore the use of the World Wide Web in business problem solving. The Web has proved itself to be a valuable research tool for business. On the Web, you can discover industry trends, statistics, growth patterns, markets, and resources—in short, all the ingredients needed to make a well-informed business plan. The Web cases in Chapter 6 will show you how to use the Web to build a business plan and also help you explore other features of the Web.

Documentation Included

Solve it! contains all the documentation you will need on how to use Office 2007 spreadsheet software like Excel and database software like Access. The documentation is provided in the form of hands-on tutorials that show you how to use the software skills required by each of the cases. The cases and documentation were written using Microsoft Excel 2007 and Access 2007 for Windows. You will find the spreadsheet data files in *Solve it!* are compatible with all versions of the software. In general, the documentation instructions work equally well for clone software with only minor changes.

If you are using earlier versions of Excel or Access (as opposed to Excel or Access 2007), be sure to check the Web site and download the Excel 97- 2003 student data files and Access 2003-2003 files. In general, Access is downwardly compatible (newer versions will open older version files) but not upwardly compatible.

Students may wish to consult the original documentation for the software being used or any one of several large reference manuals. These are generally available in your PC Lab or your corporate or college library.

Solve it! assumes students have a basic familiarity with the Windows operating system. If this is not the case, you should read through an introductory text on Windows or the Windows Users Guide.

The Skills Matrix

In order to select and develop cases, we created a Skills Matrix to identify both the software and management skills we sought to teach.

The Skills Matrix for spreadsheet software is shown on the following page (see Figure 1-1). A similar matrix is used for database problems.

Solve it! is designed to teach the management skills that allow you to organize, plan, coordinate, decide, and control. The software skills we will teach are basic (set-up and editing), intermediate (data analysis and organization), and advanced (database management, programming, and interfaces).

Management Skills

	Organize	Plan	Coordinate	Decide	Control
Software Skills					
I. Basic Skills Spreadsheet design Formulas Reporting	Cases 1—4				
II. Intermediate Skills Logical functions Graphics Statistical functions			Cases 5—7		
III. Advanced Skills				Cases 8—10	

Each *Solve it!* package contains a mix of skill levels and skill areas. Approximately one-third of the problems involve basic software skills and elementary management skills of organization and planning. The remaining cases develop intermediate and advanced software skills along with more advanced management skills.

As you proceed from beginning to more advanced cases, the problems become less structured and more analytic. More advanced cases require a written summary.

In the beginning, each *Solve it!* case identifies the specific skills involved in the case. Also included are the approximate completion times for persons at different skill levels. These estimated times are based on our experience in university classrooms and industry settings.

How to Use Solve it!

There are 13 spreadsheet cases, 12 database cases, and 9 Web cases in each *Solve it!* package. The cases are graduated in difficulty, both in terms of software skills and management skills. The cases are short enough to be answered in one computer session lasting no more than 2 to 3 hours for a novice.

Each case has an estimated completion time. Students are strongly advised not to skip early problems. If you skip early problems, you will not learn the software skills required in later cases. This will, in turn, lengthen the time required to answer later cases by several hours.

A Tutorial Documentation section that carefully describes the software skills needed to solve each case follows the case. The software skills are demonstrated using a sample spreadsheet file (Course.xlsx) and a sample database file (Friends.accdb) that you will create in the tutorial sections.

You should first read the case to understand the nature of the problem. You should then study the Tutorial carefully to be sure you understand how the software works. Finally, you should begin work on the case itself.

How to Cope With Ambiguity in Cases

Because *Solve it!* cases are derived from real world events and circumstances, they often contain ambiguities—just like the real world itself. In advanced cases, you will typically find more than one way to solve a problem, and you will find that certain assumptions and value judgments must be made to arrive at any solution.

You should first clearly identify the nature of the ambiguity. Then consider the alternative solutions. Choose the solution you prefer and specifically state the assumptions and value judgments you are making. Be prepared to defend these assumptions, as well as to learn from others who made different assumptions.

System Requirements

Solve it! assumes that you have some knowledge of IBM or IBM compatible computers, including the operating system. *Solve it!* provides specific instructions on how to start up the software in the special **Getting Started** sections of Chapters 2 and 4.

Solve it! assumes you are using an IBM or IBM compatible PC computer with at least 128 megabytes of RAM and sufficient hard disk capacity to run the application software. You must also be connected a printer with graphics capabilities.

General Instructions for Working with Student Data Files

1. Download the *Solve it!* Student Data Files. Go to **http://www.mysolveit.com/student/** and enter the **access code found on the last page of this book**. Follow the directions on the Web site for downloading and storing the files onto your hard drive.

   You will have personal access to the student files for a period of 4 months, and you can access the Student Data Files from any computer for a period of 4 months from the date of initial issue. Student Data files contain the required case data and sample tutorial files for the exercises in this book.

2. Read the appropriate case study in the case book to identify the specific data file used in the case. This will also provide an overview of the case's basic issues. On the first page of each case, the appropriate student data file is identified.

3. Start Excel (or Access) and then open the case study data file required by the case.

You are now ready to begin. Chapter 2 introduces you to spreadsheet software in general, and specifically guides you through the basics of Microsoft Excel. This is followed by 13 spreadsheet business cases in Chapter 3. Chapter 4 introduces you to database concepts and Microsoft Access. This is followed by Chapter 5, which contains 12 database business cases. Chapter 6 describes the World Wide Web and provides 9 cases for you to solve.

2

Introduction to Spreadsheet Software

An *electronic spreadsheet* is the computerized version of traditional financial modeling tools—the accountant's columnar pad, pencil, and calculator. It is organized into a grid of rows and columns. When you change values on an electronic spreadsheet, all other related values on that spreadsheet will be recomputed automatically.

Spreadsheets are especially well suited for business applications that involve numerous calculations involving interrelated pieces of data. The power of electronic spreadsheet software is the ease with which modeling and "what if" analysis can be performed. After a set of mathematical relationships has been constructed, the spreadsheet can be immediately recalculated using a different set of assumptions. As models become more complex, this capability for instant "what-if" analysis becomes even more valuable.

An Excel file is a workbook containing one or more sheets. These worksheets are considered part of the workbook similar to the pages in a spiral notebook.

This chapter will focus on the basic spreadsheet skills you will need to start solving the spreadsheet cases in the following Chapter 3.

Introduction to Microsoft Excel

An Excel spreadsheet is divided into rows and columns, with each row and each column uniquely labeled. A sample spreadsheet is illustrated in Figure 2-1.

Rows are identified numerically, with values ranging from 1 to a maximum of 1,048,576 in Excel 2007. Columns are identified alphabetically, with letters ranging from A to Z and then from AA to AZ, BA to BZ, and so on. Excel 2007 can accommodate a maximum of 167,384 columns. Earlier versions of Excel can handle a maximum of 256 columns and 65,536 rows.

Cells

The intersection of every column and row is called a *cell*. Each cell represents a unique location on the spreadsheet for storing a piece of data. Cells are identified by their column and row coordinates. For example, the cell located at the intersection of column B and row 8 is called B8. The maximum number of cells on the spreadsheet is equal to the number of rows times the number of columns. In Excel 2007, this amounts to over 175 billion cells.

Ranges

A rectangular block of cells is termed a *range*. A *range* can be a single cell, a row, a column, or several rows and columns. Many Excel commands are based on ranges. Ranges are identified by naming the cells that bound their diagonally opposite corners, thus the range occupied by the cells containing FIRST NAME, LAST NAME, QUIZ, MIDTERM, and FINAL in the following illustration would be identified as A1:E1. Range naming conventions require that you separate the cell addresses that specify the boundaries of the range by a colon, e.g., A1:E5. Ranges may also consist of nonadjacent cells and groups of nonadjacent blocks of cells that are selected by holding down the control key while highlighting them.

Another way to specify a range is to use a *range name*. Naming ranges can be easier than the other ways of specifying a range if you need to select the same range frequently for different tasks or if the range is very large. For instance, we could name the range E2:E5, which contains the final grades, FINAL. You will learn how to name ranges later on in this book.

When you work with your spreadsheet, your cursor will always be positioned on one of its cells. The cell where the cursor is presently located is termed the *active cell*. The cell pointer—a rectangular highlight that appears on the active cell—identifies the current cell. You can move the cell pointer from one cell to another by clicking the mouse pointer on another cell, or by pressing the arrow keys or other keys defined for movement such as [Tab] or [CTRL]+[Home]. Pressing the [CTRL]+[Home] keys together will move the cell pointer to the upper left-most corner of the spreadsheet, cell A1.

The Excel 2007 Window

Across the top of the Excel window is the **Ribbon**, a central part of the new Office 2007 user interface. The Ribbon replaces the Menu bar and Standard Toolbar of previous editions and contains buttons and drop-down lists for almost all of the Excel commands, grouped into separate tabs according to the general category of task being performed. For example, you make an entry bold by selecting the entry and then clicking the *Bold* button on the Home tab. When you point to a button on the Ribbon, a ScreenTip appears that explains the function of the button.

Above the Ribbon is the **Title bar**, which displays the program name ("Microsoft Excel") and the active file name in the center. At the far right of the Title bar are, in order from leftmost, the *Minimize, Restore Down/Maximize,* and *Close* buttons. At the far left of the Title bar is the **Microsoft Office button**. Clicking on this button opens a drop-down menu similar to the File menu in previous versions of Excel. This Office menu contains commands used for working with the current Office document as a whole: for opening, closing, saving, printing, finalizing, publishing, and e-mailing a file. To the right of the Office button is the **Quick Access toolbar**, which contains by default the *Save, Undo,* and *Redo* buttons. The *Undo* and *Redo* buttons undo (or redo) your last action. For example, if you delete a range of cells by mistake and you want to undo your action, you can click the *Undo* button to restore these cells. You can specify which buttons included on the Quick Access toolbar by clicking the down arrow to the right of the toolbar. This opens the Customize Quick Access Toolbar menu with a list of commonly used commands you can add to the toolbar. You can also click *More Commands* and select any Excel command to add to the Quick Access toolbar.

Below the Ribbon, at the far left of the window, is the **Name box**, which displays the name or address of the current selection. To its right is the **Formula bar**, which displays the label, number, formula, or function in the active cell.

Figure 2-1 shows an Excel worksheet screen for a course roster with data entered in the range A1:E5.

Figure 2-1

At the very bottom of the Excel window is the **Status bar**, which displays error and status messages or indicators. To the right of the Status bar are three Page View buttons—*Normal*; *Page Layout*, which allows you to see how the spreadsheet would look on the printed page; and *Page Break Preview*, which shows where on the spreadsheet page breaks will be made. To the right of the Page View buttons is the **Zoom slider** which you use to magnify or reduce the view of the current spreadsheet.

Just above the Status bar along the bottom is the **Sheet tabs line**, where you can see tabs for the different worksheets within the file. By default, an Excel workbook opens with 3 worksheets. Additional sheets may be added by clicking the *New Tab* icon to the right of the sheet-tabs; the number of worksheets permitted is limited only by your computer's available memory. Multiple worksheets allow you to organize the data in the worksheet in meaningful ways. For instance, you could create a Company Payroll Workbook with separate sheets for each Department. Data can easily be entered into multiple sheets simultaneously, and it is easy to reference a cell or range on one sheet in another worksheet.

Moving Around the Spreadsheet

Spreadsheets are usually too large to be viewed on the screen in their entirety. To view other parts of the spreadsheet, you must *scroll* the cell pointer up and down the worksheet or across it using the mouse, the arrow keys, or other cursor movement keys. When the cell pointer reaches the edge of the current screen, the screen will shift to follow the cell pointer in the direction in which it is moving.

Clicking the mouse pointer on any cell makes that the current active cell. At the right and at the bottom of the Excel worksheet window are the vertical scroll bar and the horizontal scroll bar. Clicking on the arrow buttons on these scroll bars moves your window one row up/down or one column right/left. You can also click on any point inside these scroll bars or drag the scroll box itself, to scroll faster.

You can also use the keyboard to navigate around the spreadsheet. When Excel is in READY mode (the current mode is displayed on the Status bar), various keys will behave as follows:

Excel Keyboard Pointer-Movement Keys

Key	Function
LEFT ARROW	Moves left 1 cell
RIGHT ARROW	Moves right 1 cell
UP ARROW	Moves up 1 cell
DOWN ARROW	Moves down 1 cell
[SHIFT]+[TAB]	Moves left 1 cell
[TAB]	Moves right 1 cell
[PAGE UP]	Moves up 1 screen
[PAGE DOWN]	Moves down 1 screen
[CTRL]+[HOME]	Moves to upper left corner
[CTRL]+[END]	Moves to lower right corner of the active area

Using the Mouse

Like the keyboard, you can use the mouse to choose commands, highlight ranges, resize windows, and perform many other tasks. There are some actions that you perform only with a mouse, such as dragging the border of a cell to increase column width. Whenever a selection is to be made with the mouse, use the left mouse button. Clicking the right mouse button brings up a shortcut menu with an abbreviated set of commands that are relevant to the current selection or active element.

Spreadsheet Commands

Commands are tools provided by spreadsheet software to manipulate the spreadsheet in various ways. For example, there are commands for copying data, formatting your worksheet, or printing your worksheet. Some commands affect the entire worksheet, but others only affect certain cells or ranges.

Some commands are performed by clicking a button, others by selecting an item in a drop-down menu or panel, or by selecting a check box or radio button.

Each tab on the Ribbon contains commands related to a different aspect of working with spreadsheets, and within each tab, commands are further organized into related groups. The **Home tab** contains the most commonly accessed commands: for formatting fonts, text, numbers, and cells; for applying styles to cells, and for editing, inserting, and deleting rows, columns, and cells. The **Insert tab** contains commands for adding tables, illustrations, charts, links, and special text elements and objects to a spreadsheet. The **Page Layout tab** contains commands for managing the overall appearance and layout of your spreadsheet. The **Formulas tab** has commands for working with formulas and functions, and the **Data tab** contains commands for managing your raw data as well as any data sources linked to your spreadsheet. Commands for proofing, commenting, and handling changes are located on the **Review tab**, while the **View tab** allows you to modify the workbook view, zoom levels, and the Excel window. Some tabs are context sensitive, and hidden unless you are working with a specific type of spreadsheet element. For example, tabs with commands for manipulating charts will not appear unless a chart is inserted into your spreadsheet and selected. If you are working with special Excel add-in modules, such as Adobe Acrobat, you may also have tabs with commands for working with these modules.

Some of the buttons on the Ribbon have arrows, indicating that a menu of commands or gallery of options will appear when you click on that arrow. For example, if you click the arrow beside the *Underline (U)* button on the Home tab (in the Font group), a short menu will appear allowing you to apply a standard underline to the currently selected text or a double underline.

Some commands on the Ribbon include text boxes that you can type values directly into, and these may also include an arrow, indicating there are values you can select from a drop-down menu. To the bottom right of some groups of commands you will also see a small, diagonal arrow. This is a dialog box launcher, and clicking it will open a dialog box with a full set of options and commands related to that group of commands. For example, clicking the dialog box launcher in the Font group on the Home tab opens the Font section of the Format Cells dialog box, which allows you to select multiple options for formatting the font within a cell.

You can choose a command from a menu by using the mouse to click on the command or by using the arrow keys on the keyboard to select the command and pressing [Enter]. Some commands can be executed by pressing a series of keys, called a keyboard shortcut, such as [CTRL]+[C]. The keyboard shortcut for a command is listed beside the command in a menu or displayed in the command's ScreenTip when you mouse over the button. Using a keyboard shortcut will activate the command without your needing to select it from the menu. For example, the *Paste* command button on the Home tab displays "Ctrl + V" in its ScreenTip. Pressing the keyboard sequence [CTRL]+[V] (the [Ctrl] key followed by the [V] key) will execute the Paste command.

When you choose a command on a menu it is performed immediately, unless an ellipsis ("…") or arrow is displayed beside it. If the command includes an ellipsis, clicking on that command will open up a dialog box or window that includes additional settings or commands to choose from. If the command includes an arrowhead, pointing to that command will reveal a submenu that includes related commands or options.

In addition to using the mouse to press buttons and select menu items and options, or using keyboard shortcuts, you can also execute commands by using Office 2007's Key Tips. Key Tips allow you to locate and execute any command on the Ribbon by pressing a sequence of keys on the keyboard. To use Key Tips, you first press [ALT] on the keyboard to display the Key Tips for each tab. These Key Tips are displayed in small boxes on the Ribbon. You then press the key for the tab you wish to open. The selected tab then displays Key Tips for commands or groups of commands. You then press one or more keys to locate and execute a command on that tab. For example, to execute the Double Underline command, you first press [ALT] on the keyboard to activate and display the Key Tips in the Excel window. You then press [H] to select the Home tab, then [3] to select the Underline menu, and then [D] to select the Double Underline command. Pressing [ESC] at any time you are working with Key Tips will return you to the previous command, and you can press [ESC] multiple times to bring you out of Key Tips mode altogether.

Setting up a Worksheet

Consult with your technical support specialist about how to install and configure Excel for your particular computer system and whether you are allowed to make a backup copy of the program.

To illustrate how spreadsheet software works, we will be developing a simple spreadsheet with which you are very familiar. Let us start by creating a course roster containing the information of student names and grades for a quiz, a midterm, and a final exam. The final product will look like Figure 2-1.

Assuming Excel has been properly installed, and you are using Windows XP as the operating system, you start by clicking the *Start* button, pointing to *All Programs*, pointing to *Microsoft Office*, and then finally clicking on *Microsoft Office Excel 2007*. In some cases, Excel will already be placed on the Quick Start Menu, which is a list of programs that you commonly use. In this case, click on *Start* and you will see a list of programs above. Click on *Excel* if it is present. Excel will open up with a blank worksheet. You can now start working with your worksheet.

How to Enter Data into a Worksheet

The student roster illustrated in Figure 2-1 is a very simple list. You need only enter data regarding the student's names and grades. No calculations are required. You can start at cell A1 and enter your column headings. Enter FIRST NAME in cell A1, LAST NAME in B1, QUIZ in C1, MIDTERM in D1, and FINAL in E1.

You enter data into a cell by moving the cell pointer to the cell, typing in the entry. The insertion point indicates where the next character you type will appear. Each character you enter also appears in the Formula bar. When you are finished typing in the entry, press [ENTER] to move to the next cell down or [TAB] to move to the next cell across.

In addition to pressing [ENTER] or [TAB], you can complete a cell entry by clicking on another cell or by pressing one of the arrow keys on the keyboard. This will complete the entry and move the cell pointer to another cell as directed by the mouse or the arrow key. You can also click the

Enter button on the Formula bar (this only appears after data has been entered into the current cell.) If you do this, the cell entry will be confirmed, but the cell pointer will remain in the current cell.

You can complete your roster by entering the student names in cells A2 through B5, the quiz grades in cells C2 through C5, the midterm grades in cells D2 through D5, and the final grades in cells E2 through E5.

How to Change Column Widths

You will notice that the first two column headings, FIRST NAME and LAST NAME, are truncated. This occurs because the column widths are at the default width of 8.43 characters. Both of these headings have more characters than this and Excel cuts off both entries at the right edges of the cells. (However, had the cell to the right of Column A or B been empty, the heading would carry over to display in the next blank cell.)

Sometimes pound signs (#####) will appear in a cell containing a numeric value. This happens when the column width is too narrow to accommodate the number of places in the numeric value plus additional punctuation for decimal points, commas, dollar signs, etc.

You can make column widths smaller or larger by using the **Column Width** command. Let's reset the column for student names in our example to 20 positions.

First, select the range for which you would like to adjust the column width. You can select a range by first clicking at the center of the cell and then holding the mouse button down while dragging the mouse pointer to the opposite corner of the range. To select more than one range at a time, keep the [CTRL] key pressed while selecting the next range. In our example, we need to select an entire column, which can be done in an easier manner. Every column in the worksheet has column headings (A, B, C, etc.) just above the first row of the worksheet. Clicking on a column heading selects the entire column. Click on Column A and you will find the whole column highlighted.

On the Home tab of the Ribbon, click *Format* in the Cells group and the Format drop-down menu will appear. Click *Column Width*. This opens the Column Width dialog box. Enter the desired width, *20* (for 20 characters), in the *Column width* text box and then click the *OK* button.

You can also change column widths by using the mouse. Position your mouse on the border between two column headers (such as B and C) to show the horizontal resize pointer ✛ and drag to the right or left. If you position the mouse directly on the line between the two letters and rapidly double-click, the column will be auto fitted to the exact size needed to display the contents of all the cells in the row or column.

Values and Labels

Excel has two types of cell entries: *values* and *labels*. Values are numbers, functions, or formulae. Labels are used for text entries within your spreadsheet. Labels cannot be used in calculations.

As long as there is a letter in the cell, Excel will recognize the entry as a label, even if the entry begins with a numerical character. The entry will always be treated as a value if the beginning character is one of the following:

= + - $

Position the cell pointer on the student first name *Heather*. Then position it on the column heading FIRST NAME. You will notice that the formula bar displays Heather or FIRST NAME. Any cell containing a letter is considered a label. The entries can be aligned left, right, or center, but labels are left-aligned by default.

Aligning Labels

You can right-align the labels above the grades by selecting them and clicking the *Align Text Right* button or center them by clicking the *Center* button, both located in the Alignment group on the Home tab. Alternatively, you can click the Alignment group's dialog box launcher to open the Alignment tab of the Format Cells dialog box. Practice aligning labels by selecting QUIZ, MIDTERM, and FINAL and right aligning them within their cells.

Numbers in Excel

In Excel, a number cannot contain spaces and is limited to only one decimal point. The method for changing cell formats for displaying a number will be discussed later. A number can be entered in scientific notation, or it can end with a percent sign (%) to indicate percentage. When a number ends with a percent sign, Excel will divide the number that precedes the sign by 100.

Let's review the student roster you've entered. At this point, the labels will all be right-aligned except for FIRST NAME and LAST NAME, and the numbers will be right-aligned as well. The width of columns A and B will be 20 characters, and the width of the rest of the columns will remain at the default value of 8.43 characters. The worksheet will look like Figure 2-1.

How to Edit Data

There are three ways you can edit a cell entry:

1. You can enter data into a cell that already contains information using the same procedure for entering data into an empty cell. This will cause the new data to replace the earlier entry.

2.   You can also use the [F2] (Edit) key to edit data in a cell. Position the cell pointer on the cell you wish to edit and press the [F2] key. This will switch Excel into EDIT mode. The easier way to switch into the EDIT mode is to click inside the Formula bar on the edit line (where the contents of an active cell appear). You may also double-click a cell to edit its contents.

3.   Position the cell pointer on the cell you wish to edit and then position your cursor in the Formula bar at the point where you want to make the change. Press the [ENTER] key when you have finished making the correction.

Erasing Worksheet Data

To delete data in a cell, click inside the cell and then click the *Clear* button in the Home tab's Editing group. In the menu that displays, click *Clear Contents*. You can also simply press the [DELETE] key or right-click a cell and then select *Clear Contents* from the shortcut menu.

If you want to delete an entire range of cells, you first have to select the range that you want to delete. If the range you want to delete is A1:B2 (4 cells), click cell A1, hold the mouse button down, and drag the mouse pointer to B2. This procedure highlights the range selected. Once the range is selected, you can press the [DELETE] key or use the *Clear Contents* command.

If you wish to delete both the contents and the formatting of the cell, it is necessary to click the *Clear* button on the Ribbon and then select either *Clear Formats* or *Clear All*. If you do not clear the formatting when you delete the contents, you may occasionally create errors—such as numbers being displayed as dates. This can happen because certain formatting occurs implicitly, i.e., keying a date into a cell will cause that cell to be formatted for a date even after the date itself is deleted.

Moving Data

It is a good idea to document each worksheet you create. Figure 2-2 illustrates how the worksheet we just created could be documented. Cell A1 explains the purpose of the worksheet. Cell A2 provides the name and location of the worksheet file. Cell A3 identifies the author of the worksheet and the date it was created.

Figure 2-2

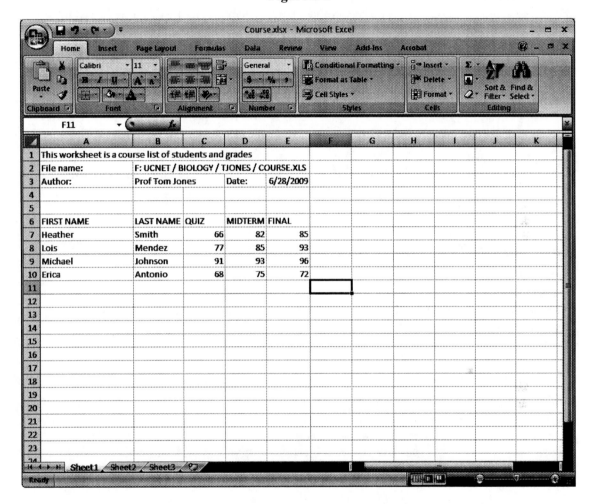

We need to make room for this documentation at the top of the worksheet by moving the worksheet down five rows. To do this, first highlight the range A1:E5 using the mouse. On the Home tab of the Ribbon, in the Clipboard group, click *Cut*. This will send the data in the selected range to the Clipboard so it can be pasted elsewhere using the Paste command. Then click in cell A6 (which is where you want the upper-left corner of your selected range to be) and click the *Paste* button on the Ribbon (also in the Clipboard group).

You could also move the grades data down by inserting rows above. To insert one row at a time above a selected cell, click *Insert* on the Home tab of the Ribbon, in the Cell group, and then click *Insert Sheet Rows*. To insert multiple rows at a time, you can first highlight the number of rows you would like to insert. For instance, if you want to insert three rows at the beginning of your worksheet, you would select the first three rows using the mouse and click *Insert* and then *Insert Sheet Rows*, and this will add three rows above the selected rows. You can use the same procedures to insert single or multiple columns using the *Insert Sheet Columns* command.

Once you have moved the worksheet down, you can enter the documentation in cells A1 through A3 so that your worksheet looks like Figure 2-2. Note that the contents of these cells seem to extend into the blank cells in Columns B through F because the cells to the right of A1 to A3 are empty.

How to Save Files

You will learn more about formatting and organizing the worksheet in the case problems later in this book. Let's save the practice worksheet for future use. To save a file, you use the Save or the Save As command. These Save commands will make an exact copy of your worksheet on disk, including any special formats and settings you have specified.

First, click the Microsoft Office button. On the drop-down Office menu that appears, click *Save*. If this is the first time that you are working on this file and saving it, this will open the Save As dialog box. Excel will provide a default filename (book1.xlsx) in the *File name* box. You can click inside this box, delete the default name, and type in a name (such as *Course*) that you choose for the worksheet. The *Save in* box indicates the drive and folder in which Excel will store the file. (The drive and folder are established during configuration, but they can be changed.) You can change the folder in which you want to save the file by clicking the *Save in* list arrow.

Enter the name you have assigned to your worksheet file in the *File name* box and click *Save*. Let's call the worksheet *COURSE*. The file name can contain uppercase or lowercase letters, numbers, and most symbols. When you save a file, Excel 2007 will automatically assign a three or four character extension, depending on the type of file you are saving. The extension *.xlsx* is used for an Excel 2007 workbook. You could choose to save the file in a new location or using other formats (including Web page or XML format) using the *Save As* command. If you want your file to be compatible with earlier versions of Excel, click the arrow at the right of the Save as type box and select Excel 97-2003 workbook (*.xls) as the file type.

> *Be sure to save COURSE.xlsx after you use it for a tutorial. You can save it under the same name after each tutorial session. Most of the changes you make to your worksheet during a tutorial will be required by subsequent sessions. Follow tutorial instructions to determine what changes to your worksheet must be saved or erased.*

Ending Your Excel Session

To exit Excel, click the *Close Button* X at the far right of the Title bar. It is a good practice to save all your files and close them before quitting. If you have not saved a file, Excel brings up a dialog box that asks if you want to save the file before the program closes. Click the *Yes* button to save the file or the *No* button to discard the changes and exit. Clicking on *Cancel* takes you back into Excel in READY mode.

Spreadsheet Design Principles

Like any helpful tool, Excel worksheets can be abused and misused, especially if worksheets are carelessly built, poorly documented, and based on false assumptions. These problems can be minimized by following a few basic principles of spreadsheet design that have emerged over the last decade.

Your spreadsheets can be more easily understood by using a five section design. In the first line on top put the company name and the title of the spreadsheet that accurately reflects the subject matter of the spreadsheet. After the title, the spreadsheet is organized into four sections: *Documentation*, *Assumptions*, *Input and calculations*, and *Ranges*. These sections are illustrated in Figure 2-3.

Figure 2-3

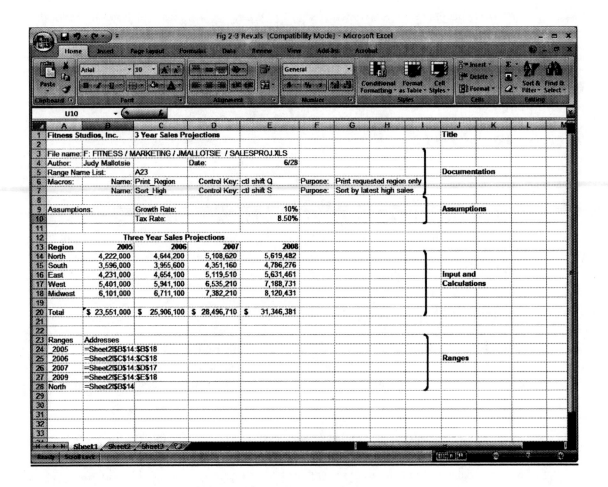

The purpose of the *Documentation* section is to describe where the spreadsheet is stored, who created it, when, what ranges are used, and what macros are used. Try to keep your descriptions simple and to the point. You can divide the *Documentation* section into five separate lines. In companies, spreadsheets and other documents are often stored on network drives, or special project drives.

The next section in a spreadsheet is used for *assumptions*. Assumptions are used throughout spreadsheets to drive the calculations in formulas. It is important that all the basic assumptions used to create the output are clearly identified. In Figure 2-3, we are assuming an annual sales growth figure of 10%. This could, of course, change, and assumptions are frequently changed in spreadsheets to test various "what-if" scenarios. For instance, the results of this worksheet will be different if we change the assumption for annual sales growth to 5% or to 15%. By isolating the assumptions in a specific section, it is very easy to change the spreadsheet as conditions change.

The third section is the *Input and calculations* section. The input data are the raw data that are supplied by the author of the spreadsheet. In the spreadsheet illustrated here, the data consist of the names of the sales regions and the actual sales figures for 2005. *Calculated results* are also displayed in this section. For instance, in this spreadsheet, the sales for 2005 are raw data that reflect actual sales in 2005. Sales numbers to the right for years 2006 to 2008 are calculated based on the assumed 10% sales growth rate. Also, the totals for all columns are calculated results produced by Excel.

The fourt section in a spreadsheet, *Ranges*, provides a list of the ranges used in the spreadsheet and their address locations.

The worksheet files on your data disk are designed to encourage you to use these spreadsheet design principles. The first five lines of each worksheet file are reserved for documentation. The *Solve it!* worksheet files provide much of the data for the input section of the worksheet. You will then complete the input and calculation sections of the worksheet to develop the solution for the spreadsheet case. If required by the problem, you can add an assumptions section by inserting rows above the input section or by moving the input section down several rows.

3

Spreadsheet Management Software Cases

Spreadsheet Case 1

Whistle Cleaners

Problem:	Develop a client prospect tracking system
Management skills:	Organization Controlling
Excel skills:	Entering Labels, Dates and Hyperlink Fields Worksheet formatting Printing
File:	WHISTLECLEANERS_Q.xlsx

Jesse Williams is a sales representative with Whistle Cleaners, a small industrial cleaning firm located in Dearborn, Michigan. Her boss has instructed her to increase sales by 12% by attracting new clients. Williams locates the names of small businesses by using telephone directories, mailing lists, and the Internet. She makes a list of these sales prospects, noting the company name, telephone number, and the owner's name and email address if available. Then she starts telephoning or emailing them to describe Whistle Cleaners' services.

If Williams's prospects are interested but not ready to sign up, she contacts them again one week later. Sometimes, Williams forgets whether she has called or emailed a prospect and either contacts them again or forgets to follow up at all. Therefore, Williams needs a way to keep track of prospects and contacts that she can easily consult and update.

Load the worksheet file WHISTLECLEANERS_Q.xlsx. This worksheet contains a list of some of Williams's prospects and information. Use your spreadsheet software to create a prospect tracking system that Williams can read on screen and print out.

The worksheet should list each prospect's name, telephone number, email address, and the date and manner of the last contact. It should also include a column for *Follow Up* in which Williams can enter a *Yes* or *No* to indicate whether additional contact is required. To locate names more easily, organize the prospect list in alphabetical order by last name.

A spreadsheet's appearance and structure are both extremely important if you want to effectively use the information it contains. Professional-looking spreadsheets are formatted in ways that allow you to quickly locate and digest their information. The format should also allow you to easily make changes and update data. This problem shows you how to develop professional-looking, maintainable spreadsheets that can be easily understood by others.

Tasks:

There are five tasks to this problem:

1. Create new columns and appropriate column headings to capture the required information. There should be column headings for *Company*, *Last Name*, *First Name*, *Telephone*, *Email Address*, *Date Called*, and *Follow Up*. The column headings for Company, Last Name, and Date Called already appear on the worksheet. Center the title of the sheet across all of the columns.

2. Create appropriate widths for each column, and then decide whether to left justify, right justify, or center the column labels. Some of the worksheet columns have already been widened for you.

3. Be sure to format the cells containing the dates to display the name of the month. The email address should be formatted as a hyperlink field so that Williams can initiate her email program by simply clicking on the field. Williams needs to make follow-up calls to Roman Herrero and Harriet Payson.

4. Williams has just found two more prospects, Brad Stockton and Cher Royer, both of whom need follow-up calls. Stockton heads Oblong River Realty and was first contacted on 7/29/09. His phone number is 313-555-5554. Royer works for Wyse Trucking and was first contacted on 7/13/09. Her phone number is 313-555-4954. Add information about these prospects to the prospect list by inserting new rows in the appropriate places

in the worksheet to ensure that the company names remain in alphabetical order. Create fictitious data for other contacts to fill in the spreadsheet.

5. Improve the appearance of the log by bolding and underlining column labels. Print a report of the log with a footer that shows the date of printing and your name. You should be able to print this worksheet on one 8-1/2 x 11-inch page.

Time Estimates

Expert:	30 minutes
Intermediate:	45 minutes
Novice:	1.5 hours

Excel Tutorial for Spreadsheet Case 1

This case draws upon the data entry skills you have already acquired while developing COURSE.xlsx in Chapter 2 and upon new skills for formatting and printing spreadsheets. You will need to use COURSE.xlsx again for this tutorial.

How to Retrieve a Data File

Begin by starting the Excel application. When the spreadsheet screen appears, your next step will be to load the data file COURSE.xlsx. Do this by clicking the Office button at the left of the title bar and clicking *Open* in the Office menu that opens. The Open dialog box will appear.

You may need to specify various settings within the Open dialog box in order to locate and load the file. The four items that must be set are the *file name,* the *file type,* the *folder,* and the *disk drive*. A list of files of the type specified for the disk drive and folder appears in the File List window. To change the settings to retrieve COURSE.xlsx, first ensure that *All Excel Files, Excel Files,* or *All Files* appears in the *Files of type* list box. If it does not immediately appear, it can be changed by clicking the *list arrow* next to the *Files of type* list box, revealing a list of file types Excel can open. To move up and down the list, click the arrows on the scroll bars next to the list. Select the required file type with the mouse pointer.

Use the *Look in* list arrow to select the Folder and Disk Drive where COURSE.xlsx is stored and display it in the *File name* box. The files are listed alphabetically, so if the desired file is not visible, you can move down the list using the scroll bar. Double-click the COURSE.xlsx file to open it. Alternatively, you can simply select the file or type *COURSE.xlsx* directly in the File Name box. When the settings are correct, click the *Open* button or press the [Enter] key.

How to Insert or Delete Columns and Rows

Suppose you wanted to add lines under the column headings in your student roster. You can insert columns and rows in an Excel worksheet in either of two ways: (a) through the Ribbon command *Insert Sheet Rows* (accessed through the *Insert* button in the Cells group of the Home tab), or (b) clicking the right mouse button to open the shortcut menu and then selecting *Insert*. This opens the Insert dialog box with four options:

1.   Shift Cells Right

2.   Shift Cells Down

3.   Entire Row

4.   Entire Column

By selecting *Entire Row* from the options presented and clicking *OK*, you can insert a blank row.

You can also select an entire row and then select *Insert* from the shortcut menu or open the *Insert* menu on the Home tab of the Ribbon and click *Insert Cells*. To select an entire row, move the mouse pointer over the row number at the left of the worksheet and press the left mouse button. To select multiple rows, keep the left button depressed and drag up or down.

You will now insert the blank line into your student roster. To do so, select any cell in the row immediately below the column headings—that is, move to row 7; it doesn't matter which column the active cell is in. In the Cells group on the Home tab of the Ribbon, click the arrow on the *Insert* button. On the menu, *Insert Sheet Rows*. You will notice that a blank row is inserted in row 7 and the data that was previously located in rows 7 through 10 has been moved to rows 8 through 11.

You can delete one or multiple rows and columns using the same principles used in inserting rows and columns. There are two ways of accessing the *Delete* command in Excel: (a) through the Delete menu on the Home tab of the Ribbon (also in the Cells group) or (b) through the shortcut menu activated by the right mouse button. If entire rows or columns are highlighted when these commands are selected, the effects will be immediate: the row(s) or column(s) will disappear.

To make the worksheet documentation section conform to the spreadsheet design principles introduced in Chapter 2, let's add a fourth line to the documentation section. Use the first four cells in Row 4, starting in cell A4, to enter *Ranges: none Macros: none*. (We will add macros and range names in later tutorials.) Then insert a row so that there are two rows between the documentation section and the course list itself. Your worksheet screen now looks like Figure 3-1.

Figure 3-1

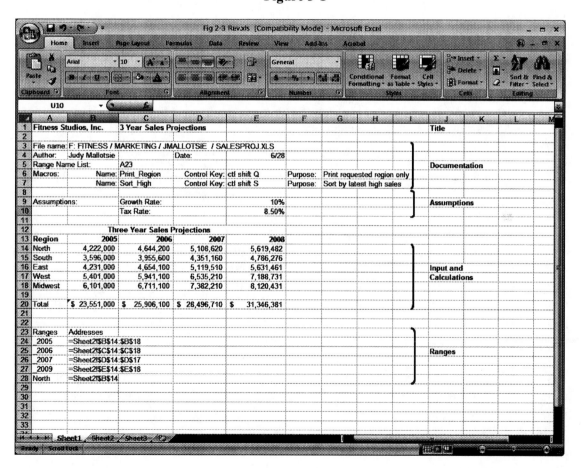

Moving and Copying the Contents of Cells

After using the *Insert Rows* command again, Row 8 will be blank. You can now add separator lines in this row to further set off the column headings from the data on the list.

This is a convenient time to explain some commonly used and helpful operations:

A *move* is referred to as a *cut and paste* in Excel. This involves simply relocating the contents of one or more cells. A *copy* reproduces the contents of the cells. The cut and copy commands are designed to be accompanied by a paste operation. The cut or copy designates *from where* the cells are cut or copied, while the paste designates *to where* they are being placed.

As with most operations in Excel, there are several ways to cut and copy:

1. Using the *Cut*, *Copy*, and *Paste* buttons on the Ribbon, located in the Clipboard group on the Home tab
2. Using the *Cut*, *Copy*, and *Paste* functions on the shortcut menu
3. Using the keystrokes for Cut (CTRL-X), Copy (CTRL-C), and Paste (CTRL-V)
4. Using the mouse pointer to drag and copy

Each of these is worth exploring at least once, and you can decide which method you find to be the most convenient. Generally speaking, most users use two of the methods listed. For example, some users will cut and copy using the mouse to drag and copy within a small area in a spreadsheet, and then use one of the other techniques to cut and copy between larger areas. Once you become familiar with each method, you will see that they are very similar. They all require you to specify a source range of cells, an operation (cut or copy), a destination or target range, and the Paste function.

It is worth explaining the mouse method of cutting and copying since it is extremely useful. This method applies to a single cell or a multiple selection. When you move your mouse pointer to the border of a selection on the worksheet, it transforms from a white cross to the Move pointer, a four-headed arrow. This is the signal that you can now perform the drag or copy.

To drag (or cut) the contents of the selection, depress the left mouse button, continue to hold it down, and move the pointer. As you move the pointer across the worksheet, a shadow of the selection will also be moved until the mouse button is released to designate the destination of the drag. This operation may require some practice, but it will become second nature very quickly and you will find it to be an important editing function.

To perform the mouse copy, the actions are nearly identical to the drag (cut). The mouse pointer is moved to the border of the selection and the cross turns into an arrow. At this time, press and hold down the [CTRL] key. A small tell-tale plus sign will appear next to the arrow, indicating that we are performing a copy rather than a move. Drag the selection as we did for the move; when the mouse button is released, you will see that the copy operation has been completed.

With practice, you will realize that each of the different cut and copy methods results in identical results.

Returning to COURSE.xlsx, we now want to insert some decorative separators into the cells in Row 8 to distinguish the headings from the body of the table. To do this, we will enter the equals sign [=] and select the *Alignment Fill* command to fill the cell width with this symbol.

First, type = and click the *Enter* button on the Formula bar to enter = in cell A8. Now click *Format* on the Home tab of the Ribbon and then click *Format Cells* to open the Format Cells dialog box. This box has six formatting tabs: *Number*, *Alignment*, *Font*, *Border*, *Fill*, and *Protection*. Select *Alignment* by clicking on the tab label at the top of the dialog box. In the Text Alignment section, select *Fill* from the *Horizontal* drop-down menu and then click the *OK* button or press [ENTER]. The cell will be filled with the = sign.

Once you have set up the first cell, you can replicate it in all the cells in Row 8 below the column heads. Do this by using the Copy command. First, click the *Copy* button on the Home tab of the Ribbon. Notice the moving "marching ants" border around cell A8, indicating a copy or cut source. Next, select cells B8, C8, D8, and E8 (referred to as range B8:E8). Do this by moving the mouse pointer to cell B8, depressing the left mouse button, and dragging to the right until the desired range is selected. Now click the *Paste* button on the Ribbon. This will copy the formatting and contents of cell A8 to the range selected. When you are finished, press [ENTER] to finalize the copy and paste action. Your worksheet should look similar to Figure 3-2. In Excel 2007, the *Paste Options* button permits you to set formatting options for the data you have just pasted. Since you do not need to consider additional formatting, you may disregard the button.

Printing Your Worksheet

To print a simple worksheet such as your student roster, which is one page or less, you need only know the basic printing commands. Select the *Print* command on the Office menu to display the Print dialog box. The various options in this dialog box can be explored later, however, for our purposes, simply accept the default settings and click the *OK* button.

Figure 3-2

	A	B	C	D	E	F	G	H	I	J	K	L
1	This worksheet is a course list of students and grades											
2	File name:	F: UCNET / BIOLOGY / TJONES / COURSE.XLS										
3	Author:	Prof Tom Joi	Date:	6/28/2009								
4	Ranges:	None	Macros:	None								
5												
6												
7	FIRST NAME	LAST NAME	QUIZ	MIDTERM	FINAL							
8	=====	=====	=====	=====	=====							
9	Heather	Smith	66	82	85							
10	Lois	Mendez	77	85	93							
11	Michael	Johnson	91	93	96							
12	Erica	Antonio	68	75	72							
13												
14												
15												
16												
17												
18												
19												
20												
21												
22												
23												
24												
25												
26												
27												

In this case, Excel will just print the page containing the student roster. Features can be adjusted, including paper size, page orientation, scaling, margin sizes, alignment, header and footer contents and options, print titles, page print sequence, and print area. You will find many of these settings in the Page Setup group of commands on the Page Layout tab of the Ribbon. To access the full set of Page Setup commands, click the dialog box launcher for the Page Setup group to open the Page Setup dialog box. Before printing, the appearance of your page can be observed in Print Preview so paper need not be wasted. To open Print Preview, click the Office button, point to *Print* in the Office menu and click *Print Preview* on the submenu. .

As Excel is printing your page, a small message box appears stating which page is currently being printed. This box contains a *Cancel* button, which you can choose if you want to stop the printing.

Changing Excel's Printer Options

The printing options in Excel can be changed in the Page Setup dialog box. The Page Setup dialog box has four tabs: *Page, Margins, Header/Footer,* and *Sheet.*

On the Page tab, you can choose specific features pertaining to individual pages being printed. The first option is Orientation—that is, whether the page is printed in landscape (horizontal wide, vertical narrow) or portrait (horizontal narrow, vertical wide) mode. The second option, Scaling, permits you to scale the size of the print up or down a specific percentage, or scale to fit a certain number of pages where the computer determines the percentage scaling. The Paper size option permits you to change the paper size between various standard sizes (e.g., Letter, Legal, Executive, A4, etc.). The next option allows you to change the print quality. The final option, First page number, permits you to specify the starting page of printing. To print from the start, enter *1* or *Auto*; otherwise enter the page number from which you wish to begin.

On the Margins tab, you can change the margins that border the pages. The size of the margins on each page's edge can be specified in particular units (inches, centimeters). At the top right and top bottom are the Header and Footer settings, which specify the distance between the edge of the page and the header or footer. The last options are whether to center the print subject horizontally or vertically on the page.

On the Header/Footer tab, you can change the appearance of the headers and footers of the printed pages. The operation and options of headers (appearing at the top of every page) and footers (appearing at the bottom of every page) are the same. Each includes a number of default sample headers, a list to which you can add. Selecting *Custom Header* or *Custom Footer* permits you to change the header/footer. Each is split into thirds: left, center, and right. In each or any of these sections, you can enter text or click a button to insert any of the following: current page number, total number of pages, date, time, file path, file name, sheet name, or picture. You can change the fonts of any text using the *Format Text* button and format an inserted picture by using the *Format Picture* button.

On the Sheet tab, you can change the print features pertaining to the worksheet. First, you can specify precisely the range on the worksheet you want to print. This is done by clicking the *Collapse Dialog* button to the right of the *Print Area* list box, and then highlighting the range on the worksheet. The next option lets you specify Print Titles, which are either rows or columns that are to appear on every printed page. These are useful for lists or tables that extend beyond the confines of a single page. The next group of options allows you to select whether or how to print the following sheet elements: *Gridlines*, *Black and white*, *Draft quality*, *Row and column headings*, *Comments*, and *Cell errors*. The final option is the *Page Order*—that is, whether to print down and across or across and down.

Save COURSE.xlsx with the changes you made during this tutorial session. You will need it for the next spreadsheet case.

Spreadsheet Case 2
Athena Beauty Products

Problem:	Evaluate the effectiveness of an e-commerce company's Web site and advertising sites
Management skills:	Analyzing Organizing
Excel skills:	Formulas Absolute and Relative Addressing Formatting Printing
File:	ATHENABEAUTY_Q.xlsx

Athena Beauty, headquartered in Macon, Georgia, manufactures and sells trendy, inexpensive cosmetics. They have been in business since 2001 and have 13 store locations in the south-eastern United States. Annual revenue from all the stores has been increasing each year, with 2008 revenues totaling $9,750,000. Lillian Castleman, President of Athena Beauty, recognized the potential market in online sales two years ago and had an outside Web development firm create an e-commerce site for her company. The site has had moderate success, but Castleman would like to increase its effectiveness by turning more visitors into shoppers and decreasing the number of attempted buyers.

The company has been attempting to increase the number of on-line customers by placing advertising for their Web site on other Web sites. When users click on these ads, they are automatically transported to Athena Beauty's Web site. Data on Athena Beauty's Web advertising campaign is summarized in the weekly Marketing Trends Reports (MTR) produced by their Web site analysis software, which appears in the ATHENABEAUTY_Q.xlsx file.

5. *Visitors* are the number of people who visited Athena Beauty's Web site by clicking on an ad for their site that was placed on an affiliated Web site.

6. *Shoppers* are the number of visitors referred by ads who reached a page in their Web site designated as a shopping page.

7. *Attempted buyers* are the number of potential buyers referred by ads who reached a Web site designated as a page for summarizing and paying for purchases.

8. *Buyers* are the number of buyers referred by ads who actually placed an order from their Web site.

9. *Source* indicates the specific Web site from which visitors came to Athena Beauty's Web site.

In trying to increase the number of on-line customers, Castleman must determine the Web site's success in converting visitors to actual buyers. She must also look at the abandonment rate—the percentage of attempted buyers who abandon the Web site just as they were about to make a purchase. Low conversion rates and high abandonment rates are indicators that a Web site is not very effective and needs work.

Castleman also wants to increase the effectiveness of her advertising dollars by increasing the size of the Athena Beauty ads on the sites where it advertises. .

Tasks

There are five tasks in this problem:

1. Create new columns for the percentage of visitors who became shoppers, the percentage of shoppers who became attempted buyers, and the percentage of attempted buyers who became buyers. Also, create a column that shows the percentage of visitors from each advertising source. Create meaningful headings and display them wrapped above the columns and in bold.

2. Create formulas to total each column so you can determine the total number of Visitors, Shoppers, Attempted Buyers, and Buyers, as well as the Percentage of Visitors from each Source.

3. Create formulas to calculate the percentage of visitors who became shoppers, shoppers who became attempted buyers, and attempted buyers who became buyers. Calculate the percentages on the totals of these categories as well. Calculate the percentage of total visitors who came from each source, utilizing absolute addressing so that the results of the formulas can easily be copied down each column.

4. Format the spreadsheet so the percentages are displayed with the percent sign.

5. Print the spreadsheet with the data *centered* both horizontally and vertically on a single page, and include a centered header with Castleman's name. Include your name and today's date in the footer.

Excel Tutorial for Spreadsheet Case 2

This case draws upon all of the skills acquired in Spreadsheet Case 1, plus new skills for using formulas, formatting, and absolute and relative addressing. You will once again use COURSE.xlsx for this tutorial.

Suppose you want to expand your worksheet by including each student's final grade. You must add an extra column and label for FINAL GRADE, and you must calculate the final grade for each student. The final exam counts for 50% of the final grade, the midterm for 35%, and the quiz for 15%.

Formulas

To compute the final grade, you must use a formula. A *formula* tells Excel what manipulations to perform on specific cell contents. The cells are specified using their cell references (e.g. A11, C3). Mathematical operators specify arithmetic operations. They are:

^	Exponentiation
*, /	Multiplication, Division
+,-	Addition, Subtraction
%	Percent (i.e. 75% represents 0.75)

Operations are always performed left to right within a formula in their order of precedence. The order of precedence in Excel corresponds to the order of the above list. Exponentiation will always be performed first, followed by multiplication and division, and then addition and subtraction. Percent amounts are evaluated when they are encountered.

Parentheses can be used to override the order of precedence. Operations inside parentheses will be performed before those outside the parentheses. The order of operations remains the same within the parentheses. When multiple sets of parentheses are employed, the operations within the innermost set of parentheses will be performed before those within the next set.

Thus, the formula for Heather Smith's final grade would be:

=C9*.15+D14*35+E9*.5

Note that the first character in the formula is preceded by an = sign. To be treated as a formula rather than a label, a formula must begin with an equals [=] sign. (The reason for the $ symbol and use of these cells is explained below.) Thus, a formula to add the contents of cells A6 and B6 must be expressed as =A6+B6. If you try to type this formula as A6+B6, it will be treated as a label.

Formula Errors

If you try to enter a formula with a logical or mathematical error, Excel will display a message box stating what error has occurred. To proceed, you must click the *OK* button. If you want further information on the error, you can select the *Help* button, which will provide a broader explanation of the error. Once the problem is corrected, you can continue.

Another common problem is the circular reference, which is a formula that directly or indirectly refers back to the same cell in which it resides. For example, if you try to enter the formula =A12+B12 into cell B12, an error box will appear stating a circular reference has occurred. This is because cell B12 is an operand in the operation, as well as the cell that holds the result of the calculation.

Absolute and Relative Addressing

Suppose we want to make our worksheet more flexible for future changes. The professor may decide that the quiz should only contribute 10% toward the final grade and the midterm will not count for 50%. In that case, the formula for the final grade must be adjusted to change the percentage weight applied to the midterm and the quiz.

You could, of course, re-enter the new formulas, but an easier way to keep track of the percentage weight assigned to each grade would be to list the percentages assigned to each grade in an unused portion of the spreadsheet. Formulas would reference the cell addresses where these percentages reside rather than the percentages themselves.

Set up an Assumptions section in the upper left-hand corner of your worksheet. First, move the course list down so that the column labels are in Row 14. Then, enter the label "ASSUMPTIONS" in cell A7, and format cell A8 in the same manner as cells A15:E14. Below the underlining, in cells A9 through A11, enter the labels "Quiz," "Midterm," and "Final Exam."

In cells B9 through B11, enter the percentage weights for each of these grades: .15, .35, and .5.

Develop a formula for a student's final grade to reference the cells where these percentages reside. It is never good practice to use the percentages themselves in a formula; always use a cell reference. Enter the formula for Heather Smith's grades into cell F16.

=C16*$B$9+D16*$B$10+E16*$B$11

The $ designates an absolute address. An *absolute address* is one that will not change when that address is copied. Excel's default is to treat an address as a *relative address*, meaning that when you copy or move a formula, the addresses of the cells in the formula will be automatically adjusted to fit the new location. A relative address has no $ symbols. Any formula with multiple cell references can have absolute, relative, and mixed addresses (see the next section) all in the one formula.

Relative addressing means that you can copy the formula in cell F14 for Heather's grade to cell F15 for Lois, and the formula will automatically adjust to add the proper cell addresses (the addresses without the $ sign) for Lois's grade. The formula bar will show the formula in F15 to be =C17*$B$9+D17*$B$10+E17*$B$11.

Mixed Addressing

There will be certain situations where you will want to combine relative and absolute addressing; that is, you will want to create a cell reference that is part relative and part absolute. Either the column letter or the row number remains constant.

For example, an address of $B21 means that absolute addressing will be used on the column portion of the address, but relative addressing will be used on the row portion. Conversely, an address of B$21 means that absolute addressing will be used on the row portion of the address, and relative addressing on the column portion. You will need to use relative, absolute, and mixed addressing throughout your *Solve it!* Spreadsheet Cases.

Formatting

Suppose you want to express the percentages in your Assumptions section as 50% rather than .5. You can change the format in which numeric information appears by using Excel's *Format Cells* commands.

First, select the cells you want to change by selecting the range *B9:B11*.

On the Home tab of the Ribbon, click Format and then click Format Cells to open the Format Cells dialog box. This box has six formatting tabs: *Number, Alignment, Font, Border, Fill*, and *Protection*. To change the format of numbers, select the Number tab. The *Category* list box displays the different types of numerical formats. Select *Percentage* in the *Category* list box. Type *0* into the *Decimal places* spin box, and click the *OK* button.

You should see the effects of this formatting on the three figures in the Assumptions area of the worksheet. They will be displayed as percentage figures: 15%, 35%, and 50%. Excel often provides shortcuts to frequently used commands and operations by allocating buttons on the Ribbon. In this case, Excel has a *Percent Style* button in the Number group on the Home tab. To format selected cell(s) with a percent style, you can simply press the *Percent Style* button:

The different Number categories listed on the Numbers tab of the Format Cells dialog box are:

10. *General* format is the default format for all new worksheets. With the General format, the values are displayed in their natural state. No suppression or compression of formatting is permitted. Scientific notation will be used to display numbers that are too large or too small to be displayed normally. The General format displays up to 11 digits.

11. *Number* format displays a fixed number of decimal places, negative values in red, negative values in brackets, and combinations of these characteristics.

12. *Currency* format places a dollar sign before each number and uses commas to separate hundreds from thousands, etc. There are options for zero or two decimal places, and for red or black negative values.

13. *Accounting* format displays four accounting formats, keeping the dollar sign to the left of the cell, showing negative values in brackets, and displaying zero values as hyphens.

14. *Date* format displays dates in a variety of different ways and can be used by Excel in mathematical calculations. Default date formats include:

    d/mm/yy   (Example 2/02/80)

d-mmm-yy	(Example 2-Feb-80)
d-mmm	(Example 2-Feb)
mmm-yy	(Example Feb-80)

To use date and time formats, you must use one of the Excel date and time functions (such as =DATE, =DATEVALUE, =TIME, =TIMEVALUE, or =NOW) to enter dates and times into your worksheet. Excel date functions will be treated in more detail in Spreadsheet Case 8. A date can also be entered as a label if it is not involved in any calculations.

15. *Time* formats can represent times in a number of formats where they can be used by Excel time functions in mathematical calculations.

16. *Percentage* format displays numbers as percentages. The default decimal places are zero and two.

17. *Fraction* format displays numbers as fractions, separating whole numbers and the fractional parts.

18. *Scientific* format displays data in exponential scientific notation.

19. *Text* format displays the values as labels rather than values.

20. *Special* format displays zip codes, zip codes + 4, phone numbers, and social security numbers.

21. *Custom* format can be used to create custom formats for numbers such as product codes.

Copy the final grade formula to the rest of the student entries. Add a column heading "FINAL GRADE" to cell F14, and match the formatting of cell F15 to the other cells in the row. Your worksheet should look like Figure 3-3.

Totaling the Values in a Range

This case requires totals of gross pay, net pay, and all deductions for the payroll register so that the employer can determine the total amount paid out for each of these categories during a particular pay period. The =SUM function of your spreadsheet software can help you do this. The =*SUM* function calculates the sum of all of the values in a specified range. The form of the =SUM function is:

=SUM(range)

For example, if you want to total the percentages in the Assumptions section of your sample worksheet to make sure they add up to 100 percent, you could use the =SUM function instead of the formula =B9+B10+B11. The values in range B9:B11 can be totalled much more easily by entering in cell B12:

=SUM(B9:B11)

Excel provides a shortcut for this formula: the *Sum Function* button $\boxed{\Sigma}$.

This button appears in the Editing group on the Home tab, and if clicked, the =SUM function will be placed in the current cell and a sample range will be assumed, typically above or to the left of the current cell. All you have to do is press [Enter] to complete the operation. Try the button as well as entering the function yourself. When entering the function, select the range to sum using the cursor keys or the mouse rather than typing the range. This tends to be easier and more accurate; typing is more prone to error.

Save COURSE.xlsx with the changes you made during this tutorial session. You will need it for subsequent Spreadsheet Cases.

Figure 3-3

Spreadsheet Case 3
Guardian Roofing Payroll

Problem:	Develop a payroll register
Management skills:	Organization
Excel skills:	Formulas
	Absolute and relative addressing
	Creating an Assumption Area for variables
File:	GUARDIAN_Q.xlsx

Guardian Roofing is a family-owned company in Lafayette, Louisiana, that produces roofing materials. It has 4,000 employees and an operating budget of $19,000,000. All employees except the eight members of the company's founding family are on the firm's automated payroll system. The family members are paid through a separate confidential payroll, which is processed manually because it contains highly sensitive information, such as salaries and bonuses. Like other salaried employees, they are paid monthly.

Timothy Schell, executive assistant to the founder, Jim Landry, is in charge of preparing this confidential payroll. He must make all of the calculations for salary changes, deductions, and net pay using a calculator. He then enters the results onto a Payroll Register sheet. A Payroll Register is a report prepared for each payroll period that lists the names, gross pay, deductions, and net pay of all employees, and the total gross pay, deductions, and net pay for that payroll period as well as the net amounts deducted and paid to date. Schell writes out the checks by hand.

This is a very time-consuming process that prevents Schell from fulfilling other responsibilities. Jim Landry would like to use his time more productively for coordinating meetings and managing correspondence. Also, there is a danger of miscalculations, which would incite the wrath of the family members. Landry and Schell would like to automate the process as much as possible while maintaining strict confidentiality.

Schell feels there are so few checks to write that this part of the process could remain manual. However, many hours could be saved if all of the payroll calculations and the preparation of the Payroll Register report could be automated.

Load GUARDIAN_Q.xlsx, which displays the names of the executive family members, their social security numbers, and annual salaries. You should develop a worksheet that creates a Payroll Register report for these employees. The worksheet should automatically calculate monthly gross pay, net pay, and all deductions. It should also provide totals for each of these categories for the current pay period and add this period's amounts to the year-to-date totals.

Monthly gross pay can be computed by dividing annual salary by 12. Federal withholding tax should be set to 26% of gross pay. State withholding tax should be set to 9% of gross pay. For the tax year 2009, FICA (the employee Social Security deduction) is 7.65% of the first $94,200 earned during the year. The Medicare deduction is 1.45% of gross pay for all wages earned during the tax year. Since this is the first pay period of 2009, FICA and Medicare deductions must be taken for all employees for this payroll. Group health insurance is $100 per month. All of these family members have elected to participate in a profit sharing plan to which they contribute 7.5% of their gross pay each month.

Tasks

There are five tasks to this problem:

1. Complete the column labels to include gross pay, all deductions, and net pay. Also, include a column for gross pay to date that will be used in future months.

2. Make all appropriate format changes for numbers and percentages. Columns containing numbers should be formatted to show two decimal places to the right of the decimal point.

3. Create an assumptions section for all deductions and other variables in the upper left of the worksheet and label it Assumptions. This way, you can easily make changes in deductions and formulas using the addressing function of spreadsheet software. By keeping all assumptions in a clearly defined assumptions section, you can make changes rapidly in the worksheet to respond to changing tax laws or other regulations. Listing variables also allows all assumptions to be clearly visible and reported.

4. Use formulas to calculate monthly gross pay, all deductions, and net pay. Be sure these formulas reference the appropriate cells in the assumptions section of your worksheet (e.g., $A$56) rather than actual values (e.g., 20%). Provide totals for gross pay, net pay, and each deduction category so that Schell can track the company's expenses for the pay period. Widen columns if necessary.

5. Print the spreadsheet on a single sheet. Include your name and today's date in the footer.

Additional Problems

1. The family members have decided to contribute 2% of their gross pay each month to the local United Charity Appeal. Modify the Payroll Register Worksheet to implement this plan.

2. The company feels it should be withholding 35% of gross pay for federal tax. Modify your worksheet to change the federal withholding tax deduction and print the new version.

Time Estimates

Expert: 30 minutes

Intermediate: 1 hour

Novice: 1.5 hours

There is no tutorial for this case because it uses skills introduced in earlier chapters.

Spreadsheet Case 4
Dabney Financial Services

Problem:	Analyze financial ratios
Management skills:	Decision Making
Excel skills:	Formulas
	Spreadsheet control
	Reporting
File:	DABNEY_Q.xlsx

Dabney Financial Services is a small-investment advising firm that has just opened in Des Moines, Iowa. It is trying to take market share from large brokerage houses by offering custom advice to clients on long-term investing, rather than recommending the stock-of-the-week strategy touted by its competitors. Dabney focuses on wealthy families and retirees who have financial assets to invest.

Clients may call or visit to seek expert advice about specific stocks in which they are interested. Estelle Tessier, a young pediatrician, has expressed interest in two firms in the drug retail sector, and she wants to know which one, if either, would be a good investment. These firms are CVS and Walgreens, both of which are listed on the New York Stock Exchange.

CVS Corporation operates in the retail drugstore industry in the United States with over 6,900 retail and specialty pharmacy stores in 44 states, the District of Columbia, and Puerto Rico. The company also does business online under the CVS.com name. It is a Fortune 500 company, and for 2008, sales of the CVS retail drugstore division were $13.8 billion.

The Walgreen Company is the nation's leading drugstore chain. Walgreens has 4953 stores in 45 states and Puerto Rico and also does business online. In 2008, sales were $4.2 billion.

To make sound recommendations, Dabney analysts must carefully examine a company's financial statements. The purpose of financial statements is to identify the major sources, uses, and flows of funds within an organization. The three principal financial statements used in business are income statements, balance sheets, and cash flow statements.

Income statements (also called operating statements) summarize the income, expenses, and profits of businesses for a specified period. The purpose of income statements is to show the profitability or unprofitability of firms during a specified period, usually a year, quarter, or month.

Balance sheets identify the assets, liabilities, and owners' (or shareholders') equity of a firm at a particular point in time. The difference between assets and liabilities is net worth or equity (literally what the organization is worth net of all other factors). Cash flow statements provide detailed information on total receipts and disbursements of cash. Cash flow statements are like checking account registers for individuals.

Certain financial ratios based on figures from financial statements have been traditionally used to assess a company's financial health and performance. There are 5 kinds of financial ratios that you can apply to assess the financial position of a firm.

1. Liquidity Ratios

Various liquidity ratios measure a firm's liquidity, its ability to draw on cash and other current assets to pay its financial obligations. Two commonly used liquidity ratios are the *current ratio* and the *quick ratio*, or *acid test*.

(a) Current Ratio = $\dfrac{\text{Current Assets}}{\text{Current Liabilities}}$

(b) Quick Ratio, or Acid Test = $\dfrac{\text{Current Assets - Inventory}}{\text{Current Liabilities}}$

The current ratio is the most commonplace measure of short-term solvency. If current liabilities are rising faster than current assets, this may be a harbinger of financial difficulty. The quick ratio measures the firm's ability to pay off short-term obligations without relying on the sale of inventory, which is the least liquid of the firm's current assets.

2. Asset Management Ratios

Another group of ratios measures how effectively a firm is managing its assets. One of these is the *total assets utilization ratio*, which measures the utilization or turnover of all of the firm's assets.

(c) Total assets utilization= $$\frac{\text{Sales}}{\text{Total Assets}}$$

3. Debt Management Ratios

These ratios determine the extent to which a firm uses debt financing. If equity, or owner-supplied funds, accounts for only a small portion of a firm's total financing, the risks of the firm are borne mainly by creditors. On the other hand, by raising funds through debt, owners can control the firm with a smaller investment of their own. If the firm returns more on the borrowed funds than it pays in interest, the return on the owner's capital is magnified, or leveraged. An important ratio is the *debt ratio*, which measures the percentage of a firm's total funds provided by creditors.

(d) Debt ratio = $$\frac{\text{Total Liabilities}}{\text{Total Assets}}$$

Creditors prefer low debt ratios, whereas it may be advantageous for owners to seek higher debt to leverage their money and earnings. However, a debt ratio that is too high signals trouble repaying loans and too much reliance on borrowed money to pay for the firm's operations.

4. Profitability ratios

Profitability ratios illustrate the combined effects of liquidity, asset management, and debt management on profits. Important profitability ratios measure the *return on total assets (ROA)*, the *return on common equity (ROE)*, or return on stockholders' investments, and the *profit margin on sales*.

(e) Return on Total Assets (ROA) = $$\frac{\text{Net profit after taxes}}{\text{Total assets}}$$

(f) Return on Equity (ROE) = $$\frac{\text{Net profit after taxes}}{\text{Net worth (equity)}}$$

(g) Profit Margin = $$\frac{\text{Net profit after taxes}}{\text{Sales}}$$

5. *Market Value ratios*

These ratios help indicate what investors think of the company's past performance and future prospects. The market value ratios (and stock price) will be high if a firm has strong liquidity, asset management, debt management, and profitability ratios. The most widely used market value ratio is the *price/earnings ratio*.

(h) Price/Earnings Ratio = $\dfrac{\text{Price per share}}{\text{Earnings per share}}$

To evaluate a firm's financial ratios properly, you must compare its ratios to ratios for comparable businesses. You can find financial ratio data on comparable businesses in publications like Dun and Bradstreet's *Industry Norms & Key Business Ratios* and Robert Morris's *Annual Statement Studies*. Both publications group businesses and provide financial ratio data classified by standardized industry classification codes.

Tasks

There are five tasks in this case:

1. Examine the 2008 income statements and balance sheets of CVS and Walgreens, which can be found by loading the file DABNEY_Q.xlsx. All data are based on the publicly available 2008 annual Form 10K reports of these firms. You can find the 10K reports either at the EDGAR database maintained by the Securities and Exchange Commission (www.sec.gov) or from the firms' Web sites (usually in a section called Investor Relations).

2. Print out the financial statements so you have a hard copy to work with. Review them very closely.

3. Assign range names to the balance sheet and income data that will be used to calculate the financial data. Create a table of range names below the worksheet. Format the ranges with the income statement and balance sheet data to display a comma with one decimal place. Format the ranges with the financial ratios, earnings per share, and stock price to display two decimal places.

4. Calculate the eight financial ratios outlined above for each company at the end of the financial statements. Print out the ratios for both companies.

5. In a single paragraph, write an analysis of both companies. Based on the information provided in this case, is each firm financially sound? Which would make the better investment? Review the financial statements of both companies for any items that might help explain their financial position.

Additional Problems

1. Obtain the current stock price for each of these companies and recalculate the Price/Earnings ratio.

2. Use a search engine on the Web to get additional information on these companies from their home sites and also from two financial sites that cover these stocks. Some good sources are Hoover's (www.hoovers.com), Google Finance (finance.google.com), and Yahoo Finance (finance.yahoo.com). How do professional analysts feel about investing in these companies? Do you agree?

Time Estimates

Expert:	45 minutes
Intermediate:	1 hour
Novice:	1.5 hours

Excel Tutorial for Spreadsheet Case 4

You do not need to use range names for the solution to this case, but you may choose to use them when you use different formats for different ranges in your worksheet.

In COURSE.xlsx, name the range with the student grade data as GRADES. Also name each of the cells holding the percentages.

Naming Ranges

You can name a range the with the *Define Name* command. To name the range of student grades as GRADES, highlight the cells from C16:F19, open the Formulas tab on the Ribbon, and click

Define Name in the Defined Names group. This opens the New Name dialog box with the percentage range reference already inserted into the *Refers to* text box. Type the name *GRADES* in the Name text box and click the *OK* Button.

You can alternatively click the *Define Name* button, select the range once within the dialog box, and type the name. Use either procedure to name cell B9 *Quiz*, cell B10 *Midterm*, and cell B11 *Final_Exam*.

Creating a Table of Range Names

You can document your range names in a table in your worksheet using the *Use in Formula>Paste Names* command. Place the table in an unused portion of the worksheet where it will not overlay any data. The spreadsheet design principles introduced in Chapter 2 suggest placing the range name table below the left-most portion of the worksheet. For the table's column heads, type RANGES into cell A22 and ADDRESSES into cell B22. Copy cell A15 into cells A23 and B23.Now, to create the range name table, click inside cell A24. On the Formulas tab on the Ribbon, in the Defined Names group, click *Use in Formula* and then click the *Paste Names* command. The Paste Name dialog box opens listing the named ranges.

The purpose of this dialog box is to paste a selected name in the formula bar. However, we are using the alternative purpose of the dialog box—pasting a list of range names and their references onto the worksheet. To do this, click the *Paste List* button. Your worksheet should resemble Figure 3-4. The pasted list of range names is static, so if you add or delete range names, you will have to paste the list again. Also, be careful that the pasted list does not overlay existing data.

Figure 3-4

	A	B	C	D	E	F	G	H	I	J	K
1	This worksheet is a course list of students and grades										
2	File name:	F: UCNET / BIOLOGY / TJONES / COURSE.XLS									
3	Author:	Prof Tom Jo	Date:	6/28/2009							
4	Ranges:	None	Macros:	None							
5											
6											
7	ASSUMPTIONS										
8	=============										
9	Quiz	15%									
10	Midterm	35%									
11	Final Exam	50%									
12											
13											
14	FIRST NAME	LAST NAME	QUIZ	MIDTERM	FINAL	FINAL GRADE					
15	===============	===========	====								
16	Heather	Smith	66	82	85	81.1					
17	Lois	Mendez	77	85	93	87.8					
18	Michael	Johnson	91	93	96	94.2					
19	Erica	Antonio	68	75	72	72.45					
20											
21											
22	RANGES	ADDRESSES									
23	===========	===========									
24	Final_Exam	=Sheet1!$B$11									
25	GRADES	=Sheet1!$C$16:$F$19									
26	Midterm	=Sheet1!$B$10									
27	Quiz	=Sheet1!$B$9									
28											

Spreadsheet Case 5

The Town of Clintwood

Problem:	Prepare a budget for a small municipality
Management skills:	Planning
	Decision Making
Excel skills:	Formulas
	Spreadsheet control
	Reporting
File:	CLINTWOOD_Q.xlsx

The town of Clintwood has a population of 6,108 and is located in McDowell County, West Virginia. Each November, Curtis Brown, the town manager, works with the Mayor and the Board of Trustees to develop the town's budget for the forthcoming year. The town's main source of revenue is the local property tax, but it also receives some aid from the state government and some revenue from miscellaneous licenses and fees.

The town leaders want to hold to their campaign promises of raising taxes by only 4%. Their community has become very environmentally-conscious, and they do not want to encourage new businesses that would add to the traffic congestion or pollute the air. They fear revenues may be declining because the state of West Virginia is facing severe financial problems and wants to cut the state aid it provides to local governments.

Curtis Brown wants to develop a budget that can be supported by anticipated revenues. Anticipating continued cutbacks in state aid, Brown would like to develop preliminary budgets for the next two years. That way he can plan ahead if major changes are required. If planned expenditures exceed revenues, Brown, the Mayor, and the Trustees must develop an alternative budget that is balanced. Can they develop a balanced budget without raising local property taxes?

Load the file CLINTWOOD_Q.xlsx, showing the actual receipts and disbursements for the Town of Clintwood in 2008. Brown wants to use this budget as the basis for projecting the town budget for the next two years.

One way to analyze a budget is to estimate the amount of each category of cash receipts and disbursements. The projected outflow of funds is subtracted from the projected inflow. If the amount of outflow is greater than the amount of inflow, the town must secure additional funds to pay for its expenditures or it must reduce its spending. For instance, the town could raise taxes or borrow money to meet its costs, or it could reduce some of its expenses.

In projecting the next two years' budgets, Brown wants to use the following assumptions: He expects the state will reduce its aid to the town by 6% each year. Historically, expenditures for employee salaries and benefits have been rising 13% annually. He expects all other expenditures to rise at a rate of 6% annually and miscellaneous receipts to rise 5% annually. The town's expenditure for debt service to pay off previous loans will remain constant. Can the town balance its budget if it keeps its promise not to raise taxes beyond 4% or go further into debt?

Tasks:

There are five tasks in this case:

1. Print out and review CLINTWOOD_Q.xlsx.

2. Create an Assumptions section of the worksheet to identify factors in your calculations of receipts and disbursements. Make sure formulas reference cells in the Assumptions section wherever possible.

3. Calculate the receipts and disbursements for each of the categories on the worksheet for 2009 and 2010. Calculate total receipts and total disbursements. The case has been simplified so that all revenue is collected in the year it is due.

4. Complete the worksheet by subtracting total receipts from total disbursements in 2009 and 2010. Print the results.

5. Write a brief analysis of the projected 2009 and 2010 budgets for the town of Clintwood. If these budgets don't balance, what steps would you recommend be taken by the town? Revise your worksheet to incorporate your recommendations, save it under another name, and print it out again. Keep revising the worksheet until you have developed a balanced budget. Is there some way for the town to come up with a balanced budget without raising taxes?

Additional Problem

1. What if state aid is not reduced but instead increases by 5% for the next two years? What impact would this have on the budget? Revise your worksheet and save it under a different name. Print out and analyze the results.

Time Estimates

Expert:	30 minutes
Intermediate:	1 hour
Novice:	1.5 hours

There is no tutorial for this case because it uses skills introduced in earlier chapters.

Spreadsheet Case 6
Badger Jams

Problem:	Develop a breakeven analysis model for a start-up venture
Management skills:	Planning Decision Making
Excel skills:	Formulas Graphics Worksheet organization
File:	BADGERJAMS_Q.xlsx

Badger Jams, Inc. is a newly formed, one-person company located in Badger, Minnesota, that produces organic jams and spreads from local ingredients. The jams and spreads are packaged in traditional jelly jars with hand-drawn labels. Its founder, Pat Lindstrom, has arranged to sell this new collection of spreads in a network of organic food stores and supermarkets, as well as local tourist shops. Lindstrom believes that a huge demand for natural homemade style products makes this a promising business opportunity.

Before Lindstrom invests heavily in advertising, cooking equipment, warehouse rental, and office space, he must know if there is a future for this type of business and at what point he can expect it to produce a profit. Lindstrom has not done any formal market research, but he would like to sell each twelve-pack of jars to retailers for a wholesale price of $39.95.

This is a classic problem for all businesses—determining what objectives they must meet to produce a profit or to minimize losses. What Lindstrom must do is utilize the managerial accounting concept of breakeven analysis. *Breakeven analysis* establishes the *breakeven point*, which is the number of units that Lindstrom must sell to yield no profit and incur no loss. Any units sold beyond the breakeven point will represent profit, and a sales volume below the breakeven point will put the firm at a loss.

To perform breakeven analysis, a company must examine its operating costs. Some of these costs are fixed and do not change over the range of the operations activity regardless of how many units of an item the company produces or sells. Variable costs, on the other hand, increase as production increases and decrease as production decreases.

In the case of Badger Jams, Inc., fixed costs are Lindstrom's rent for a large office-storage-preparation area ($12,000 per year), the cost of a commercial stove ($7,200), the cost of large cooking equipment, such as bowls, pots, and sterilizers ($950), and the cost of an initial advertising campaign ($5,550). Lindstrom's variable costs are the cost of supplies like fruit, sugar, jars, packaging, and shipping. Lindstrom has calculated that the cost of preparing and packaging each twelve-pack of jars is $15.60 and the cost of shipping each package is $1.95. He has decided not to pay himself a salary right away. Until the business starts producing a profit, he plans to live off his savings, which amount to $64,000.

Once a product's costs have been determined, the contribution margin per unit must be calculated. The contribution margin per unit is the difference between the selling price per unit and the variable costs per unit. (The contribution margin per unit = average selling price per unit - variable costs per unit.) Once the contribution margin per unit has been determined, one can then calculate the breakeven point. In a company such as Badger Jams, Inc., which produces only a few products, the formula for the breakeven point would be calculated by dividing the total fixed costs by the contribution margin per unit.

Often the best way to display the results of breakeven analysis is in graphic form. It is also useful to use breakeven analysis to generate pro forma income statements that convert unit data to dollars and display projected sales revenue.

Tasks:

There are four tasks in this case:

1. Load the data file BADGERJAMS_Q.xlsx. Create a worksheet that displays the total fixed cost and the total variable cost per unit for one package of jam from Badger Jams, Inc. Calculate the contribution margin per unit and the breakeven point. Include an

Assumptions section that identifies variable factors used in calculations. Assign range names to the variables to be used in the calculations.

2. Use your results to generate pro forma income statements using the framework supplied on the data file. A pro forma income statement is a projection of future incomes, not actual incomes earned. Include two projections of sales and income below the breakeven point and two above it. Include a projection of sales and income right at the breakeven point. The income data below the breakeven point should reflect zero sales and sales at half of the breakeven units. The income data at the breakeven point should reflect sales at 1.0 times the breakeven units. The income data above the breakeven point should reflect sales at 1.5 and 2.0 times the breakeven units.

3. Create a line chart (graph) to display the most important data from the pro forma income statements and the breakeven point. The X-axis of the chart should display the range, indicating units sold in your pro forma income statements. The first data series should display fixed cost (which will be constant). The second data series should display total cost figures. The third data series should display revenue figures. Give your chart (graph) a title, and supply titles for the X and Y axes. Supply legends for all of the data series. The point on the chart where the data lines for total cost and revenue intersect is the breakeven point.

4. Be sure to name and save your chart as well as your worksheet. Print both the chart and the worksheet including your name in the footer. Examine your output. Write a one-paragraph statement analyzing the results of the breakeven analysis. Is Badger Jams, Inc. a worthwhile business venture for Lindstrom?

Additional Problem

1. Lindstrom has been told that the cost of the glass jar will rise 7% in a few weeks. Jars account for approximately 15% of the baking and packaging cost for each case shipped. What impact will this have on Lindstrom's breakeven analysis?

Time Estimates

Expert: 45 minutes

Intermediate: 1 hour

Novice: 2 hours

Excel Tutorial for Spreadsheet Case 6

This case draws upon all of the skills acquired in previous Spreadsheet Cases, plus new skills for creating and printing graphs, or charts as they are known in Excel. You will need to use COURSE.xlsx again for this tutorial.

Creating Charts with Excel

Excel provides excellent functions for generating charts to graphically display data on your worksheets. An Excel chart can be stored on a separate sheet or it can be embedded in the same worksheet as the data. With the chart embedded in the worksheet, you can instantly observe the effects of changing the data in the worksheet. The steps to achieve each of these graphs are identical.

We want to graph the grades of each test for every student. It is easier to select the range containing the data before selecting the Insert Chart command. Select the range *A16:F19*. This range contains the values representing the students' final grades as well as the students' names and their test grades. Open the Insert tab on the Ribbon. In the Charts group are 7 button commands for adding different types of charts: Column charts, Line charts, Pie charts, Bar charts, Area charts, Scatter charts, and Other (Stock, Surface, Doughnut, Bubble, and Radar).

Different types of charts emphasize different qualities or aspects of data, so it is important to choose the right chart type for the data and for your purposes. Displaying comparisons among different elements or changes over time are two of the most common uses of charts.

The most important chart types are:

Major Excel Chart Types

- The **Area Chart** shows each data series as a shaded area, each added onto the previous area.

- The **Bar Chart** shows the values as solid horizontal bars of differing lengths. This type is ideally suited to categorized data.

- The **Column Chart** is similar to the Bar Chart except that the bars are vertically aligned. Again, this type is ideally suited to categorized data.

- The **Line Chart** shows trends and values, typically over a time horizon at even intervals, representing each series as points connected by a line.

- The **Pie Chart** shows values as a proportion of a whole or total. The values are represented as a slice of a circular pie. This is only used when there is a single data series.

- The **Scatter Chart** shows the degree of a relationship between the numeric values on both the X and Y axes for several data series. This chart type is useful since it represents data with uneven intervals on the axes.

Click the *Line* button on the Ribbon to open a menu of options. The options include various types of line charts, some with 3-D visual effects. Hover the mouse over the types of line charts to view their Screen Tips, which explain more about each type of chart and how it is best used. Click *Line with Markers* to create this type of chart using the selected worksheet data.

Excel automatically recognizes the first and last names of the students as labels and creates a chart with a legend distinguishing each student. The chart is inserted over the selected data. At the same time, three Chart Tools tabs, specific to working with charts, display on the Ribbon: Design, Layout, and Format. The Design tab contains commands for working with the chart as a whole: changing the type of chart, selecting the data it is based on, the basic chart layout and style used. The Layout tab includes commands for modifying the layout of the chart: whether or not to hide elements, such as labels, axes, background, etc.; and the Format tab contains commands for applying styles: colors, fills, and more to chart elements and text.

To move the chart to its own sheet, click *Move Chart* in the Location group on the Chart Tools: Design tab. This opens the Move Chart dialog box. Select the *New sheet* option, leave the default sheet name of *Chart 1*, and click the *OK* button. This creates a new sheet entitled *Chart 1* in your workbook that displays just the chart.

Notice the Chart1 tab at the bottom of the screen. This is where the newly created chart is stored. To move between the chartsheet and the worksheet, simply click the respective tab at the bottom of the screen.

Graph Formatting

Excel provides extensive features for formatting objects within charts. Although the Insert Chart command has produced an attractive chart, further enhancements can be made to improve some of its aspects. You can select virtually any object in an Excel chart and adjust its features. You can select objects in a chart using the arrow keys to step through each of the objects that can be changed or simply select the object with the mouse.

Objects that can be selected are: Axis (X and Y), Axis Title, Chart Title, Chart Area, Plot Area, Data Series, Data Point, Legend, Legend Key, Legend Entry, and <Chart Type> Group.

Once the object is selected, you can choose open the Format tab and click the Shape Styles dialog box launcher to open the Format <Object> dialog box. Alternatively, you can right-click an object and select the Format <Object> command on the shortcut menu to open this dialog box.

The *Format <Object>* dialog box contains different tabs for adjusting different aspects of the object.

For example, select the Y axis by clicking on it. A gray outline, with circles at each corner and small squares along each side appears to indicate the object is selected. Open the Format tab on the Ribbon. In the Shape Styles group, click the Shape Styles dialog box launcher on the Ribbon. This opens the Format Axis dialog box, which contains tabbed sections. The tabs displayed depend on the object selected: The tabs for the Format Axis dialog box are Axis Options, Number, Fill, Line Color, Line Style, Shadow, 3-D Format, and Alignment.

Select the Axis Options tab. The settings here permit you to change the minimum value, the maximum value, the major interval value, and the minor interval value (unit) of the axis. Other settings also let you specify where the X axis crosses, whether the scale is logarithmic, whether the values appear in reverse order, and whether the X axis crosses at the maximum value.

Currently the graph has all the data points congregating at the top of the chart. It would be preferable for the data to be spread more evenly up the chart. To do this, we would adjust the minimum value of the Y axis to 60. To do so, first select the *Fixed* radio button beside Minimum. This permits manual entry of fixed values. Now enter *60* in the Minimum value text box and click the *Close* button. Your chart should now resemble that in Figure 3-5.

Figure 3-5

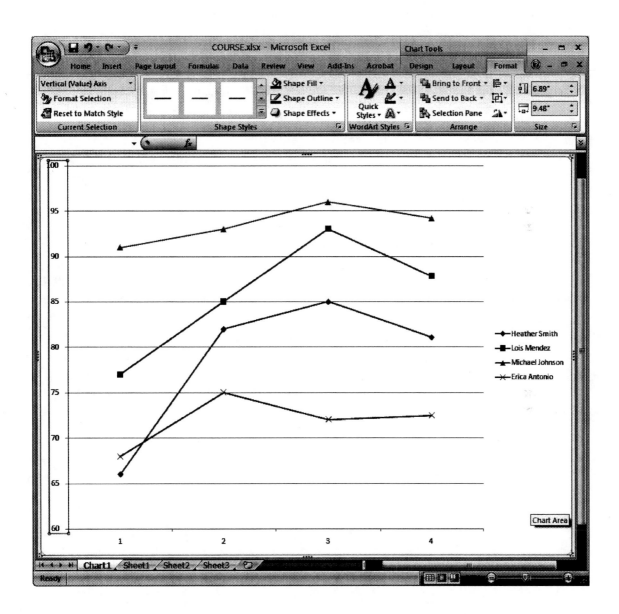

Other tabs used in Format <Object> dialog boxes include:

- **Number:** Lets you change the presentation of values
- **Fill:** Lets you apply a fill (interior color or pattern) to an object
- **Alignment:** Lets you change the arrangement and orientation of objects
- **Border (or Line) color:** Lets you apply and modify object borders or lines
- **Border (or Line) styles:** Lets you modify the style (width, dashes, arrow settings, etc.) of borders or lines
- **Shadow:** Lets you apply and modify a shadow effect
- **3-D Format:** Lets you apply and modify a 3-D effect
- **Marker Options/Fill/Line Color/Style:** Lets you format and modify the type of marker or icon used for data points

Embedding a Chart in a Worksheet

All the features discussed for a chart in a separate chartsheet apply equally to a chart embedded in a worksheet. Charts are embedded by default in the worksheet when they are created.

You can move a separate chart back to its worksheet by clicking *Move Chart* on the Chart Tools: Design tab and selecting *Object in* in the Move Chart dialog box. Do so now to move the chart back to Sheet 1. When you do so, the workbook opens Sheet 1 with the chart selected. You can tell that the chart is selected, or active, because of the pale blue border around the chart. At the corners and along the sides of this border are three dots, indicating places at which you can drag the border to increase or decrease the size of the chart. A selected chart can be seen in Figure 3-6.

Figure 3-6

When a chart is deselected, the blue border disappears and is replaced by a thin border. To select an embedded chart, simply place the mouse pointer over the chart and click the left mouse button. To resize the chart, grab the border at one of the sizing locations (with the three dots) and drag it in the desired direction. To move the chart, grab the selected chart anywhere inside the border and drag to the new location. To delete the selected chart, simply press the [DEL] or [Delete] key. Use the Move Chart command to move the chart back to a separate sheet titled Chart1.

Printing and Saving a Chart

Excel chartsheets can be printed in exactly the same way as Excel worksheets can as described in the Tutorial for Spreadsheet Case 1. The *Print Preview* and *Page Setup* operations apply in the same way as for a worksheet also.

A chart is saved when the workbook in which it resides is saved, as described in the Tutorial for Spreadsheet Case 1.

Spreadsheet Case 7
Hardware Nuts

Problem:	Develop an inventory control system
Management skills:	Organizing Controlling
Excel skills:	Spreadsheet control Logical functions
File:	HARDWARENUTS_Q.xlsx

Hardware Nuts, Inc. in Chico, California, wholesales small hardware items like bolts, nuts, and washers to local builders and contractors. The hardware business is highly competitive, but Hardware Nuts has acquired a long list of clients by always stocking high quality items within the budgetary limits specified by clients.

Because the company is relatively new, Tim Kokura, the general manager, has been tracking the supplies kept in inventory by using a traditional, manual ledger sheet. This process is time-consuming, and errors have sometimes resulted in missed production deadlines due to inadequate inventory. In response, Kokura has increased the level of safety stock to avoid running out in the future. This increase, however, raises operating costs, and Hardware Nuts needs to keep these down to remain competitive. Kokura has decided to implement his own inventory control system using a PC and spreadsheet software.

To ensure efficient use of funds, a good inventory control system will maintain an inventory level that is neither overstocked nor understocked. It will match existing inventory levels against desired levels so that understocked items can be reordered.

There are two basic models for accomplishing this. The first is to use a *reorder level system*, which merely ensures that required items are ordered with sufficient lead time to arrive when needed in the production process. The second is to use a system that determines the least expensive quantity to order, or most economic quantity. This approach, based on the *economic order quantity model*, strikes a balance between carrying costs (e.g., taxes and insurance) and procurement costs (e.g., ordering, shipping, and receiving costs).

Ordering in large quantities reduces procurement costs, but it also raises carrying costs. The *economic order quantity* represents the number of units where procurement costs equal carrying costs. The exact size of the economic order quantity depends upon the estimated amount of the product needed each year, its unit cost, the fixed cost of placing and receiving an order for the item, and the carrying cost for the item in inventory, expressed as a percentage of inventory value. The formula for calculating an item's economic order quantity is:

$$EOQ = \sqrt{(2FU/CP)}$$

where:

- EOQ = the item's economic order quantity
- F = the fixed cost of ordering the item
- U = the amount of the product needed each year
- C = the item's carrying cost, expressed as a percentage of inventory value
- P = the item's unit cost

The calculation of the economic order quantity often results in a fractional amount that must be rounded to the next whole number to determine the economic order quantity.

Load the data file HARDWARENUTS_Q.xlsx. This file contains a list of items that Hardware Nuts keeps in its warehouses, the balance on hand, the balance on order, unit cost per item, estimated annual usage per item, and the order point. The order point is the number of units of an item in inventory that triggers the decision to order more items. There is usually a lead time period (for example, two weeks) between the time an order is placed and the time it is actually fulfilled. Reordering while some inventory is still in stock reduces the possibility of an out-of-stock situation.

Assume that the order cost is a fixed cost of $115.00 for all items in this problem. Also, assume that the inventory carrying cost is 25% of the inventory value for all items in this problem.

Tasks:

There are four tasks in this case:

1. Above the table of data, insert rows to hold Assumptions for carrying costs and order costs.

2. Add the following columns to the worksheet to track:

a. *Balance Available* that can be calculated by adding balance on hand + balance on order

b. *Order Quantity* for those items in need of reordering; if the balance available is less than the order point, calculate the economic order quantity. If the balance available is greater than the order point, put a zero in the column for order quantity. Use the =IF and the =SQRT functions, and be sure to use absolute cell references when referring to the fixed and carrying costs.

3. Develop a method for identifying any stock items that need reordering on the worksheet. (**Hint:** One way is to add a column containing a formula to print an asterisk next to needed stock items.)

4. Write a short paragraph suggesting some enhancements to this application to make it a better management tool.

Time Estimates

Expert:	1 hour
Intermediate:	1.5 hours
Novice:	2 hours

Excel Tutorial for Spreadsheet Case 7

This case draws upon all of the skills acquired in previous Spreadsheet Cases, as well as new skills for using the logical functions of your spreadsheet software and the =SQRT function. You will once again need to use COURSE.xlsx for this tutorial.

Excel includes a set of logical functions that enable the software to perform conditional tests and evaluate a condition in your worksheet. Depending on whether the condition is true or false, different values will be returned to cells.

The most important conditional function in Excel is =IF. The =IF function enables you to test one or more conditions in your worksheet and perform different tasks depending on the outcome of the test. The form for the =IF function is:

=IF(condition, action if true, action if false)

This formula tests the *condition* to determine if specific results or cell contents are true or false. The *action if true* portion contains specific instructions to execute if the result of the test is true. The *action if false* portion contains another set of instructions to execute if the result is false. The instructions to be executed can return cell contents that are labels as well as values.

To perform conditional tests, the =IF function and other conditional functions require logical operators. These operators help establish the relationship between two numbers, strings, or cell references.

Logical Operators	
Operator	**Meaning**
=	Equal
<	Less than
>	Greater than
<=	Less than or equal to
>=	Greater than or equal to
<>	Not equal

To establish relationships between two or more conditional tests, Excel provides Logical Functions.

Logical Functions	Description
AND (*logical1, logical2, ...*)	Returns TRUE if each *logical* condition is true; returns FALSE otherwise
OR (*logical1, logical2, ...*)	Returns TRUE if any *logical* condition is true; returns FALSE otherwise
NOT (*logical*)	Returns TRUE if *logical* is FALSE; returns FALSE otherwise
TRUE()	Returns TRUE always
FALSE()	Returns FALSE always

The logical functions NOT, AND, and OR contain conditional tests to result in a single TRUE or FALSE. The following are examples of logical statements using =IF, using the logical operators, and using the logical functions:

=IF(A5>20,B5,0) means that if the value in cell A5 is greater than 20, you will use the value in cell B5. Otherwise, assign the number zero.

=IF(AND(B11<>0,G11=1),10,0) means that if the value in cell B11 is not equal to zero and the value in cell G11 equals 1, you will assign the number 10. Otherwise, assign the number 0.

=IF(OR(E13="Profit",F15>=G15),"Surplus","Deficit") means that if either cell E13 contains the label "Profit" or the contents of cell F15 are greater or equal to the contents of cell G15, you will assign the label "Surplus". Otherwise, assign the label "Deficit".

The second and third examples just above show that logical functions can have more than a single condition as the =IF conditional test.

For your student roster, you can develop a conditional test to print an asterisk (*) after the name of any student whose final grade is less than 80. In cell G16, add a formula that will examine the student's final grade. If the grade is less than 80, an asterisk will appear in the cell next to the final grade. If the grade is greater than or equal to 80, a character string consisting of a blank

space will be placed in the cell. The formula for this would be as follows:
=IF(F16<80,"*"," ")

Copy this formula into range G17:G19. Observe on your screen and in Figure 3-7 that the final grade for Erica Antonio will be followed by an asterisk. The final grades for the other students will be left blank.

Figure 3-7

The =SQRT Function

The =SQRT function is one of a series of functions that perform mathematical, statistical, and trigonometric operations. The =SQRT function calculates the square root of a positive number. The form of this function is:

=SQRT(number or cell reference)

For example the square root of the average of Heather Smith's quiz and midterm grades would be =SQRT((C14+D14)/2)

You do not need to save COURSE.xlsx with the modifications you made during this tutorial session.

Inserting Functions

Excel provides a facility that makes it easier to retrieve or enter functions. You can activate it by pressing the *Insert Function* button on the Formula tab of the Ribbon, located in the Function Library group of commands.

Press the *Insert Function* button now. This will display the Insert Function dialog box. Select the function that you want to use. In the *Search for a function* text box, you can enter a question describing what you want to do. Otherwise, you can use the *Or select a category* list box to select a major category of formulas (e.g., Financial, Statistical, Logical, etc.). For example, if you want the IF function, select *Logical* from the *Or select a category* list box, and then scroll down the list in the *Select a function* list box until IF appears.

Select *IF*, and then press the *OK* button to open the Function Arguments dialog box. In this second and final dialog box, you type your logical test in the top box, your desired output for a true result in the middle box, and your desired output for a false result in the bottom box. When you have completed the Function Arguments dialog box, click the *OK* button to close the dialog box and enter the desired formula in the selected cell.

Nested functions use a function as one of the arguments within another function. (Arguments are the values that functions use to perform operations or calculations.) To create a nested function, follow the same general procedure as described above for creating a formula with the IF function.

First, click in the cell where you want to place a formula. Second, open the Insert Function dialog box and select your desired function. Third, enter the arguments required for the nested function and then click *OK* to close the dialog box.

When entering arguments for nested functions, you can type the desired cell references into the relevant text boxes in the Function Arguments dialog box. However, to avoid typographic errors, click the *Collapse Dialog* button at the right end of an argument's text box to collapse the large dialog box to a small rectangular one and then do the following: (a) Select the worksheet cell(s) needed to create the first part of your formula. (b) Click the *Expand Dialog* button at the right end of the small dialog box to return to the Function Arguments dialog box. (c) Tab to the second argument box, collapse the dialog box, select the desired cells for that part of the formula, and re-expand the dialog box. (d) When you have filled in all the required argument boxes in the Function Arguments dialog box, click *OK* to close it.

Spreadsheet Case 8
Action Plastics

Problem:	Develop an employee benefits billing reconciliation program
Management skills:	Organizing Controlling
Excel skills:	Nested functions Spreadsheet control
File:	ACTIONPLASTICS_Q.xlsx

Action Plastics, Inc., located in Cincinnati, Ohio, manufactures plastic parts for the toy industry. Action Plastics sells these specialized parts to toy manufacturers for incorporation into their products. Action Plastics is a subsidiary of a multinational corporation that has its headquarters in Mumbai, India, its manufacturing plants in India, the United States, and Taiwan, and its sales offices in India and the United States. The corporation employs more than 8,000 people worldwide. Action Plastics, Inc., employs 340 people and has annual revenues of $46,600,000.

Each subsidiary location is in charge of the selection and administration of health insurance benefits for its employees. Health insurance premiums are tiered by the number of dependents insured under each employee. Action Plastics pays for the cost of health insurance premiums for each employee, and employees must contribute to the cost of dependent care.

Daniel Lehman is responsible for reconciling the monthly insurance invoice issued by Action Plastic's health insurance provider, Zeitgeist Healthcare. Each month, he must add new employees and delete terminated ones. He must also ensure that the total amount billed from Zeitgeist matches his records. Lehman has been processing the invoice manually and has encountered an increasing number of discrepancies over the past few billing cycles. He spends a considerable amount of time going through the invoice employee-by-employee, trying to rectify the difference between the invoice issued by Zeitgeist and his own records.

His boss, Ria Pradit, has suggested that Lehman automate the billing reconciliation process by creating a spreadsheet that automatically calculates the monthly premium based on the number of dependents each employee insures. The rates for insurance year 2008 are: $240 for 0 dependents (employee only), $312 for 1 dependent (employee plus 1 spouse or child), and $440 for 2 or more dependents (employee plus 2 or more dependents).

Action Plastics pays for the employee portion ($240) of the health insurance premium, while the employee is responsible for the dependent portion through a payroll deduction. Lehman must inform Payroll if an employee is responsible for a portion of his or her health insurance premium so it can be deducted monthly from the employee's paycheck. His spreadsheet must also include this amount.

Load the file ACTIONPLASTICS_Q.xlsx. It has employee names and the number of dependents they insure. Lehman will use this data, as well as additional data listing new hires and terminations for the month, to calculate the monthly insurance cost. He will also calculate the amount of payroll deductions for the month.

Tasks

There are four tasks in this case:

1. Add the heading *Premium* to the headings row and create a formula that will calculate the amount of premium based on the number of dependents. (**Hint:** This formula is comprised of nested IF functions.) Since premiums usually rise annually, remember to use absolute addressing in the formula.

2. Add two more employees: Devonne Jackson and Pavan Kumar. Devonne has a husband and two daughters she wants to cover under Action Plastic's insurance, and Pavan wants to insure his wife.

3. Add the heading *Emp Contribution* (Employee Contribution) to the headings row and create a formula that will calculate the amount of premium for which each employee is responsible.

4. Sort the data in order by Number of Dependents and then by Employee Last Name.

Time Estimates

Expert: `	1 hour
Intermediate:	1.5 hours
Novice:	2 hours

Excel Tutorial for Spreadsheet Case 8

As discussed in Tutorial for Spreadsheet Case 7, nested functions use a function as one of the arguments within another function. You do not have to use distinct functions when you nest. You can also nest the same function. In this tutorial, we will discuss how you can nest the IF function to create powerful functions that display a range of variables.

Let's review the structure of the IF function. The form for the =IF function is:

=IF(condition, action if true, action if false)

This formula tests the *condition* to determine if specific results or cell contents are true or false. The *action if true* portion contains specific instructions to execute if the result of the test is true. The *action if false* portion contains another set of instructions to execute if the result is false. The instructions to be executed can return cell contents that are labels as well as values.

Up to seven IF functions can be nested as *value_if_true* and *value_if_false* arguments to construct more elaborate tests. For this tutorial, we will be nesting four functions to calculate the letter grade of each student.

Notice that the simple IF statement uses parentheses in its argument:

=IF(condition, action if true, action if false)

When you create a nested IF statement, you must use everything in this argument except the closing parenthesis and the equal sign. A sample nested IF argument would look like this:

=IF(condition, action if true, action if false, IF(condition, action if true, action if false, IF(condition, action if true, action if false, IF(condition, action if true, action if false)))

Notice that the end of the argument contains all of the closing parentheses for each of the nested arguments.

In this tutorial, we will use the COURSE.xlsx file. We have previously calculated the numerical value of the final grade as the FINAL GRADE column. Now we will calculate the final grade as a letter grade. The breakdown of the letter grades is as follows:

A	90 – 100 points
B	80 – 89 points
C	70 – 79 points
D	60 – 69 points
F	< 60 points

In cell G14, create a heading called *LETTER GRADE*, and below it insert separator marks as in cells A15 through F15. Clear the contents of cells G16 through G19. In cell G16, type in the following formula:

=IF(F16>90,"A",IF(F16>80,"B",IF(F16>70,"C",IF(F16>60,"D","F"))))

Use the Fill Handle to copy the formula into cells G17 through G19. Your spreadsheet should look like Figure 3-8. Save COURSE.xlsx with the changes you made during this tutorial session. You will need it for the next Spreadsheet Case.

Solve it!

Figure 3-8

Spreadsheet Case 9
Karma Digital

Problem:	Determine a relationship between defects and production volume
Management skills:	Controlling Planning
Excel skills:	Regression analysis Graphics
File:	KARMADIGITAL_Q.xlsx

Karma Digital in Albuquerque, New Mexico, is a medium-sized DVD replicating company. Karma Digital has been able to take advantage of a growing market, and its business has expanded dramatically. Since opening fifteen years ago, the company has doubled its workforce and more than quadrupled its production.

Karma Digital's customers are radio program syndicators and small recording companies. Many defective DVDs go undetected until people try to use them. Karma Digital's customers feel that any incidence of defects threatens their reputation and credibility, and has set high quality standards to ensure their viability in the marketplace.

A zero defect rate is an impossibility, but Karma Digital management has mandated a rate below one defective DVD per ten thousand. Unfortunately, Karma Digital's defect rate has been steadily rising. Silvana Sandoval, Karma Digital's Quality Control Supervisor, wonders if the rise in defects comes from the company's growth and increased production volume.

To meet production demand, Karma Digital has had to double its labor force. Its recent recruits tend to be fresh out of high school or job retraining programs. Karma Digital's own internal training has been minimal because many of its positions, such as pressers and packagers, do not involve special technical skills. Sandoval feels many workers do not pay close attention to quality control procedures, nor do they operate equipment as carefully as they should.

Senior management has ordered Sandoval to curb the rise in DVD defects. Karma Digital's sales targets are to obtain orders for 15,000,000 DVDs by 2009 and 20,000,000 by 2010. Sandoval wants to institute a stronger training program and higher quality controls, but she needs some data to convince Senior Management that, if unchecked, the frequency of defective DVDs will worsen. In addition to predicting future defect levels, Sandoval also wants to use this data as a baseline to gauge the success of her quality control problems.

Load the data file KARMADIGITAL_Q.XLS. It shows Karma Digital's production volume and defects per 10,000 DVDs from 1999 to 2008. Sandoval will use this data to determine the historical relationship between frequency of defects and production volume so she can predict the level of defects in the future.

You can predict the level by performing a regression analysis, a statistical method for measuring the relationship between two or more variables. If the relationship is between only two variables, the method is called *simple regression*. If the relationship is between more than two variables, the method is called *multiple regression*. We have simplified this case for instructional purposes so that only two variables—incidence of defects and production volume—will be analyzed.

A regression analysis results in an equation that describes the behavior of one dependent variable in terms of other variables, called *independent variables*. In this case, there is only one independent variable, production volume, and one dependent variable, incidence of defects. The regression analysis also produces statistics that measure the strength of the relationship between the independent and dependent variables. You can visualize regression analysis as a way of drawing the "best line" through a series of data points.

You can then use the regression equation to forecast future incidence of defects given projected production volumes. Some popular business applications for regression analysis are determining the relationship between a product's price and cost of production, or determining the level of sales to be generated by an advertising campaign.

Tasks

There are four tasks in this case:

1.   Carefully examine the data file, KARMADIGITAL _Q.xlsx, which you have just loaded. Use the regression analysis commands of your spreadsheet software to perform a simple regression analysis. In Excel, the Regression dialog box allows you to perform regression analysis. (To open this dialog box in Excel 2007, first open the Data tab on the Ribbon, and in the Analysis group, click Data Analysis. In the Data Analysis dialog box that opens, select Regression in the Analysis Tools list box and click OK. In earlier versions of Excel, you must load the *Analysis Tool Pack* and then select *Data Analysis* from the Tools menu.)

For the dependent variable (Input Y Range), select the level of defects range. For the independent variable (Input X Range), select the production volume range. For your Output Range text box, select a cell to the right of your data so that the regression analysis does not overwrite any existing cell contents.

2. To the right of your data, create a column for the *Regression Line*. Calculate the Regression Line as follows:

    (a)   Multiply the value of the X Variable 1 Coefficient by each value of the independent variable (Pieces Produced).

    (b)   Add the value of the constant (i.e., Intercept of Coefficients).

    (c)   Be sure to apply absolute cell referencing to the X Variable 1 Coefficient and Intercept of Coefficients.

    (d)   Copy the formula into the remaining rows (i.e., down to the final year of known data). Print out the worksheet and the Regression Output. Put your name in the footer of all printouts.

3. Construct an XY (Scatter) type chart showing the independent variable (Pieces Produced) on the X-axis, the dependent variable (Percent Defective) on the Y-axis, and the Regression Line. Entitle the graph as *Production Volume vs. Defects, 1999-2008*. If needed, add an explanatory legend. Print out this graph.

4. Extend the independent variable range with values of 15,000,000 for 2009 and 2,000,000 for 2010. Then extend the regression line to predict future levels of defects. Revise your graph to incorporate this data and print again. Entitle this graph *Production Volume vs. Defects, 1999-2010*.

Time Estimates

Expert: 45 minutes

Intermediate: 1.5 hours

Novice: 2.5 hours

Excel Tutorial for Spreadsheet Case 9

This case expands on graphics and other spreadsheet skills that you have previously used and introduces the use of an Excel command for regression analysis. You can use your sample student roster (COURSE.xlsx) if you expand it to include a column for the students' ages.

The professor and school administration want to see if there is any correlation between student age and academic performance. In cell H14, enter the column heading *AGE*. Copy cell G15 to cell H15. Place ages in corresponding cells in range H16:H19. Assign the age of 27 to Heather Smith, 25 to Lois Mendez, 23 to Michel Johnson, and 18 to Erica Antonio.

The number of students on this worksheet is too small a sample to be statistically valid in actual life. Nevertheless, the worksheet will illustrate the concept of regression analysis and the Excel Regression Analysis tool. Excel provides a variety of Analysis Tools that can be accessed through the *Data Analysis* dialog box. To open the dialog box, open the Data tab on the Ribbon and click *Data Analysis* in the Analysis group.

Note: if *Data Analysis* does not appear in the Tools menu, the Analysis ToolPak add-in has not been loaded. (An *add-in* is a file that provides additional functions, commands, and menus.) To add the Analysis ToolPak, click the Office button and then click *Excel Options* to open the Excel Options dialog box. Click *Add-Ins* in the left pane of the dialog box. At the bottom of the right pane, make sure *Excel Add-ins* is selected in the Manage list box and click *Go*. In the Add-Ins dialog box that opens, place a check mark beside *Analysis ToolPak* and click *OK*. In the alert window that opens, asking if you should install the add-in now, click *Yes*. It may take a few minutes for Microsoft Office to complete the installation (**Note :** To install the Data Analysis add-in file on a stand-alone computer, you may need the Office 2007 or Excel 2007 application disks. In a networked environment, the file may already exist on the network. Consult your instructor if you have difficulty installing the file.)

In the Data Analysis dialog box, scroll down the list as needed, click *Regression* and press the *OK* button. To determine the relationship between students' ages and final grades, you will want to make age the independent variable (x) and final grade the dependent variable (y).

The Regression dialog box (see Figure 3-9) requires that you specify the ranges that hold the dependent values and the independent values.

Figure 3-9

At the *Input Y Range* setting, specify your dependent variable. In the window provided, enter the range *$F$16:$F$19*(the range for final grades). Alternatively, since this dialog box also permits you to select ranges on the worksheet, select the Final Grades range using your mouse.

At the *Input X Range* setting, specify one or more independent variables. In the window provided, enter the range$H$16:$H$19 (the range for students' ages). As with the Y range, ranges on the worksheet can be selected with the mouse.

Select the *Labels* check box to indicate that the selected ranges include the Labels in the first row. (Another input setting available is the *Constant is zero* check box, which lets the user force the Y intercept to zero. We will not use this setting for this problem.) If you wanted to apply confidence intervals to the regression in addition to the default 95% levels, you would click the *Confidence Level* check box. Leave this box unselected.

The Output options section of the dialog box contains several option buttons and check boxes. Three output options are available: (1) The *Output Range* deposits the output on the same sheet and asks for the upper-left cell reference of the output range. (2) The *New Worksheet Ply* creates a new worksheet in the same workbook and (optionally) asks you to name the new worksheet. (3) The *New Workbook* creates an entirely new workbook and places the output in cell A1 of its first worksheet. Select the *Output Range* option button and enter the cell reference *$K$1* in the available window. (Generally, you should allocate a blank worksheet area so that the resulting analysis does not overlay existing data.)

Excel provides four check boxes for residual values: *Residuals, Standardized Residuals, Residual Plots*, and *Line Fit Plots*. *Residuals* are the differences between the actual values and predicted values using the regression coefficients for the same dependent values. The plots will be embedded charts in the worksheet where the output tables will appear. Choose the *Line Fit Plots* setting to compare the actual values and the predicted values.

The final check box is for *Normal Probability Plots*. You would add a check mark here to create a chart to plot normal probability. Leave this check box unselected. Click the *OK* button to start the regression calculations.

Figure 3-10

Spreadsheet Case 10
Blue Sky Computer Services

Problem:	Develop an accounts receivable system
Management skills:	Organize
	Control
Excel skills:	Date Math
	Database querying and extraction
	Lookup Functions
	Data Functions
File:	BLUESKY_Q.XLS

Blue Sky Computer Services, based in Utica, New York, provides assistance to computer and cable users who have hardware, software, or connectivity problems with their electronic equipment. Blue Sky was founded in 1996 by four Electronic Engineering majors who were frequently asked to help their family and friends with installing, upgrading, and connecting their game machines, TVs, and computers. At first they served only local people, but news of their skill spread, and today Blue Sky employs 87 people, including a full-time administrative assistant and a part-time accountant. Gross revenues now total almost one million dollars annually!

Blue Sky has remained essentially a small, friendly business. Three of the original founders have gone on to careers with large corporations, but one, Ralph Alterman, has taken over and he is now trying to build the business even more. Blue Sky's customers now include several small businesses as well as individuals. Alterman fears that the firm does not generate as much revenue as it could to pay the bills and maintain a healthy growth curve. He suspects that one of the reasons for this is that too many bills are outstanding. The business has been run on a largely goodwill basis. They have maintained some of their key accounting records manually, and they have had to remember the names of the people who had not paid up.

Now Alterman would like his accounts receivable organized and automated so he can easily locate late payers. Load the data file BLUESKY_Q.xlsxto see the outline of the accounts receivable file. It contains a sample of Blue Sky's accounts receivable list as of January 1, 2009. Alterman would like to type in the date (today's date) whenever he accesses the file and then automatically calculate the days outstanding for each account. He also would like to produce an aging report that automatically classifies the records according to 4 aging categories of lateness: Current (30 days or less), 31-60 days, 61-90 days, and Over 90 days.

Alterman would also like some reporting mechanism to identify the most seriously late payers (over 90 days) so he can contact them and, if necessary, provide their names to a collection agency. He wants to sort the accounts receivable file first by Overdue Category and then by Invoice Amount. He would also like to have a listing of customers who are more than 90 days late with outstanding balances.

Tasks

There are five tasks to this problem:

1. Calculate the number of days each invoice has been outstanding. This is the difference between the invoice date and today's date. Format the results as a number.

2. Classify the invoices using formulas into the four aging categories shown on the worksheet. (**Hint:** Use a lookup function to classify the invoices.) Display overall invoice totals.

3. Sort the database in descending order using the using the *Days Overdue Category* as the primary sort key and in descending order using the *Invoice Amount* as the secondary sort key. Print the sorted database (including the information you just provided on categories of lateness).

4. Using the sorted database from Task 3, use the Advanced Filter command of your spreadsheet software to extract (copy) a report that shows the relevant information on customers more than 90 days overdue. Print this report.

5. Use the math function SUMIF to total the invoice amounts by *Overdue Category*.

Time Estimates

Expert: 1 hour

Intermediate: 2 hours

Novice: 3 hours

Excel Tutorial for Spreadsheet Case 10

This case requires new skills utilizing Excel data management capabilities, along with math, lookup, and date functions. Save a new version of the COURSE.xlsx file for this tutorial that does not include the regression analysis data or the range name table.

Excel Date Functions

To determine how many days an account is overdue, you must be able to calculate the difference between today's date and the date of a customer's invoice. You can calculate the difference by subtracting the earlier date from the later one and by formatting the result of the date calculation in **numeric** format.

Excel can represent any 20th or 21st century date as a serial number equal to the number of days after December 31, 1899. For example, January 1, 1900 is serial number 1 because it is the first day after December 31, 1899. Likewise, January 1, 2000 is serial number 36526 because it is day 36,526 in the number sequence. (Excel supports two date systems: the *1900* for the PC and the *1904* for the Mac.)

You can enter today's date by using the function =Today(). The date provided by the Today() function is updated to the current date whenever the spreadsheet is modified. The function =Now() is similar, but it provides the time as well as the date. Note that although these functions have no arguments, you must include the parentheses after the function name.

For practice purposes, modify your COURSE spreadsheet to include data about due dates for students' library books. You will then calculate the number of days overdue by subtracting the date due for each student's books from the report date.

Create a new range for book due dates in H14:H19. The first cell (H14) should contain the column label DUE DATE, and H16:H19 will contain date information for each student as follows:

Heather Smith:	2/27/08
Lois Mendez:	6/30/08
Michael Johnson:	4/16/08

Erica Antonio: 5/25/08

Enter the due dates for the students. In cell E21, enter the label REPORT DATE. In cell G21, enter the date of this student roster report (6/25/08). Enter a label for DAYS OVERDUE in I14. Using the Report Date and the student book due dates, calculate the number of days each student's book is overdue. Perform the calculation by subtracting each student's due date from the report date. Be sure to format the cells in the DAYS OVERDUE column as *Numeric*. A negative number indicates that the book has that many days left before it becomes overdue. Your worksheet should look like Figure 3-11.

Figure 3-11

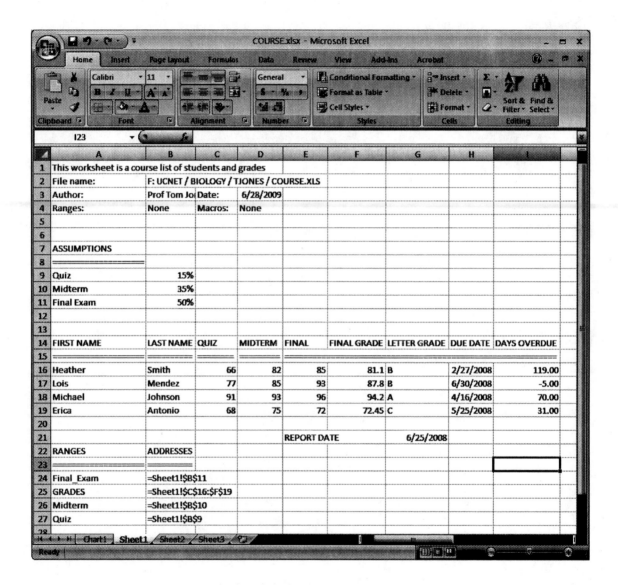

Mathematical Function =SUMIF

=**SUMIF** is a quick way to sum only those cells that meet a particular condition (e.g., all the unit sales on a specific day, such as Saturday). The format of the =SUMIF function is:

=SUMIF(range to be tested, criterion, range to be summed)

Note that the criterion may either be a cell, in which case the contents of the cell are matched, or an actual value in quotes. This would include text. For instance, in Figure 3-12 below, you can find out how many sales are made on Saturday by using the SUMIF function in cell B16.

Figure 3-12

If you are asking Excel to match a text criterion, put the text you want to match in quotes when using this function.

Lookup Functions

The =*VLOOKUP* function is often used to translate one set of values into another set of values based on a lookup table you create. For instance, let's say you want to translate students numerical test grades into letter grades. VLOOKUP can do that for you automatically.

The =VLOOKUP function obtains data from a list in much the same way one would manually look up information in a table. Often VLOOKUP is a simpler alternative to a complex =IF function. Note that the column containing the item being searched for must be sorted in ascending order and any lookup value outside the range of the table will return =N/A (not available). The format of the =VLOOKUP function is:

=VLOOKUP(Value to be looked-up, range in which to look, column with the result)

To see how the VLOOKUP function works, let's modify your COURSE.xlsx file to provide a comment for each student based on their final GPA (grade point average). Beginning in cell E25 create the VLOOKUP table of Teacher Comments shown below:

0	F	FAIL
60	D	OK
70	C	GOOD
80	B	BETTER
90	A	BEST

Format the lookup table so that it is distinct from the rest of the worksheet.

Enter the label *COMMENT* in Cell J14. Now enter in Cell J16, the VLOOKUP argument: =VLOOKUP(F16,$E$25:$G$29,3) to display the comment based on the student's final grade reported in E16...E19. Copy this function down to J17:J19 so that comments will be provided for each student. Your spreadsheet should look similar to Figure 3-13.

On your own, you could also translate the students GPA into a letter grade using the same LOOKUP table. Note that with this lookup table, you could also replace the =IF functions used to display the letter grades.

When using =VLOOKUP, always be sure use an absolute address or named range for the look-up table. Test the results of any lookup function to be sure that all possible cases are covered, like a grade of zero or no grade at all.

Figure 3-13

	A	B	C	D	E	F	G	H	I	J
1	This worksheet is a course list of students and grades									
2	File name:	F: UCNET / BIOLOGY / TJONES / COURSE.XLS								
3	Author:	Prof Tom Jo	Date:	6/28/2009						
4	Ranges:	None	Macros:	None						
5										
6										
7	ASSUMPTIONS									
8										
9	Quiz	15%								
10	Midterm	35%								
11	Final Exam	50%								
12										
13										
14	FIRST NAME	LAST NAME	QUIZ	MIDTERM	FINAL	FINAL GR	LETTER GRADE	DUE DATE	DAYS OVERDUE	COMMENT
15										
16	Heather	Smith	66	82	85	81.1	B	2/27/2008	119.00	BETTER
17	Lois	Mendez	77	85	93	87.8	B	6/30/2008	-5.00	BETTER
18	Michael	Johnson	91	93	96	94.2	A	4/16/2008	70.00	BEST
19	Erica	Antonio	68	75	72	72.45	C	5/25/2008	31.00	GOOD
20										
21					REPORT DATE		6/25/2008			
22	RANGES	ADDRESSES								
23										
24	Final_Exam	=Sheet1!$B$11			LOOKUP TABLE					
25	GRADES	=Sheet1!$C$16:$F$19			0	F	FAIL			
26	Midterm	=Sheet1!$B$10			60	D	OK			
27	Quiz	=Sheet1!$B$9			70	C	GOOD			
28					80	B	BETTER			
29					90	A	BEST			
30										

Database Management with Excel

The student roster you have created in A14:J19 in the COURSE.xlsx spreadsheet can be treated as a database where data can be extracted, sorted, and analyzed. Consider each row with data about a student as one *record* in the database. Within each row, each cell represents a *field* of that record. The headings at the top of each column, such as LAST NAME or QUIZ, represent *field names*.

With Excel, you can treat any collection of data organized into records and fields as a database. Fields in an Excel database may contain either labels (such as the student names in our roster) or numeric data (such as the student grades).

You can use various data commands with an Excel database to sort its records in numeric or alphabetical order, or to find and list records that match criteria that you specify. There are also several powerful database functions that help you analyze your data.

To streamline the data in the student roster database, delete the row that includes the separator marks, Row 15. Doing this will allow Excel to properly distinguish between the headers and the data in your database. Now, sort the student roster database and arrange it by the number of days overdue in ascending order. To sort, select any cell in the range A14:J19 that contains the data and the column headings. Open the Data tab on the Ribbon and click *Sort* in the Sort & Filter group. In the Sort dialog box that opens, you can add multiple levels of sorts. For example, you could sort by Letter Grade, and then alphabetically. To do so, you would first select LETTER GRADE in the *Sort by* list box under Column. To add a second level of sort, click the *Add Level* button. In the second row, select *LAST NAME* in the *Then by* list box. You can remove a level by clicking the *Delete Level* button.

For this exercise, perform a sort based on the Days Overdue column. In the *Sort by* list box, select *DAYS OVERDUE*, and then select *Largest to Smallest* for the order.

Notice a check box setting at the top of the Sort dialog box indicates whether the list includes or excludesheaders (containing field names). The dialog box should already indicate that a headers are present. If it does not, select the *My data has headers* check box. If you specify that the list does not contain a header row, the heading row will be sorted with the data.

To execute the sort, select the *OK* button. Your course roster will then sort so that Heather Smith, with 119 days overdue, will be first on the list, and Lois Mendez, with 5 days left before his due date, will be last on the list (see Figure 3-14).

Figure 3-14

Filtering a Database

You can search an Excel database for specific records, and copy or extract records using the *Filter* or *Advanced Filter* commands. For example, you can filter your student database to produce a list of all students whose books are more than 45 days overdue.

The Filter and Advanced Filter do the same thing in different ways. An Excel filter enables the user to dictate criteria that will include some records and exclude others. The Filter command performs the filter operation on the list at the same location. The Advanced Filter command gives the user the option to filter on the same location as the list or to copy to a new location. The Advanced Filter also permits more complex criteria than the Filter, although the Filter satisfies most demands.

The Filter command is a simple but extremely effective tool to distill large amounts of data very quickly. To demonstrate its usefulness, highlight the range A14:J18. Now open the Data tab on the Ribbon and click *Filter* in the Sort & Filter group. This action places drop-down list buttons next to each of the field names (column headers). It is with these buttons that the query is achieved. Press the list arrow on the *QUIZ* field. The top level of the *QUIZ* drop-down menu for each field contains options for sorting the values in the column, and selecting or excluding specific values. Selecting one of these specific values will display those records with that entry only. Click *Select All* to remove all checks beside specific values. Then click *77* on the *QUIZ* drop-down list and click *OK*. All entries other than those with 77 in the QUIZ field are hidden and the row numbers of the remaining entries are colored.

Open the *QUIZ* drop-down menu again and click *Select All* to return to a full list. Click *OK* to close the *QUIZ* drop-down menu. Select the *DAYS OVERDUE* drop-down menu and point to *Number filters* to open the submenu. The submenu contains options such as: Equals, Greater than., Between and Custom filter. These options allow you to specify a condition or criterion for displaying a record. For example:

- The **Equals** option allows you to specify a value that a record must have for the Quiz field in order to display.

- The **Custom** option lets you enter a criterion for the current field.

- The **Between** option displays all rows that fall between the upper and lower limits you specify.

Select *Custom Filter*. The Custom AutoFilter dialog box permits one or two simple conditions connected with an OR or an AND. If the field being queried is text, the box for the first logical operator on the left should be an *equal to* or = sign. For our purposes, select *is greater than or* equal to (>=) as the logical operator. Then type *45* in the value window to the right of this logical operator box to represent DAYS OVERDUE >= 45 (greater than or equal to) 45 days. Press the *OK* button to execute the query. The list should have two records displayed now: Heather Smith and Michael Johnson. If you wanted a separate permanent copy of the results of an AutoFilter query, you would have to copy them manually. To turn off the Filter, click *Filter* on the Ribbon.

The Advanced Filter command permits more advanced criteria than the Filter command. It requires criteria in a separate location on the worksheet. This is best done by copying the field names from the original list so no typing error can creep in. Copy the headings to A31:I31. Type *>=45* under the DAYS OVERDUE heading in the criteria (cell I32).

Select any cell in the student grades list (A15:J18). Open the Data tab on the Ribbon, and in the Sort & Filter group, click *Advanced*. In the Advanced Filter dialog box, select *Copy to Another Location* to provide a separate list for the result of the query. For this Action setting, the *Copy to:* text box becomes active. Three references are now required for this dialog box: the *List Range*, the *Criteria Range*, and the *Copy to Range*. Select the ranges:

List Range	A14:J18
Criteria Range	A31:J32
Copy to Range	A33

It is not necessary to specify the end of the Copy to Range since you do not know the number of rows that will be copied. However, be careful because the copied rows will overlay any preexisting data in these cells.

The Criteria Range setting in the Advanced Filter dialog box tells Excel which records to search for in the database. Your search criteria may include one or several fields in the database. The criteria range will have at least two rows: one for the heading and one for the selection criteria.

The first criteria row **must** be the field names of all of the fields that will be referred to in your search criteria. The second row of the criteria range is where the various selection criteria are entered. You must enter each criterion directly below the field name to which it applies. Criteria may be numbers, labels, or formulas. A criteria range can be two or more rows long. For this example, there are two critera rows: 31 and 32.

Select the *OK* button to execute the query. The resulting screen should look like Figure 3-15.

Figure 3-15

To search for exact matches of labels, enter the label used as a criterion exactly as it appears in the database. You can also search for similar, but not identical, label entries using special characters called *wildcards*. You can use wildcards in both Advanced Filter criteria and Filter criteria:

- "?" instructs Excel to accept any character in that specific position and can be used only for fields of the same length (for example, "b?t" matches "bit" or "bat," but not "beet").

- "*" instructs Excel to accept any and all characters that follow and can therefore be used for fields of unequal length (for example, "bat*" matches "batch" or "batter," but not "butter").

- The Copy to Range determines the destination of the extracted records and the field names are copied as well. This option is only active when the Copy to Another Location has been selected. The Copy to Range should be an unused area of the worksheet.

- The rows copied by the Advanced Filter will not reflect any subsequent changes to the original list.

Spreadsheet Case 11
Morgan Wagner Machinery

Problem:	Develop a sensitivity analysis for capital budgeting
Management skills:	Planning
	Deciding
Excel skills:	Two Input Data Table building
	Financial functions and Formulas
File:	MWM_Q.xlsx

Morgan Wagner Machinery, Inc. (MWM) of Decatur, Illinois, makes bearings and metal parts for the farm machinery industry. To increase productivity and profits, the company has started investing in new computer numerically controlled machine (CNC) tools, enabling it to design and make parts faster and with fewer defects. CNC machine tools have multiple tools and multi axes that operate under the control of a computer program entered by the machinist. Most machine shops today employ these sophisticated tools that can carve complex shapes out of solid metal. In keeping with the investment strategy, the company's production manager, Kris Shillings, wants to spend $640,000 for a new CNC programmable machine. Shillings estimates that the new tool will increase the firm's after-tax income by $130,000 each year over five years by reducing production costs. At the end of six years, Shillings hopes to sell the tool for a total of $210,000. The sale price of the tool at the end of its useful life to the firm is the *salvage value*.

Purchasing new, expensive equipment or upgrading plant facilities often requires substantial investment to produce future benefits. Such investments are *capital expenditures*. The process of analyzing and selecting various proposals for capital expenditures is *capital budgeting*. A capital expenditure is not worthwhile unless it produces at least the same rate of return on the investment as if the expenditure were invested at a certain rate of interest that the firm specifies. Businesses use several methods for evaluating the desirability of capital expenditures. One widely used method is the *net present value method*.

You must compare the initial cost of the investment to the total cash flow from the investment. The total cash flow is the sum of the additional income produced by the investment plus the salvage value of the machine tool. You must discount the cash flow from the investment to account for the declining time value of money. A dollar earned ten years from now will not be worth one of today's dollars because you could invest today's dollar at a certain rate of interest.

Ten years from now, you would have not only the dollar, but also the interest income from the period. For instance, $1000 invested at a 7% interest rate, compounded monthly, would be worth $2,010 at the end of 10 years.

To arrive at the return from the investment in today's dollars, first calculate the present value of the total cash flow from the new machine tool discounted at the target interest rate for borrowing money. This targeted discount rate is the minimum return on the investment desired by the company. MWM wants a minimum return of 10% on its investment. Subtract the initial purchase price of the tool in today's dollars from the present value of the total cash flow from the investment to arrive at the net present value of the investment. If the net present value for the investment is positive, it is a worthwhile investment. If it is negative, you should reject the investment.

Since investments vary greatly with changes in interest rates, Shillings wants to see whether or not the new machine tool makes a good investment under a wide range of situations. What if the interest rate and annual income from the new tool are lower (or higher) than originally assumed? Shillings can perform a *sensitivity analysis* in a data table that shows how interest rate changes and annual income from the investment affect the net present value.

Tasks

There are five tasks in this case:

1. Review the data file MWM_Q.xlsx to see the assumptions for the problem and the basic outline of the template. Calculate the total additional income from the investment for the years 2009-2014.

2. Calculate the cumulative cash flow from the investment for 2009-2014. Use the =NPV function to calculate the present value of this amount. (**Hint:** In the Function Arguments dialog box, the Rate equals the interest rate required by the firm. Value 1 equals cumulative cash flow from the investment. You do not need data in the Value 2 text box.) Calculate the net present value of the investment by subtracting the cost of the investment from the present value.

3. Calculate the profitability index by dividing the present value of the cash flows by the cost of the investment, displaying 4 decimal positions for the profitability index. The profitability index is another capital budgeting method that helps firms compare the profitability of different potential investments. (For instance, if the present value of the total cash flow from an investment is 24,000 and the initial cost of the investment was 22,500, the profitability index would be 1.066.) Using this method, firms can compare

various capital investment projects and select those with the highest profitability indices. You should reject any investment with a profitability index of less than one.

4. Develop a data table showing the impact of different interest rates and different annual additional incomes on the profitability index. In the top left corner of the data table range, key the formula in which the variables are to be tested. In this problem, it is the formula used to obtain the Profitablity Index. **Note:** Copying and pasting the value of a cell or manually typing in a value will cause the data table to yield incorrect data. The data table command uses the formula in the top left cell to create the values in the table. This cell must therefore contain a formula.

5. Enter the interest rates on the X axis beginning in the cell immediately to the right of the cell containing the Data Tables' formula. The interest rate should begin with a value of 7% and end with 13% in half percent increments. The interest rate is the X variable and should increment across the row. Enter the annual incomes from the investment on the Y variable down the column beginning immediately below the cell containing the formula. The annual income should begin with $100,000 and end with $160,000 in $10,000 increments. (**Hint:** Use the *Edit/Fill/Series* command of your spreadsheet software to set up these values on the data table.)

6. Finally, use the *Data/Table* command to open the Table dialog box, insert the appropriate values in the Data Table Dialog box, and then close the dialog box. To make comparisons more accurate, format the resulting Profitablility Indices with 4 decimal positions.

7. Write an evaluation of the proposed purchase. Should Shillings make the investment? Should it be rejected at all costs? Are there conditions under which it would be worthwhile? If so, what are they? Utilize the information created by the Data Table command to support your conclusion.

Time Estimates

Expert:	1 hour
Intermediate:	1.5 hours
Novice:	2 hours

Excel Tutorial for Spreadsheet Case 11

This case requires knowledge of spreadsheet software's table-building features and Excel's =NPV function. You do not need the COURSE.xlsx file for this tutorial.

Sensitivity analysis is the process of exploring various *what-if?* situations to determine the impact of one or several variables on a model. Table-building automates the what-if? process so that sensitivity analysis need not be performed manually. Instead of performing repeated what-if? analyses, the Excel table-building function allows various values to be substituted for existing values in your worksheet. Excel will then generate a table to detail the results.

To demonstrate, create a new Excel worksheet that calculates sales commissions. Save the worksheet as CASE9_TUTORIAL.xlsx. See Figure 3-16 to view the spreadsheet format. You want to see the impact on commissions on sales of $5000 when they are based on different percentage rates. To fully display the data table on your worksheet screen, we will not enter documentation into the first four rows.

Set up your worksheet so that the labels PERCENT, SALES, and COMMISSION appear in cells A1, B1, and C1, respectively, and the values for percent (5%) and sales ($7500) that we want to use in our calculation are in cells A2 and B2, respectively. In cell C2, place the formula, =A2*B2, for calculating the commission. In cell A5, type *DATA TABLE 1*. In cell A7, type *Percent*, and in cell B7, type *Commission*.

You could enter different percentages in the A column and then copy the formula for commission calculation to appropriate cells in the C column. However, you can also use the *Data Table* command to perform this analysis automatically.

The Edit/Fill/Series Command

Before using these commands, you must enter the different percentage values in a column. Rather than enter each value individually, use the *Edit/Fill/Series* command. This command fills a range of cells with a series of numbers or dates that increase or decrease by aspecified increment or decrement, or increase or decrease with a multiplicative growth factor.

First, in cell A9, type *.05*, and press *[Enter]*. Reselect cell A9, and on the Home tab, in the Editing group, click Fill and select *Series*. In the Series dialog box, select the *Columns* option button, and be sure that the Type is *Linear*. In the *Step value* text box, type *.01*. In the *Stop value* text box, type *.10*. Press *[Enter]* or click the *OK* button when finished. Format the cell range A9:A14 as percentages with no decimal points.

Alternately, if you did not have a required Stop value, but you did have a desired range for the series, you could select the range with the first cell containing the starting value and select *Fill>Series*. You would not specify a Stop value in the dialog box; instead, Excel would finish filling the series when it reached the end of the selection.

Data Table Command

After generating the column of interest rates in range A9:A14, you must enter either the formula for calculating commissions or the cell address from which to draw the formula. *This entry goes next to the column of percentages and one row above the first entry.* In cell B8, enter the formula =C2. (You could have also entered the formula for computing commission in cell B8.)

Select the range *A8:B14*, the range containing the percentage values, the formula, and the blank cell where the results will go. Next, open the Data tab on the Ribbon, In the Data Tools group, click *What-If Analysis* and click the *Data Table* command on the menu. The Data Table dialog box has two available settings: the Row input cell and the Column input cell. Since you are examining only the impact of changes in one variable—percentage—you will enter a cell reference in only one of these. The variable numbers you are examining are in a column, so you should enter the cell reference for the percentage variable. Enter the reference *A2* in the *Column input cell* and click the *OK* Button.

By entering only a single input cell reference in the dialog box, you are examining the impact of changes to one value in a formula. (If, instead, you had entered data in both the Row input cell and Column input cell, you would have shown the impact of changes to two values in a formula.) The results should look like Figure 3-16.

Solve it!

Figure 3-16

Now examine the impact on commissions if the sales amount, as well as the percentage, is variable. What happens when sales are $7500, $12,500, and $17,500? You would enter the values for our second variable (Sales) in the row just above the first entry of our first variable (Percentage). First, in cell D5, type *DATA TABLE 2*. In cell F7, type *Sales*. Then in cell range

E8:G8, enter the Sales values: *7500*, *12500*, and *17500*. In cell range D9:D14, copy and paste the Percentage values that appear in cell range A9:A14. *You also must enter the address of the formula (=C2) in the cell directly above the first entry of the first variable.* (In your tutorial file, this would be in D8.)

Select the range of the table (D8:G14) and then, on the Data tab of the Ribbon, in the Data Tools group,click *What-If Analysis* and then *Data Table* . In the Table dialog box, choose cell reference *B2* as the Row input cell and cell reference *A2* as the Column input cell. Click *OK*. The two-dimensional data table should resemble Figure 3-17:

Solve it!

Figure 3-17

Spreadsheet Case 12
Truman Assembly

Problem:	Develop a parts inventory scheduling system
Management skills:	Controlling
	Deciding
Excel skills:	Sorting by Multiple Keys
	Macro Creation
	Creating Command Buttons
File:	TRUMAN _Q.xlsx

Truman Assembly is a moderately-sized assembly company in Michigan, North Dakota. The company specializes in assembling parts into various types of lawn mowers for larger companies. Neils Truman founded the company 13 years ago.

Business has grown steadily over the last few years, and scheduling both the supply and production sides of the business has become more complex than in the early years. Truman's small amount of factory space limited the amount of inventory the company could keep on hand and restricted assembly operations to only one or two jobs at a time. The company has a difficult time getting all of its vendors to ship items on a timely basis. Production-job due dates also caused problems. For example, an order with a two-month deadline might take three months to complete. There simply was no system in place that linked outstanding orders to fulfill with the production of lawn mowers in the factory.

With uncertainty on both the supply and production sides, shipments of many of their component parts sometimes arrive late with little or no penalty to the supplier. However, Truman Assembly knows that maintaining superior customer loyalty in such a competitive industry requires that the company minimize the number of late shipments.

Thankfully, the company has solved its basic problems on the assembly side of the business. Better worker training, more space, and more efficient shipping services have enabled Truman to deliver products at the quality level that its customers desire and on time. However, Truman still has problems getting its vendors to deliver the small items it needs in a prompt and reliable manner. These delays make it hard to keep storage space needs and essential inventory as low as possible and have reduced profit margins.

Truman's purchasing director, Lee Chiang, recently started using spreadsheet software to track vendor inventory, inventory costs, and delivery performance. She laid out the worksheet, set up the fields and records that the company needs to track, and entered the main data about its vendors. However, Chiang now needs your help to make sorting the worksheet to make better use of the information.

Tasks

There are four tasks in this problem:

1. Create a macro that sorts the entire spreadsheet in ascending order by Vendor Name, then in ascending order by Item No., and then in descending order by Cost per Order. Name the macro "*VendorSort*". Assign this macro control key sequence of [Ctrl] + [Shift] + [V].

2. Create two additional macros. The first should sort the spreadsheet column "DAYS OVERDUE" in ascending order to indicate which shipments arrived quickest. Name the macro *FastArrival*. The second should sort the same column in descending order to indicate the slowest shipments. Name the macro *SlowArrival*. Include a secondary sort to organize VENDOR NAMES alphabetically in ascending order in both macros. Assign these macros control key sequences of *[Ctrl] + [Shift] + [F]* for fast, and *[Ctrl] + [Shift] + [S]* for slow.

3. Create three *Command* buttons above the data area. Assign a macro to each button and label them appropriately as *Sort by Vendor, Sort by Slow Delivery,* and *Sort by Fast Delivery*.

4. Write a one-paragraph summary that identifies the fastest and slowest suppliers. Determine if your conclusion should change based on the additional factors of Item Cost and A/P (accounts payable) terms.

Time Estimates

Expert: 1 hour

Intermediate: 1.5 hour

Novice: 2 hours

Excel Tutorial for Spreadsheet Case 12

This case requires that you use Excel to build a *macro* to perform a sort on a list. A macro is, in essence, a recorded sequence of commands. The commands are contained in a module that can be stored in the current workbook or in a workbook of macros. You can execute a macro through the *Macro* menu on the View tab of the Ribbon or via an assigned control key sequence.

For this exercise, you will need COURSE.xlsx with some of the changes you made during the Spreadsheet Case 8 tutorial session.

Excel includes an extensive scripting language called Visual Basic. Several Microsoft applications can use this language. Excel allows macros to be recorded by transcribing a series of operations performed by users to the equivalent Visual Basic commands. The commands are stored in a module and can be edited using the Visual Basic Editor. Macros can be stored in the current workbook or in a Personal Macro workbook, making them accessible by any workbook.

You can record a macro by accessing the command *Macros>Record Macro* on the View tab of the Ribbon and naming the macro.

You can create a macro, for example, to automate the sorting of your student roster spreadsheet by number of days overdue in ascending order, the same task you performed during the tutorial for Spreadsheet Case 8.

To record an Excel macro, click *Macro* on the View tab, in theMacros group. This opens a menu with more choices. From the Macro menu, select *Record Macro* to open the Record Macro dialog box.

Recording a New MacroAssign a meaningful name to the macro. The *Macro name* text-entry box is highlighted with the default name *Macro* followed by a number. Type *SortMacro* as the name of the macro to replace the selected default name. Macro names must begin with a letter and cannot contain spaces or punctuation marks. Otherwise, they can include letters, numbers, and underscores.

Assign a letter for the keyboard shortcut that a user can type to start the macro running. Type *K* into the *Shortcut key* text box. Notice that Excel changes the shortcut to Ctrl+Shift, so as not to overwrite an existing shortcut using Ctrl + K.

From the *Store macro in* list, select *This Workbook*. If you are creating multiple macros to be used in more than one file, they can also be stored in a Personal Macro Workbook.

Describe the macro. In the *Description* text box where ,type *Sorts by the number of overdue days in ascending order.* (See Figure 3-18.)

Figure 3-18

To start recording, click the *OK* button. While you are recording, be careful to include only those commands, keystrokes, and typed items that are absolutely necessary to create the macro. Avoid mistakes, as Excel will include them in the macro if it is still recording. To turn off macro recording function, click *Macro* and then click *Stop Recording* on the View tab of the Ribbon. Excel will not record the Stop Recording command as part of the macro.

One of the most common problems when recording a macro is forgetting to stop recording! If this occurs, immediately select *Stop Recording*, delete the macro (on the Macro menu), and start over. To halt a macro that seems to be running forever (perhaps because you forgot to stop recording), hit the *[ESC]* key.

To automate the sorting of your student roster spreadsheet, record the following actions:

1.   Select the range A14:J18.

2.   Open the Data tab on the Ribbon and click *Sort*.

3.   In the Sort dialog box, select *DAYS OVERDUE* in the *Sort by* list box.

4.   In the Order column, select *Smallest to Largest* for the sort.

5.   Make sure that the *My data has headers* check box is selected.

6.   Click the *OK* button to execute the sort.

7.   To finish, open the View tab on the Ribbon, click *Macro* and then click *Stop Recording*. The macro stops recording.

To test the macro, first undo the changes you made while creating the macro so you can see if it works correctly. It is also a good idea to save a worksheet before running a macro for the first time. This way, if the macro has any problems that affect the data, you can revert to the saved version of your workbook.

To run the macro, open the *View* tab, click on the *Macro* command, and select *View Macros* from the menu. The Macro dialog box opens. Beneath the *Macro name* text box is a larger box listing all available macros. Click on your macro's name in this box. The name displays in the text box above, and the macro's description appears at the bottom of the dialog box. Click the *Run* button. You can also run the macro by hitting the control key sequence assigned to it. If the macro runs correctly, the spreadsheet will sort in ascending order.

Assigning a Macro to a Command Button

To make it even easier to run a macro, you can add it as a button on the Quick Access toolbar, and the button will appear every time you call Excel. (However, if you specify that a macro is saved for only the current workbook, the macro will not run in other workbooks.)

To create a Quick Access button, click the down-arrow to the right of the Quick Access toolbar, and click More Commands. This opens the Customize section of the Excel Options dialog box, which allows you to modify the Quick Access toolbar. From the *Choose Commands* drop-down list, select *Macros*. In the list box on the left, scroll down to select *SortMacro*. Click the *Add* button to add *SortMacro* to the right pane, which lists the buttons in the Quick Access toolbar. (Notice that you can change the button that is used on the Quick Access toolbar by pressing the *Modify* button and selecting a new button icon to use in the Modify Button dialog box that opens.) Click OK to add the SortMacro macro to the QuickAccess toolbar and close the Excel Options window. Clicking on the *SortMacro* button will now cause the macro to run.

Viewing the Macro

Recording a macro and then viewing and editing it is a great way to learn Visual Basic. You can view your macro commands by opening the View tab, clicking *Macro* and then *View Macros*, and then selecting the *Edit* option from the Macro dialog box. The Visual Basic module for the macro will appear and can be edited. The module for the macro to sort the student roster spreadsheet would look like Figure 3-19.

Figure 3-19

```
Course.xls - Module1 (Code)                                    [_][□][X]
(General)                                 ▼  Macro4                      ▼
    Sub SortMacro()                                                  ▲
    '
    ' SortMacro Macro
    ' Sorts number of overdue days in ascending order
    '
    ' Keyboard Shortcut: Ctrl+Shift+K
    '
        Range("A15:J18").Select
    End Sub
    Sub Macro3()
    '
    ' Macro3 Macro
    '

    '
        Range("A14:J18").Select
        ActiveWorkbook.Worksheets("Sheet1").Sort.SortFields.Clear
        ActiveWorkbook.Worksheets("Sheet1").Sort.SortFields.Add Key:=Range("I15:I18") _
        , SortOn:=xlSortOnValues, Order:=xlAscending, DataOption:=xlSortNormal
        With ActiveWorkbook.Worksheets("Sheet1").Sort
            .SetRange Range("A14:J18")
            .Header = xlYes
            .MatchCase = False
            .Orientation = xlTopToBottom
            .SortMethod = xlPinYin
            .Apply
        End With
    End Sub
    Sub Macro4()
    '
    ' Macro4 Macro
    '                                                                ▼
```

As you can see, modules have a non-tabular format, and they lack the rows and columns typical of regular worksheets. Instead, data displays as lines of text against a white background.

Managing Your Macros

To easily write and edit macros, you should become familiar with the Visual Basic Editor. With the help of this editor, you do not have to learn Visual Basic itself to make simple edits to your macros. The editor enables you to edit macros, copy macros, rename macros, etc. Note also that recent versions of Excel have increased safeguards against computer viruses transmitted by macros. To set the level of security most appropriate for your spreadsheet activities, click the Office button and then click *Excel Options*. Select *Trust Center* in the left pane of the Excel Options window. In the right pane, under Microsoft Office Excel Trust Center, click the *Trust*

*Center Settings*button. Select *Macro Settings* in the left pane of the Trust Center window. The Macro settings you can choose from are:

- Disable all macros without notification

- Disable all macros with notification

- Disable all macros except digitally signed macros

- Enable all macros

To edit a macro in your worksheet, open the View tab, click <u>*Macro*</u> and then click *View Macros*. Select the macro you wish to work with in the list box, and then click *Edit* to display the editing window. (Notice that you can also delete a macro in this dialog box by selecting the *Delete* button.) In the editing window, make the desired changes, and then click the *Close* button at the right end of the blue Title bar.

Troubleshooting Macros

When troubleshooting macros, you will generally come across one of three different problems. First, if you click the *Refresh* button, a message may display telling you that your macro changes will be lost. (This message displays if you have edited a macro in the Visual Basic Editor and have changed the copy of your workbook in the Microsoft Script Editor.) In such cases, click *No* in the message box, switch to the Visual Basic Editor, and export any modules you have changed. Then in your workbook in Microsoft Script Editor, click *Refresh* on the Refresh toolbar. Finally, click *Yes* and then import the desired modules to restore the changes to your macro.

Second, while recording a macro, you may accidentally record an undesired action. To delete that action, open the Visual Basic Editor, remove the unwanted steps, and then click the *Close* button. Alternately, you can delete the defective macro and re-record it with the correct steps.

Third, a recorded macro may display an error message in some situations, but not in others. (For example, a macro that looks for a certain column header will run properly if the column header is displayed, but it may malfunction if the header is not displayed, thereby prompting the error message.) In these inconsistent situations, write down the number of the error message. Open Visual Basic Help, search for *error messages,* and find information about the message number you received.

Spreadsheet Case 12
Pacific Trading

Problem:	Develop a faster method of data analysis
Management skills:	Support management decision making Prepare ad hoc reports
Excel skill:	Creating and Using Pivot Tables
File:	PACIFIC_Q.XLS

Pacific Trading, an importer of organic fruits and vegetables, was formed only one year ago by Oregon investors Kieran Peters and Matt Staley. With more and more Americans concerned about eating a healthy diet that includes plenty of vegetables and fruits, grocery stores that emphasize health foods and organic foods have experienced rapid growth. Good food is not inexpensive, and upscale grocery chains like Trader Joe's and Whole Foods charge premium prices for their products. Although it is less well known than its competitors, Pacific Trading has also grown beyond its founders' expectations.

As is often the case with quick success in business, Pacific Trading is having severe growing pains. They are frequently out of stock of the most in-demand items in one city, but are overstocked with the same item in another city. Because of the perishable nature of their products, it is impossible to reship the items to where they are needed.

Fortunately, their Business Manager, Maria Galambos, has kept very accurate weekly sales records over the last year. Peters and Staley realize that this data could help them better predict the areas and timing of future product demand.

They frequently ask Galambos what she considers "off the wall" questions, and she spends hours rearranging her spreadsheets and using the data commands to give them the reports they want. However, every day they want more information and different reports, and as a result, Galambos can't concentrate on her regular work of paying bills and salaries!

She has recently taken an advanced Excel course and learned about pivot tables. Galambos thinks these may be the answer to her prayers. Using a pivot table, she could quickly and easily rearrange the data to provide the answer to "today's question"!

Using the file PACIFIC_Q.xlsx, create a pivot table that would answer some of the questions posed by Galambos's managers.

Tasks

There are four tasks in this case. Each of these tasks can be solved with a pivot table. Do not make four separate pivot tables. Pivot tables consume considerable memory, and it is not necessary. Instead, rearrange the fields in the table to get the answer you need, format your table using one of the Autoformats, and then print it out. Write a short paragraph to support your reports.

1. During what month are peaches most in demand in Eugene?

2. Who is the least productive salesperson? From the information provided by the pivot table, can you suggest any reasons for this person's poor performance?

3. Sales to restaurants entail more labor than sales to other venues. Is it worthwhile to continue marketing to restaurants? (**Hint:** To have the total show as % of column, select *Field Settings/Options/Show Data/as percent of column*.)

4. Pacific Trading may be growing too fast and be spread over too wide a geographic area. Peters and Staley want Galambos to choose a city where closing down or decreasing marketing would have the least negative impact on the company's revenues. What city should she choose?

Excel Tutorial for Spreadsheet Case 13: Pivot Tables

This case asks you to use Excel for more than the routine tasks of entering and formatting data and using formulae and functions to calculate answers. In this case, you are being asked to look at existing data to discover correlations and predict trends.

Excel's data management commands provide some of this functionality, but often several commands and combinations of commands are needed to look at and compare the data you want to analyze. To look closely at one segment of data, like the first month of the year, you would first need to select and extract it with a filter, perhaps sort it and then perform calculations. This process would need to be repeated for each different segment of data, i.e., for each month. Perhaps you want to look at the data by quarters and not by months? Or by product type? Or by salesperson? For each different analysis, you would need to rearrange your data and repeat the commands and calculations.

Excel's Pivot Table command accomplishes the same results as many of the data commands more easily and without the need to disturb your original data. It allows you to summarize and analyze your data in alternative perspectives merely by dragging and dropping names. A pivot table can be used on data from large external data bases, or from Microsoft Access, as well as on one or multiple ranges from an Excel spreadsheet.

For this tutorial, you will use the student data file COURSE_DEMOGRAPHICS.xlsx. This file is automatically downloaded when you download files from the Web site www.MySolveit.Com. You will use this file to create a Pivot Table, and then to answer a number of questions. Once you complete this tutorial, you will have learned the skills needed to perform the tasks in this case.

The COURSE_DEMOGRAPHICS.xlsx student data file is a list of students in Professor Tom Jones biology class at Metro State University. The file contains data regarding each student's name, major, sex, attendance, and grade information.

Excel data used in a Pivot Table must be in the form of an Excel database or list, where: (1) each column has a label, (2) there are no blank rows or columns, and (3) there are no totals in the list. See the Tutorial for Case 10 for a review of Excel database requirements and functions.

Professor Tom Jones has several questions about his students:

- Did the men miss more classes than the women?

- Were the students from Springfield absent more often than others?

- Is it true that women get better grades?

- Does the student's birth month correlate to his or her grades?

Use the Excel student data COURSE_DEMOGRAPHICS.xlsx downloaded with your student files to create a pivot table to answer these questions. Before you create a pivot table, it is a good idea to give a range name to the list data. Here we have named cells A7:K107 as tblSTUDENT.

A pivot table consists of 4 areas:

- *Data* items are what you want to measure.

- *Columns* are usually the fields in which you are looking for a trend.

- *Rows* are usually the fields by which you want to categorize.

- *Pages* are often used for major categories.

In order to create a pivot table you must use the Pivot Table Wizard.

Creating a PivotTable

To create a Pivot Table:

1. Select the top left cell of data in your table, in this case, cell A8. This allows Excel to recognize the beginning of your data set.

2. Open the Insert tab on the Ribbon, and in theTables group, click *PivotTable*. This opens the PivotTable dialog box.

3. In the PivotTable dialog box, Excel automatically recognizes the data table to use (the range from A7:K106). Select *New Worksheet* for where you want the PivotTable report to be placed (Figure 3-20) and click *OK*.

Figure 3-20

4. Excel opens a new worksheet, Sheet1 with a blank PivotTable Report ready for you to configure. On the Ribbon, two PivotTable Tools tabs display with commands for working with PivotTables: Options and Design.

5. In the PivotTable Task pane on the right of the worksheet, drag the *CITY* field down from the Field List to the *Row Labels* box. (Not you could also drag this field to the worksheet, to the *Drop Row Fields Here* area.)

6. Drag the *SEX* field to the *Column Labels* box.

7. Drag the field *DAYS ABSENT* to the *Values* box. Your worksheet should resemble Figure 3-21 below.

Figure 3-21

Voila! You have created your first Pivot Table!

Examining Your Pivot Table

One of the most common problems people have with pivot tables is figuring out what to put where to get the answers they need. The pivot table you just created answers two of Professor

Jones' questions: "Did the men miss more classes than the women?" and "Were the students from Springfield absent more frequently than those from other cities?"

To answer both of these questions, it was necessary to use the fields for SEX and for CITY. The data being analyzed was DAYS ABSENT. Examine Figure 3-21. What are the answers?

Note that the pivot table is showing the raw number of days absent for students from each city and of each gender. This could be misleading if there were more men than women, or if there were a different number of students from each city (as there are). It would be more useful to obtain an average of the days absent rather than their sum. Below, we will see how easy it is to change the function in the data area from sum to average.

The pivot table is located on a new sheet in your workbook, with the PivotTable Task pane at the right. The Task pane and the PivotTable Tools tabs on the Ribbon remain visible as long as the PivotTable in the worksheet is active. If you click away from the PivotTable, the PivotTable tabs and the Pivot Table task pane close. You can easily reopen these by clicking within the Pivot Table on your worksheet.

Filters

Any field in the Row or Column area can be filtered to display only the categories you select, and the data totals will reflect only those categories. To filter the data so that only two cities are showing, click the list arrow above the CITY column on the table. Deselect *Select All*, select both *Centerville* and *Springfield* and click *OK*. Look at the Totals (Figure 3-22). Reselect *Show All* for CITY and notice the changed totals.

Solve it!

Figure 3-22

Add/Delete/Rearrange Fields in a Row or Column

To add or delete a field, just drag it to or from the Field List. You can add sub-rows or sub-columns by adding a second field beneath or to the left of another field.

To rearrange fields, simply drag and drop them to the desired location. Move *SEX* to the Row Labels box and *CITY* to the Column Labels box. Your pivot table should now look like Figure 3-23.

Figure 3-23

Change the Field in the Data Area

To change the field in the data area, drag the new field from the PivotTable Field List into the Values box and then remove the original field. To remove a field from one of the boxes at the bottom of the PivotTable Field List pane, simply drag it back to the list of fields at the top. You can also deselect the field's check box in the field list.

To answer Professor Jones' second two questions, you must analyze the Final Grades. Drag the *FINAL GRADE* field to the Values box and remove the field *DAYS ABSENT* by selecting and hiding it. Return the CITY field to the Row Labels box and the SEX field to the Column Labels box. Remove the filter on the City column.

Change the Type of Calculation in the Data Area

The default calculation for fields in the data area is Sum. However, Professor Jones wants to see the average of the Final Grade for each category. To change the type of calculation, first select any cell in the data area of the Pivot Table. On the PivotTable Tools: Options tab of the Ribbon, in the Active Field group, click *Field Settings*. This opens the Value Field Settings dialog box. On the Summarize by tab, select *Average* in the *Summarize value field by* list box. Click *OK* to close the Value Field Settings dialog box.

Format Data Cells

To remove the multiple decimal positions that appear for Average Grades, select any cell in the data area and click the *Field Settings* button on the Ribbon again. Click the *Number Format* button to open the Format Cells dialog box. In the left pane, click *Number*, and in the right pane, select *0* decimal places. Click *OK* twice to close the Format Cell dialog box and the Value Field Settings dialog box. Examine Figure 3-24.

Do women in this table get better grades?

Figure 3-24

Pages

Unlike the Row and Column areas, Page displays only all of the data categories in the field or any one category. It is a very helpful tool when analyzing large amounts of data. Essentially, the Page Area makes the pivot table a 3-dimensional cube of information. Drag the field *MAJOR* into the Drop Page Fields Here area on the worksheet, or into the *Report Filter* box on the PivotTable task pane. Click the arrow to the right of (ALL) and select MATH in the drop-down menu to see the only Math majors.

Grouping Data

One of the most powerful features of a pivot table is its ability to consolidate large amounts of data. Data can be grouped by categories you create, or for date or time data, by standard units of measurement such as months or hours. To group data, click on the field in the pivot table that you would like to see grouped. On the PivotTable Tools: Options tab, in the Group group, click *Group Selection*. In the Grouping dialog box that opens, select the parameters you wish and click *OK*.

Does a student's birth month correlate with his or her grades? Replace the *City* field in the *Row Labels* box with the *DOB* field, and group the DOB field by months to find out. See Figure 3-25.

Figure 3-25

Refreshing the Pivot Table

When changes are made in the original data, they are not immediately reflected in the table. To update the Pivot Table with the latest data, click the *Refresh* button on the PivotTable Tools: Options tab on the Ribbon, in the Data group.

Pivot Table Formatted Reports

Excel provides over 20 table and report formats to enhance your pivot table. To select one, open the PivotTable Tools: Design tab and select one of the many styles in the PivotTable Styles gallery. You can also change the layout of the table, including how to present subtotals, grand totals, whether the layout should be in compact, outline, or tabular form, and whether to include blank lines by using the commands in the Layout group. The PivotTable Style Options group allows you to select whether or not to show row and column headers, and whether columns or rows should be banded (alternately shaded). Select a Table Style that you feel enhances the Student pivot table and print it. If you want to return your Pivot Table to its original view, select *None*, which is the first Style thumbnail in the PivotTable Styles gallery. .

Now that you are comfortable with the basic concept of Pivot Tables, take a few minutes to answer some questions of your own about these students.

1. What major has the most women? What major has the most men?

2. From what city do the best performing students come?

3. Do you think that the PivotTable Styles help to clarify the data, or do they just make it "pretty?" Why?

If you make a mistake, remember that the *Undo* button on the *Quick Access* toolbar can reverse your actions and restore the screen to its original state.

4

Introduction to Database Software

This chapter describes the elements of a computerized database and how to use database software. The name "database" sounds formidable, but you use databases every day.

Some examples of common manual databases are telephone books, address books, and recipe collections. Digital databases we use everyday are lists of songs on our iPods or other MP3 players, the home pages of Web sites like Youtube.com and Yahoo.com, and of course search engines like Google. In fact, the entire World Wide Web is a collective database with somewhere over 10 billion pages.

In the business world, some common manual databases are a list of customers and customer addresses, a list of suppliers, a list of products sold and their respective prices, a list of products in inventory, and a filing cabinet that contains invoices arranged in numerical or date order. For the most part, with the exception of very small businesses, these manual databases have been converted to digital databases.

What is a Database?

These examples of common databases can help provide an initial definition of a database as any organized list or file of information about people, places, or things (see Figure 4-1).

For spreadsheet software, the central metaphor is that of a matrix where quantitative information is organized in rows and columns, but in a database, the central metaphor is that of a list or file where information is organized in rows (records) and columns.

Any problem in the real world that can be expressed as a problem of lists or files is potentially amenable to solution by a computerized database.

There are three basic types of databases: hierarchical, network, and relational. It is recommended that you consult a textbook for a detailed description of the various kinds of databases. Here we will describe only *relational databases*.

A simple example of a database file is a customer file:

Record #	Field 1	Field 2	Field 3
1			
2			
3			
4			

As you can see, in a database file all the information you have on an entry is called a *record*. Each record is composed of a number of *fields* that constitute the information stored on each entry. A collection of records is called a *file*. Below you will learn how to create a computerized database file, but modern database packages like Access offer much more than just computerized files.

Figure 4-1

Customer addresses in an address book

Employee information forms in file folders

Product sales information in a ledger

What is a Database Management System?

A database management system (DBMS) is a software package that, at a minimum, allows the user to create several different database files *and* relate information in one file to information in another file. Second, a modern DBMS provides a number of related tools needed to develop complete information systems.

One important advantage of *relational* database management systems over a manual filing cabinet is the ability to easily combine specific pieces of information (*fields*) from several different database files into a new file.

For instance, what if you wanted to determine a daily inventory that was calculated by deducting daily sales of all products from a beginning inventory?

Here, you would want to find out from the invoice file at the end of each day exactly which items were sold. You would then want to go to the inventory file and debit the existing inventory. In a truly sophisticated system, you might want to go into a third file that contained the names and addresses of your suppliers, and then generate a purchase order and mailing label for those products where inventory was low.

In a manual record system stored in the traditional filing cabinet, a lengthy search process would be required to solve this problem. In a contemporary relational database management system, the job can be done in seconds.

A second feature of a relational DBMS is a set of powerful tools that can be used to develop a complete information management system. Included here are facilities to create and store memos, notes, data entry screens (called forms in Access), reports, labels, and programs. These features are controlled through a powerful fourth generation language or menus that require little or no programming knowledge.

Briefly, a contemporary DBMS for the PC is a system development tool that permits the user to create complete management systems suitable for a small business or an office within a large business organization.

Comparative Advantages of Database Packages

Once students learn a relational database package, they often find it more powerful and useful than spreadsheet packages, yet the programs have very different strengths (and weaknesses).

Spreadsheet programs are very good at manipulating quantitative data, but they are poor at storing and manipulating lists or extracting parts of files from a larger data set. They generally are quite poor at combining information from several different files, and they typically have very limited macro or programming languages, although recent releases of popular spreadsheets have improved.

Database packages are very good at creating and manipulating lists of information, especially text information. Contemporary relational database packages have very friendly, easy-to-learn, menu-driven command systems that permit the novice to accomplish many, if not all, of the program's functions.

In addition, relational database packages are accompanied by powerful fourth-generation languages that are easy to learn and permit intermediate users to build complete information systems suitable for a small business or an office within a larger business.

Database software is comparatively weak at manipulating quantitative data. This gap, however, is closing with the development of more sophisticated reporting tools.

To operate a contemporary business, both kinds of packages are needed. Data can be exchanged between the packages so that the most appropriate software is used.

Introducing Microsoft Access for Windows

Microsoft Access 2007 is an integral part of Microsoft's Office 2007 suite of applications. An Access database is represented as a collection of objects. One database file (a file with an MDB or ACCDB extension) contains all the tables, queries, forms, reports, and other objects associated with a particular database. A brief description of these objects, the relationships between them within the database envelope, and the graphical buttons that identify them is shown in Figure 4-2.

Figure 4-2

A Microsoft Access Database

A Microsoft Access database can contain six types of database objects:

- **Tables** store data.
- **Queries** gather data you request from one or more tables. You can View or edit the data in a form or print it in a report.
- **Forms** display data from tables or queries so you can view, edit, or enter data.
- **Reports** summarize and present data from tables and queries so you can print it or analyze it.
- **Macros** automate your database by performing actions you specify, without the need of programming.
- **Modules** store Access Basic code you can write to customize, enhance, and extend your database.

Table

Query

Form

Report

Macro

Module

Access 2007 object names are not limited to eight characters as was true in older PC databases. Access object names (and field names in tables) can be up to 64 characters in length, and can include spaces as well as a mixture of upper and lowercase letters. Access is also not case sensitive, and it will locate data within a field (as long as the spelling is correct!) regardless of the case originally used to enter it.

The Ribbon

In Office 2007, the Ribbon replaces the Menu bar as well as the Standard toolbar and other toolbars used in previous Office versions for access to commands and settings. The Ribbon runs across the top of the screen, and commands are grouped into separate tabs, according to the general type of work being performed.

The Home tab contains the most commonly accessed buttons and functions. The Create tab contains commands for creating new tables, forms, reports, queries, and macros. The External Data tab includes commands for importing, exporting, and collecting external data and for working with a SharePoint server (a Microsoft Office networking application). On the Database Tools tab are command s for managing your database, such as working with macros and analyzing performance.

A number of Ribbon tabs are contextual: they only appear when you are working with an object that requires them. For example, the three Report Layout Tools tabs (Format, Arrange, and Page Setup) are hidden until you begin working with a report. Similarly, some Office or Access add-in programs may have their own tab that is present only when the add-in is enabled. For example, if your version of Office has the Adobe Acrobat add-in installed for working with PDFs, your Office programs will include an Acrobat tab on the Ribbon.

Many of the commands on the Ribbon are presented as buttons to click; others with arrows lead to a drop-down list of related commands and options. Some commands may include a text box you can type into or be check boxes that you select to enable or disable certain settings. If you are uncertain what a button's function is, you can hover the mouse pointer over a button and a ScreenTip will appear to name and describe the button, and give its keyboard shortcut, if any.

Another new feature of Office 2007 is the Microsoft Office button: the large round button at the top left of the screen with the Office logo. Clicking this button leads to commands and settings for working with the application or with a document as a whole, and contains many of the commands formerly found on the File menu in earlier versions of Access. For example, the commands for Opening, Printing, Saving, and Closing a file are found on the Office menu.

To the right of the Office button is the Quick Access toolbar: by default it contains the *Save, Undo,* and *Redo* button commands, but you can add or remove commands as you please by clicking the arrow to the right of the toolbar.

Get Help At Any Time!

Access 2007 includes two other interactive help tools: an extensive context-sensitive help system (press **[F1]** or click the icon with the question mark at the top right of the window at any time to launch Access Help), and various of wizards that offer help in creating Access objects, such as tables, queries, forms, reports, and macros. Unlike the main help system, which you must search or browse to find answers to questions, wizards ask you relevant questions and actually create a customized version of the object in question according to your responses. A summary of Access wizards used in this edition of *Solve it!* is presented in Figure 4-3.

Other Access Wizards include the Input Mask Wizard, the Lookup Wizard, the Simple Query Wizard, the Label Wizard, the Chart Wizard, the Table Analyzer Wizard, the Database Documenter Wizard, the Import Spreadsheet Wizard, the Import Text Wizard, the Link Text Wizard, the Find Unmatched Query Wizard, the Find Duplicates Query Wizard, the Crosstab Query Wizard, the PivotTable Wizard, the Database Splitter Wizard, and the User-Level Security Wizard.

Figure 4-3

Query Wizard	Helps users construct complex queries for common database management tasks, such as the merging two tables or performing cross tabulations.
Form Wizard	A tool for creating forms in a variety of predefined formats and presentation styles.
Report Wizard	A tool for creating reports in a variety of predefined formats and presentation styles.
Macro Wizard	A tool used for creating or editing a macro from within an event procedure in a form or report.
Control Wizards	Creates code behind command buttons, option groups, and list and combo boxes used in forms or reports.

Access Setup Requirements

To use Access 2007 (Microsoft Office Professional 2007) you will need:
- A personal computer with 500 MHz or faster processor
- Available hard-disk space usage will vary depending on configuration and operating system (2 GB recommended for Office 2007 Professional).
- 256 MB of RAM
- Operating Systems: Microsoft Windows 2000 with service pack 2 (SP2) or higher, Windows Server 2003 with SP1, or later
- 1024X768 or higher resolution monitor

Terminology and Conventions Used in the Access Tutorials:

- *Double-click* means to press the left mouse button twice in rapid succession.
- *Click* means to press the left mouse button once only.
- *Right-click* means to click the right mouse button once.

- New terms, new file names, key concepts, commands and menu choices, and action words appear in *italics*.

- New object names are shown in bold (e.g., **MyContacts**).

Getting Started—Access 2007 for Windows

To Start Access 2007

1. From Windows, click on the *Start* button at bottom left of the screen, and then point to *Programs* (or *All Programs* in Windows XP).

2. Within the Programs menu, point to *Microsoft Office 2007*, and then select the *Microsoft Office Access 2007* option. This action will start the Access program. The application opens with a Getting Started window that allows you to choose a database template to begin working with, open and read articles related to Access and Office 2007, as well as create a new database or open an existing one.

Creating a Database in Access 2007

Now that you've started the program, let's create a database. Throughout Chapter 5 we will be using a practice database table called **FRIENDS** in the tutorial sessions to illustrate the various features of Access. A copy of this practice table is included in the student data files you have downloaded from the MySolveIt.com Web site). But let's build this database from scratch to show you how easy it is to work with Access.

1. With Access 2007 started, click the Office button, and then click *New*. (Alternatively, you can click the *Blank Database* button at the top of the main pane of the Getting Started window). On the right of the Getting Started window, a Blank Database section appears to help you begin a new database.

2. In the *File Name* text box, name the database **Contacts.accdb**, and then click the Folder icon to specify the file location where the new database should be stored. (Note that previous versions of Excel use a different file format, with the extension .mdb. Excel 2007 can open, work with, and save files using the .mdb extension as well as the .accdb file format. However, earlier versions of Excel will not be able to work with .accdb files.) For convenience, save the new database in the same directory where you are storing your other *Solve it!* Student Files. Now click *Create* to create and save the database.

3. After you create the database, Access opens a new, blank table for you to begin adding records to the database. It also displays the Datasheets tab on the Ribbon which contains commands for working with tables and populating them with data (Figure 4-4).

    On the left of the Access window is the Navigation Pane, which allows you to navigate to different Access objects by locating and clicking the name of the object. You can specify which types of objects are shown and how they are grouped in the Navigation pane by setting the options in the Navigation Pane menu. To open the menu, click the down arrow at the top of the pane. In the Navigate to Category section, you can specify how the objects displayed in the pane are grouped. Click *All Access Objects*. In the Filter by Group section, you can limit the objects that are viewed to certain categories. Click *All Access Objects* in this section. For now, only Table1 shows, because currently it is the only object in the database.

You can collapse the Navigation Pane by clicking the Shutter Bar *Open/Close* button – the button with two arrows to the left of the Navigation Pane Title. To open the Navigation Pane you can click either on the Shutter Bar *Open/Close* button or click directly on the shutter bar itself (the narrow, vertical blue bar that reads Navigation Pane.)

Figure 4-4

Creating Tables in Access

Access has automatically created the blank Table1 object to begin building a database because all the basic information stored in a database is stored as records in a table. A database table is a matrix of rows and columns, just like a spreadsheet. Each row in an Access table is a *record*, and each column is a *field* that describes some unique information about the records.

For instance, a telephone book is a familiar table:

Last Name	First Name	Address	Phone Number
Bell	Robert	52 Galley Road	737-3423
Bellini	Andrew	9 Francis Drive	736-9005
Bellis	Aldo	241 Albany Road	528-2007
Belotti	John	32 Forest Ave	736-9340

Each row contains the information on a unique record—in this case a person. Each column contains important information about all the records—in this case last name, first name, address, and phone number. These columns are called fields in the language of databases.

Now let's create the basic table for our practice Contacts database. In Access you can work with Tables in two different ways:

- **Design View:** In this view, you work with field names and properties. This view is useful for creating and modifying the table itself.

- **Datasheet View:** In this view, data is presented similar to a spreadsheet matrix; it is useful for entering and editing data.

Let's use the Design View because it will give you a better understanding of how tables are built and used. You can return later and practice using the Datasheet View for creating tables.

1. On the Datasheet tab on the Ribbon, click the *View* button (in the Views group) to open the View menu and then click *Design View*. You will be prompted to name the table; type *MyContacts* as the table name. The Design View appears, along with the Table Tools: Design tab on the Ribbon (Figure 4-5). The name of the table in the Navigation pane is changed to *MyContacts*.

Figure 4-5

The Design View allows you to determine what fields you want in your database. In the Contacts database you will want to keep track of all your professional and business contacts. Here's a list of fifteen basic fields you would want in a contacts file:

CUSTOMER_ID	CITY	FAX
LAST_NAME	STATE	LAST_MEETING_DATE
FIRST_NAME	ZIP	NOTES
COMPANY	BUSINESS	PROFESSIONAL
STREET	MOBILE	PERSONAL

2. Access has automatically created the first field for you, ID, which can be used as a "primary key" to uniquely identify any record in your table. Primary keys will be discussed later in this chapter. Retitle this field CUSTOMER_ID, to match the first field in our list above. Then, press [Tab] to move the insertion point into the second column, Data Type, to create a second field.

3. In the second row, under Field Name, enter the first field from the table above, CUSTOMER ID, then press [Tab]. The cursor moves to the Data Type column. Even a simple personal contacts database has many different types of data, from text for names, to dates and binary yes/no data (personal versus professional contact). There are eleven different data types in Access 2007 (see Figure 4-6).

Figure 4-6

Text	Use for text, combinations of text and numbers (such as an address), or numbers on which you don't intend to perform calculations (such as phone numbers or part numbers).
Memo	Use for longer text, such as notes and comments.
Number	Use for data on which you might want to perform calculations, unless it's money.
Date/Time	Use for dates and times.
Currency	Use for large numbers requiring rapid calculation, or numbers that require highly accurate rounding, such as money.
AutoNumber	Use to automatically assign consecutive or unique values, such as invoice numbers.
Yes/No	Use for true/false, yes/no, or on/off values.
OLE Object	Use for inserting other OLE compatible files or objects, such as pictures or Excel spreadsheets.
Hyperlink	Use to store text or combinations of text and numbers as a hyperlink address; This is typically used for connection to data stored on the public World Wide Web or a firm's internal Intranet.
Attachment	Use to attach one or more files to a record; takes up less file space than OLE Object.
Lookup Wizard	Use to create a field that allows selection of a value from another Access table or from a list of values.

You can see these different data types by clicking on the down arrow in the Data Type column. The Data Type drop down list begins with Text—alphanumeric characters. In this case—for the CUSTOMER_ID field—you will want to keep the Auto Number data type that Access has selected. This will result in Access assigning a unique consecutive number to each contact. However, for other fields you will want to store other data types. For example, for the LAST_NAME field you would select *Text* as the data type; for the NOTES field you would to select *Memo* as the data type; and for the LAST_MEETING_DATE field you would select the *Date/Time* data type. For the PROFESSIONAL and PERSONAL fields, which will be used to indicate whether the contact is a professional and/or a personal contact, use the *Yes/No* data type.

Contrary to what you might think at first, telephone numbers and zip codes are usually created as Text data types simply because there are no calculations that will be performed with these numbers. When finished, your table will use five data types: AutoNumber (CUSTOMER_ID), Date/Time (LAST_MEETING_DATE), Memo (NOTES) and Yes/No (PROFESSIONAL, PERSONAL), and Text (all other fields).

4. Now that you have created your first field CUSTOMER_ID, press [Tab] to move the cursor to the Description column. Here you can enter a description of the field, but this is not required. The description appears in the status bar when using an Access database. For now, leave this area blank.

5. The Field Properties area in the lower half of the Table Design View window allows you to specify the properties for each field, and to control the kinds of data entered into the database for each field. For instance, you might want to restrict the length of the Last Name field to 30 characters; prevent the entry of text data in a date field; or force users to enter data in some required fields before accepting any of their data. For now, accept the default values.

6. Use your mouse to place the cursor in the second row of the Table Design View, and enter the second field name: LAST_NAME and select its data type. Repeat this process for the remaining fourteen fields defined in the personal contacts table above. Your MyContacts table should look like the table in Figure 4-7.

7. When you are finished entering all the fields in the Contacts database, close the Design view window by clicking on the *Close Window* button [X] to the far right of the MyContacts tab.

Congratulations! You have defined your first table in a database!

Figure 4-7

Adding Records to the Contacts Database

Now that you've created the **Contacts** database, add records to the MyContacts table for three of your closest professional or personal contacts.

Double-click on the **MyContacts** table in the Navigation pane. The MyContacts table will open in Datasheet View, with the fields displayed across the top of the table. The cursor prompts for you to enter data into the first field. Since the first field is CUSTOMER_ID, and will be autonumbered, press [Tab] to the second field, FIRST_NAME, and begin enter your first record. When you are finished filling all fields for the first record, and press ENTER. Repeat for two more contacts.

Modifying a Database and Changing Tables

You can re-enter the design view and change a database table at any time.

1. On the Home tab of the Ribbon, click the *Design View* button in the Views group. This button changes from Design View to Datasheet View, depending on which view you are in at the moment, allowing you to toggle quickly between the two views. Alternatively, you can click the small *Design View* icon at the far right of the bottom Status bar of the Access window.

2. Add a new field MIDDLE_NAME to the list of fields between LAST_NAME and FIRST_NAME. Place your cursor in the LAST_NAME row. On the Design tab of the Ribbon, in the Tools group, click *Insert Rows*. This will add a row above the currently selected row. Now enter MIDDLE_NAME as a field.

3. You can also delete fields in Design View. Open the Table Tools: Design tab and click the *Delete Rows* button or right-click a row and select *Delete Rows* on the shortcut menu.

Primary Keys

Access uses a unique tag called a primary key to identify each record in a table. As a license plate is unique to car, or a fingerprint is unique to an individual, the primary key should uniquely identify each record. While tables can be created without declaring any field as primary, Access discourages this by prompting you every time you create a table to define a primary key.

Why are primary keys so important? Mainly because primary key fields are used to create relationships between tables. Why would you want to have multiple tables? In a simple database like **Contacts**, a single table is sufficient for the basic purpose of keeping track of friends. But in the business world matters are more complex, and a single table rarely is sufficient to capture all the information required to support a business.

For instance, consider a typical business that uses a sales force to sell products to customers. In order to keep track of customers, their orders, the parts they ordered, sales people, and shipping information, you probably will want to have at least five different tables in your sales database—one for each of the entities you want to keep track of. You will want one table for customers, another for orders, and others for order details, employees (sales people) and shippers (see Figure 4-8). And you want to be able to pull information from each of these tables in a flexible manner in order to answer important business questions.

In Figure 4-8 the primary keys for each table have been selected. The primary keys are used to build relationships between the various tables in a database so complex queries can be answered. For instance, if you want to know what sales person made a sale to a specific customer, and when was it shipped, you would have to draw information from the following tables: customers, orders, employees, and shippers.

Figure 4-8

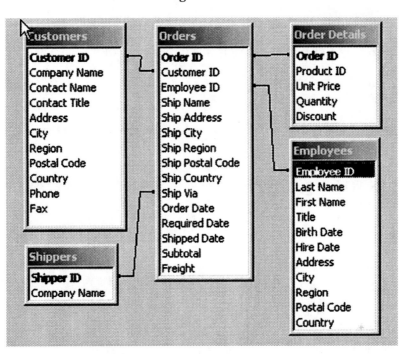

Not all fields are good candidates for primary keys. For instance, if you chose the Last Name field as a primary key, your table could not contain two records with the last name "Jones." Because many large databases have persons with duplicate last names, Last Name is not a good choice as a unique identifier of people. Telephone numbers are often unique, but sometimes two people share a single phone number.

Some number fields make good primary keys. For example, an employee ID number would uniquely identify each record in an Employee table. Similar unique numbers include a product number (SKU or stocking unit number), an order number, or employee ID number. In our case we are using the unique CUSTOMER_ID number created for each contact. But what if we wished to use another field as primary key?

Let's look at how to assign a primary key.

1. Open the MyContacts table in Design View.

2. Place the cursor in the first field CUSTOMER_ID. This is a unique number for each contact. Notice that a key symbol appears to the left of the field, indicating that this is a primary key field. On the Design tab, the *Primary Key* button in theTools group is also highlighted.

3. Click the *Primary Key* button on the Ribbon. This action removes the Primary Key status of the current field, and the key symbol beside the CUSTOMER_ID field disappears.

4. Place the cursor in the second field, LAST_NAME and click *Primary Key* again. This assigns LAST_NAME as the primary key of the table.

5. You do not need to unassign a field as primary key before you reassign another. To reassign CUSTOMER_ID as the primary key place your cursor in the CUSTOMER_ID field and press the *Primary Key* button to change the primary key of the table.

Exiting Access

You now have enough information to complete the database cases in Chapter 5. To exit Access, click

the Office button and then click *Exit Access* or click on the *Close* button at the far right of the title bar, to close the program. When you are prompted, save the changes to your Contacts database.

5

Database Management Software Cases

DATABASE CASE 1
Northampton Abrasives

Problem:	Create and modify a sales support system.
Management Skill:	Organize
Access Skill:	Data Table Setup
	Data Input and Editing
	Selecting Data Subsets
	Printing
Data Table:	NORTHAMPTON

Luisa Delgado had always been competitive. As long as she could remember, there was always something to strive for: getting better grades, achieving faster times in her long distance running, and outdoing her three sisters. It thus gave her great satisfaction to learn last week that she had been selected as "Salesperson of the Year." She had sold more abrasives, grinding wheels, and sandpaper last year than any of the other 196 sales staff at Northampton Abrasives Inc.

Northampton Abrasives was founded in Massachusetts in 1919 shortly after World War I. The founders recognized the growing need by metal and wood manufacturers for various abrasives and other finishing supplies to complete their products. Northampton's primary customers were furniture manufacturers in the northeastern United States. The family-owned business grew solidly throughout the years, and by 2009, the company was the leading supplier of abrasives and cutting tools to the furniture industry in the country.

Recent advances in computer-controlled machinery, along with robotics and flexible manufacturing systems, provided a strong growth period for Northampton. The new machines required large quantities of high quality abrasives, particularly sandpaper belts. These expensive machine tools were used on a 24/7 basis. To minimize downtime and maintain high quality, sandpapers were changed frequently, often before wearing out.

Although very profitable, the abrasive supply industry had become very competitive. Northampton Abrasives had many competitors who undercut them on particular items, but only 3M had as large a range of products. Northampton Abrasives follows a high product quality and premium pricing strategy based on excellent customer service. Their competitive advantage lies in three areas:

- A comprehensive product range

- A hard-working and knowledgeable sales force

- Guaranteed overnight delivery for stock items

Delgado has been very successful in presenting Northampton Abrasives to her customers as a provider of a full range of abrasive and refinishing supplies. Rather than approach new companies, she has concentrated on increasing the average purchase of existing clients.

In the four years Luisa Delgado has been with Northampton Abrasives, her rise to success has been rapid. It seemed that only yesterday she had started out as a trainee sales representative with old Howard "Killer" McNeeley. McNeeley preached that there were only two important things in sales: *"Get close to the customer and know the products inside-out."*

Delgado kept her client information in a large notebook ledger. The data was stored alphabetically by the client's company name. She had acquired more than 250 companies in her Midwestern territory of Iowa, Kansas, Oklahoma, Missouri, and Nebraska.

Within each company, she called on an average of four different groups of people in purchasing, engineering, production, and the workshop. She had nearly 920 names as well as details on the products they ordered and plenty of other useful information. Delgado often asked about her clients' wives or husbands by name, and she always knew the pattern of their last few orders. If the orders were decreasing, she asked why and found out if one of her competitors had more fully met any of her client's needs.

As her client base expanded, Delgado's ledger became impossibly heavy. She was also constantly trying to find information that was in the ledger but was not easily accessible. For example, last month a new low-cost sandpaper belt for soft woods had been introduced. Delgado wanted to know which of her clients had ordered the product it superseded so she could write or call on all those clients and demonstrate the new product. Locating that information in her ledger would have taken a week of searching, so she relied on her memory, but she felt sure that she had overlooked some major users.

Delgado had tried asking Northampton's overworked Information Systems department to get the information for her from past invoices, but the IS Manager replied, *"We'd love to, but we can't even finish our own work. Besides, I don't think it's possible. You'd be better off putting it on a laptop computer and using a database package like Access. It will be much more flexible than our system. It's also cheaper and portable."*

One of the perks of winning the "Salesperson of the Year" award was a new ideas budget of $35,000, which Delgado has decided to devote to her new Sales Support System. Delgado has purchased a laptop computer with Microsoft Office 2007 that includes Access. She wants you to help her build prepare a prototype database that could take the place of her manual system.

Delgado wants all of the important data to be entered into the database so she can look up information in many different ways, even while she's on the road. At night in her hotel room, she can update the database after visiting clients throughout the day. Delgado feels certain the new system will enable her to keep improving her performance and maybe even win her the "Salesperson of the Year" award a second time.

The important fields for the prototype system are:

Company Name	First Name	Product Group
Address	Last Name	Spouse Name
City	Department	Order Pattern
State	Title	CompanyID
Zip	Last Order Date	

Northampton Abrasives' products are classified into three major groups: grinding wheels (G), sandpaper (S), other refinishing supplies (O). Within each group, there are up to 99 subgroups, i.e. S01 to S99. Order patterns are coded as: increasing (I), decreasing (D), or stable (S). Each client company is assigned a 5-digit identification number.

A portion of Delgado's database has been started for you in the table NORTHAMPTON in SOLVEIT_CH5.ACCDB database. Create a new Access database and import this object now.

Tasks

There are seven tasks in this case:

1. Complete the table structure to include the information desired by Delgado.

2. (a) Enter data for the new fields to complete the existing records. (b) Enter data for three new clients into the data table.

3. Alicia Martin, the Production Manager for Martin Mechanics in Kansas City, Missouri, has retired and was replaced by Jack Stallmayer. Jack's wife's name is Judy, and he will now be known as the Production Director. Update the data in the table to reflect these changes.

4. Print a listing of the entire table.

5. Print all of the records in the table, but only include the following fields: Company, City, Client First and Last Names, and Last Order Date.

6. Delgado is traveling to Kansas City to meet Jack Stallmayer at Martin Mechanics and wants to know her other clients in Kansas City. Create a query, and then print a listing of all clients based in Kansas City. The list should only include these fields: Company, Client First and Last Names, and Title.

*7. After using the client database for three months, Delgado reports tremendous savings in time and she is able to do her job more efficiently. She has found, however, that the database does not handle customers that buy from more than one product group. For example, General Electric purchases products from the G10, S20, S35, S40, S30, O50, and O70 product groups. Find a way to incorporate this extra information into the database.

Time Estimates (excluding tasks marked with *)

Expert:	30 minutes
Intermediate:	1 hour
Novice:	1.5 hours

Tutorial for Case 1 Using Access 2007

To learn and practice the skills for this case, and many of the following cases, you will need to use the practice database table FRIENDS, which is one of the tables in the SOLVEIT_CH5.ACCDB database that you downloaded with your Student Files.

Access Help

You can use Microsoft Access Help at any time by clicking the *Help* button at the top

right of the Access window or pressing F1 on the keyboard.

To start Access:

1. Click *Start* to open the Start menu. Point to *All Programs* (or *Programs*), and then point to *Microsoft Office 2007* on the Programs menu. If you are having difficulties, ask your instructor for assistance.

2. Click on *Microsoft Office Access 2007* in the Microsoft Office 2007 submenu to launch the Access program.

3. Click the *Office* button and then click *Open*. Use the Open dialog box that opens to navigate to the SOLVEIT_CH5 database, which you downloaded from the Solve It! Web site. Once you find the database, double-click on the file to open the database. You may see a security warning below the Ribbon that alerts you that some content has been disabled. If so, click the warning's *Options* button and enable the content.

4. Double-click on the FRIENDS table in the Navigation Pane to open the table displayed in the default Datasheet View.

Note: To import a table from a separate Access database, click the External Data tab on the Ribbon, and in the Import group, click *Access*. In the Get External Data – Access Database wizard, click *Browse* and navigate to the database file from which you are importing the table. Make sure the *Import tables, etc.* option button is selected and click *OK*. In the Import Objects dialog box, select the objects you wish to import and click *OK*. Click *Close* to close the Get External Data wizard. The imported object will display in your database's Navigation Pane.

Access displays table data in columns and rows, similar to a spreadsheet. Each row in an Access table represents a *record*, and each column represents a *field*. For example, in Figure 5-1, there are 20 records in the FRIENDS table, and the *Current Record* box, at the bottom of the table's window, displays 1 of 20indicates that record 1 is currently selected. Above the rows of records are the *field selectors*, which contain the field names for each column. Fields describe various categories of information (e.g.: Last_Name, First_Name) that make up each record. To the left of each record are the *record selectors*, which are used to select a particular record. A record selector is highlighted in blue to indicate the currently selected record and highlighted in orange you click in a cell to begin editing. As you make changes within a record, a pencil icon displays. An asterisk appears in the record selector of a new record into which you can enter data

Figure 5-1

CONTACT N ▾	LAST_NAME ▾	FIRST_NAM ▾	STREET ▾	CITY ▾	STATE ▾	ZIP
	Drucker	Peter H.	345 Warren Road	Hudson	New York	12305
2	Whitney	Craig	25 Wood Lake Road	Morris	New Jersey	25059
3	Sitkin	Howard W.	17 Morace Street	Springvale	New Hampshire	49492
4	Skalek	William F.	8 Yorkshire Place	Teatown	South Dakota	39285
5	Salione	Phillip	35 Truesdale Ave	Phoenix	Arizona	35842
6	Fabian	James T.	36 Palmer Court	Chicago	Illinois	30928
7	Kohlman	Frank	35 Miller Drive	Milwaukee	Wisconsin	49740
8	Tedesco	George R.	346 Skytop Drive	Spokane	Washington	35828
9	Zito	Helen K.	64 Albany Post Rd.	Dana	Maryland	35080
10	Peterson	Jack S.	54 Elmor Ave	Barston	Ohio	39897
11	Nelson	Robert M.	1 Franklin Ave.	St. Louis	Missouri	34097
12	Buckley	Denise	23 Georgetown Rd.	Chicago	Illinois	30928
13	Roberts	James	567 Ridge Rd.	Columbus	Ohio	56778
14	Thompson	Howard	799 Tucker Ave.	Blakeley	Wisconsin	35899
15	Parker	Gina	640 Palm Tree Lane	Phoenix	Arizona	35899
16	Jones	Timothy	89945 Marydale Lane	Starkey	New Hampshire	49478
17	Kaufman	William	7654 Flamton St.	Milwaukee	Wisconsin	49788
18	Timko	Rebecca	34 Salem Ave.	Spokane	Washington	35829
19	Emerson	Douglas	789 Carmichael Ave.	Boston	Massachusetts	12345
20	Hicks	Kevin	3407 Nathrop Dr.	Chicago	Illinois	30987
*	(New)					

Tables can be displayed in two ways. Figure 5-1 shows the default Datasheet View, represented by the Datasheet View button on the status bar ▦. Datasheets are used to display, edit, and delete records, as well as to print tables. Later in this tutorial, we will also be using Design View, represented by the status bar button ◣. Design View is used for adding, editing, and deleting fields, as well as for defining field properties and indexes.

Navigating Within a Datasheet

Use your [Tab] key or click with your mouse to move to a particular column within a record. Use the horizontal or vertical scroll bars to practice viewing records and fields in the datasheet. Use the *Specific Record* box and the navigation buttons shown in Figure 5-2 to move to a specific record in the datasheet.

Figure 5-2

Resizing Columns and Rows in an Access Datasheet

To resize a column (field), position your mouse on the right edge of a column at the field selector level, (e.g.: Last_Name). When a horizontal resize pointer ✛ displays, as shown in Figure 5-3, drag horizontally until the column is the desired size. You can also double-click the right edge of any column heading to automatically resize the width to display all data in the column. You can also right-click on a selected column and click the *Column Width* command to open the Column Width dialog box. (Alternatively, on the Home tab, in the Records group, click *More* and then click *Column Width* on the drop-down menu.) Click *Best Fit* to size the column so that all data in the column displays, or enter a specific width in the *Column Width* box and click *OK*.

Record rows can be resized by positioning the mouse pointer between any two record selectors at the left side of the datasheet. When a vertical resize pointer ✛ displays, drag up or down until the rows are the desired size. *Warning: Unlike column resizing, this will resize all of the rows.*

Figure 5-3

Saving Datasheet Layout Changes

Open the Office menu and click the *Save* command, or click 🖫 on the Quick Access toolbar.

Printing a Datasheet

With the table open in Datasheet View, open the Office menu and choose the *Print* command to open the Print dialog box. If you have selected only certain records for printing, click the *Selected Records* option button in the *Print Range* section of the dialog box and then click *OK*. You can also choose the number of copies to print in the *Copies* section.

How to Change the Structure of an Access Table

Table Design View is used for establishing and modifying the field structure of a table. To switch to Design View, click the *Design View* button ◩ at the right of the bottom status bar, or, on the Home tab, in the View group, click the *Design View* button ◪ if it is available. (This button typically toggles between Datasheet View and Design View.) If it is not, you can click the arrow on the bottom half of the *View* button to open the View menu and click *Design View*.

As you move around the Design View window (see Figure 5-4), a help box on the right side of the Field Properties pane, in the bottom half of the window, describes the purpose of the currently selected property. For example, the required Data Type property is used to determine the kinds of values that can be entered and stored in a field. Let's add a new field called TITLE to the table to store titles, such as *Mrs.*, *Ms.*, *Mr.*, and *Dr.*

Figure 5-4

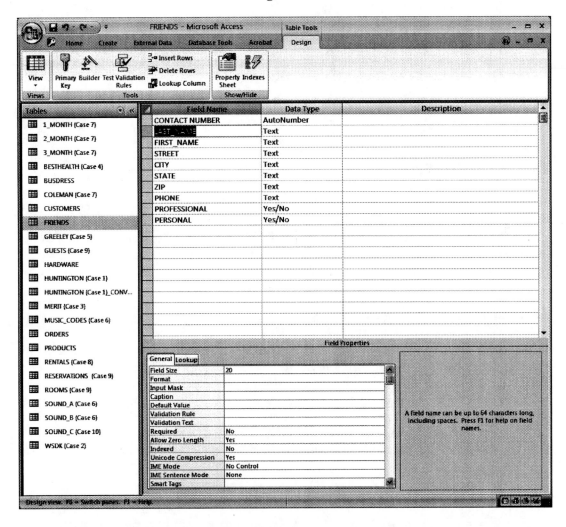

1. Add the Title field before the Last_Name field. Position your mouse pointer over the row selector for the Last_Name field, and then click once to select the field. On the Table Tools: Design tab, in the Tools group, click *Insert Rows* to insert a blank row above the Last_Name field.

2. Click in the blank *Field Name* column and type *TITLE*.

3. Click in the blank *Data Type* column to choose the kind of data the field will accept.

   In this case, the default Text data type is the one we need. Notice the list arrow on the right end of the cell. Clicking the list arrow will open a list of the other available data types. Review the Access data types section in Chapter 4 for an explanation of each data type.

4. Click in the *Field Size* cell in the Field Properties pane. The default width for text fields is 255 characters. Since the field will contain only abbreviated terms, change the field size to 5 characters.

5. Click the Office button and select *Save*, or click the 💾 on the Quick Access toolbar to save the changes.

6. On the Table Tools: Design tab of the Ribbon, click the top half of the *View* button ▦ or click ▥ in the Shortcuts section of the status bar to return to Datasheet View.

How to Enter Records

Scroll down to the end of the record set to the row indicated by the New Record symbol (*) in the record selector. Click inside the first empty field of this row. Add one record to the FRIENDS table. Move between fields using the [Tab] key. Press [Tab] once more to move to the first field of the next record. Access will automatically save your data when you leave a record either by moving to another record or by closing the table.

How to Edit Existing Records

In Datasheet View, move to the empty *Title* field and add appropriate titles for each of the records in the FRIENDS table. For example, for the record Peter Drucker, click in the *Title* field and enter the title *Dr*. Notice that the pencil symbol appears in the record selector, indicating that the record is being edited. Press the down arrow key on the keyboard to move to the Title field for the next record. Add a title and continue down the column to add titles for the remaining records. As you move down the column, the pencil symbol will appear in each record you are editing and Access will automatically save the changes.

Closing a Table

Just below the application window's *Minimize* ▬, *Maximize* ▭, and *Close* ✕ buttons at the top right of the Access window is a second set of *Minimize, Maximize,* and *Close* buttons. These are for the currently opened object in Access – in this case, the FRIENDS table. (Note that if the FRIENDS table's window is already minimized, these icons will appear on the top right of the table's window). Click ✕ to close the table.

How to Display and Print Selected Fields: Building a Query 1:

A *query* is a question that you ask about certain data in a database, such as, "How many customers live in Melbourne?" or "What were our sales figures for last month?"

Alternatively, you may just want to view selected fields of a database in a certain order. The Select Query window is a graphical query-by-example (QBE) tool. This means you can use the mouse to select and drag the fields you wish to view to the window. Then you can choose to view the data in a certain order or set criteria so that only records that meet those criteria will display (e.g. customers who live in Melbourne). In other words, you are defining an example of the records you wish to view.

Let's say that you want to display and print just three fields from the FRIENDS table: Last_Name, First_Name, and City. Here's how to create an Access query to do this:

1. Open the Create tab on the Ribbon. In the Other group, click *Query Design*. Access opens a select query window with a design grid at the bottom. The Show Table dialog box also opens above the query window (see Figure 5-5). Notice also that the contextual tab Query Tools: Design appears and opens on the Ribbon because you are working with a select query.

2. In the Show Table dialog box, select the table you want to base the query on, in this case, *FRIENDS*, and then click *Add*. This adds a field list for the FRIENDS table to the query window. Click the *Close* button to close the Show Table dialog box.

Figure 5-5

3. Select the *Last_Name* field in the FRIENDS field list. Hold down the [Ctrl] key and select *First_Name* and then *City*. (The [Ctrl] key is handy to use when selecting nonadjacent fields for a query.) Release the [Ctrl] key.

4. Use the mouse to drag the selection to the design grid. Release the mouse button when the mouse pointer is in the first Field cell in the design grid. The three fields are added in order to the design grid as shown in Figure 5-6.

Figure 5-6

5.   Click the *Run* button on the Query Tools: Design tab, in the Results group, or to generate the query results set as shown in Figure 5-7.

Figure 5-7

LAST_NAME	FIRST_NAME	CITY
Drucker	Peter H.	Hudson
Whitney	Craig	Morris
Sitkin	Howard W.	Springvale
Skalek	William F.	Teatown
Salione	Phillip	Phoenix
Fabian	James T.	Chicago
Kohlman	Frank	Milwaukee
Tedesco	George R.	Spokane
Zito	Helen K.	Dana
Peterson	Jack S.	Barston
Nelson	Robert M.	St. Louis
Buckley	Denise	Chicago
Roberts	James	Columbus
Thompson	Howard	Blakeley
Parker	Gina	Phoenix
Jones	Timothy	Starkey
Kaufman	William	Milwaukee
Timko	Rebecca	Spokane
Emerson	Douglas	Boston
Hicks	Kevin	Chicago
Hawthorn	Diane	New York

6. Click the Office button and click *Print* to open the Print dialog box and click *OK* to print the query.

7. Click the *Design View* button to return to the Query Design window.

8. Click the *Save* button ⊞, or click the Office button and then *Save* to save the query. Type *Tute1Query1* in the *Query Name* text box in the *Save as* dialog box and click OK.

On the Query Tools: Design tab, in the Results group, click *View* and then click *SQL View* to view the Structured Query Language code generated by Access for the query. You can also find the SQL View command by clicking the SQL View icon **SQL** on the far right of the window's bottom status bar, next to the Design View icon.

SELECT FRIENDS.LAST_NAME, FRIENDS.FIRST_NAME,
FRIENDS.CITY
FROM FRIENDS;

This code can be cut and pasted into an event procedure within a macro or a module and used as part of a larger program. Access provides a number of useful programming shortcuts. We will be looking at some of these in later cases. Return to Design View for Tute1Query1.

How to Display Selected Records: Building a Query 2

Now that you have constructed a simple query, let's go one step further and search the FRIENDS table for records that meet specific criteria. In this example, let's extract only those records that contain *Mr.* in the Title field.

1. Open Tute1Query1 in Design View. Select the *Title* field in the FRIENDS field list. Drag the selected field to the design grid and release the mouse button over the Last_Name field. Access automatically moves the fields to the right and inserts the Title field as the first field in the query.

2. In the *Criteria* cell for the Title field, type: *Mr.* On the Query Tools: Design tab of the Ribbon, in the Results group, click the *Run* button The query result set is displayed in Figure 5-8.

Figure 5-8

TITLE	LAST_NAME	FIRST_NAME	CITY
Mr.	Whitney	Craig	Morris
Mr.	Sitkin	Howard W.	Springvale
Mr.	Skalek	William F.	Teatown
Mr.	Salione	Phillip	Phoenix
Mr.	Fabian	James T.	Chicago
Mr.	Kohlman	Frank	Milwaukee
Mr.	Tedesco	George R.	Spokane
Mr.	Peterson	Jack S.	Barston
Mr.	Nelson	Robert M.	St. Louis
Mr.	Roberts	James	Columbus
Mr.	Thompson	Howard	Blakeley
Mr.	Jones	Timothy	Starkey
Mr.	Kaufman	William	Milwaukee
Mr.	Emerson	Douglas	Boston
Mr.	Hicks	Kevin	Chicago
*			

3. Click ▟ to return to Design View. Notice that Access has enclosed the criteria in quotation marks, indicating that this is a text criterion. Access is not case sensitive, so entering *Mr.* in either lowercase or uppercase will produce the same search result.

4. To print the new query, click the Office button, point to *Print*, and then click the *Quick Print* command.

5. Open the Office menu again and click *Save* as to open the Save as dialog box. Save the query as *Tute1Query2* and click *OK*. Exit Access by clicking *Exit Access* on the Office menu or by clicking the *Close* button on the Microsoft Access Title bar.

Database Case 2

Hudson, Palmer, Martinez & Flenderson Attorneys-at-Law

Problem:	Construct a Personnel Database
Management Skill:	Coordinate
Access Skills:	Table Setup
	Data Input
	Select Queries
	Report Design
	Printing
Data Table:	HUDSON PALMER

Hudson, Palmer, Martinez, & Flenderson (Hudson Palmer for short) is a large legal practice with offices in Allentown, Harrisburg, and Scranton, Pennsylvania, specializing in corporate law. The Hudson Palmer Allentown office employs more than 85 freelance and contract personnel, including expert witnesses (EW) from various fields and disciplines, private investigators (PI), process servers (PS), and legal researchers (LR). These people are hired on an as-needed basis to assist in the conduct of cases on behalf of the many client corporations the firm represents.

Hudson Palmer has 38 Principal attorneys who are also the main partners in the firm. Each Principal has a staff of assistant lawyers. In addition, all Principals keep separate lists of contractors and freelancers with whom they have worked successfully in the past. Typically, these lists reside on 3" x 5" cards in a file cabinet in each partner's office. Whenever a client's case requires certain outside expertise, the partners reach for these cards and select their favorite people.

The partner's remuneration is based in part on their performance—the more successful cases they litigate, the more money they make. Moreover, the more experienced and competent freelancers they know, the more likely they are to successfully litigate, and thus the more likely that attractive clients will seek them out for assistance. In this environment, there is a natural tendency to safeguard the names of good freelancers and contractors for one's own accounts. However, there is also the likelihood that by sharing this information, the firm's overall success would increase and everyone would benefit.

Jeffrey Hudson started the law firm 24 years ago with fellow Temple University graduate Bradley Palmer. Jeffrey knows how the freelancing system works. The problem is that each attorney squirrels away the names of the people that he or she thinks are really excellent.

When it comes to the talent pool, there is no sharing among attorneys. Second-rate people may be used on a case because the names of the first-rate people are only known by one or two attorneys. If a partner hires a poor freelancer, and the verdict on a case goes against the interests of a client, the client may be inclined to look for new legal representation in the future, and thus the firm's profits and reputation suffer.

Hudson wants to establish some sort of centralized repository for this information. Too much time is wasted searching for people with particular skills or knowledge that may already be known to some of the partners. The central repository could also contain comments on the performance of the freelancer or contractor on prior occasions and other relevant data. Hudson would like some sort of scoring system so that freelancers and contractors could be rank-ordered. This would ensure that only the best people would be hired to work with the firm.

The partners are not happy with this idea. Sharing these resources with the other partners may mean that their favorite people will be unavailable when they need them most. On the other hand, a central repository might help them find new resources for assistance about whom they did not previously know. Therefore, with somewhat mixed feelings, the partners have agreed to support the proposal to build a central repository of contractors. They have responded to a memo sent out by Hudson asking them to list the resources they would like to have stored in a central database.

The following fields were identified: First and Last Name, Skill, Hourly Rate, Number of Hours Employed for Each Quarter of 2008, Phone Number, Rating (Excellent, Good, OK, or Poor) and Initials of the Rater. Hudson reviewed the suggestions and added a field to store an additional free form text comment about each freelancer.

Parts of this database have been identified in the table HUDSON PALMER in the SOLVEIT_5 database. Create a new Access database and import this table now.

Tasks

There are seven tasks in this case:

1. Complete the design of the table to store the rating system devised by Hudson. Be sure to devise a way to limit the rating field to only 4 categories and to record free-form text remarks from the attorneys.

2. Fabricate and enter hours worked for the existing freelancers or contractors. Enter data for three new freelancers or contractors, such as private investigators (PI), process servers (PS), legal researchers (LR), or expert witnesses (EW). Enter data for at least the first three freelancers in the comments field. Use your initials for the partner who is contributing the remarks.

3. Create a query that shows the contractors sorted first by their skill, then by their rating, and then by their name. Include the comment field and print the results of this query.

4. Create a report to list all the freelancers and contractors with just the following fields: Last Name, First Name, Hourly Rate, the Total Number of Hours Worked, and the Total Amount Earned in 2008. Print the report.

5. Produce and print a report to list all expert witnesses who charge more than $250.00/hour. Include in this report the total number of hours this group of freelancers worked for Hudson Palmer in 2008. Print the report.

*6 There are several areas where this system can be enhanced and improved. (What will happen next quarter? What if two partners have the same initials?) Make a list of all of the improvements you would make, and then pick one and implement it into the database.

*7. Currently, with the comments in a Memo field, no analysis or data manipulation can be performed using the ratings of the freelancers. There may also be conflicting opinions on the merit of any one freelancer if they have worked for more than one partner. Devise a method to accommodate these differing opinions in such a way that meaningful analysis can be performed. Note that this may mean redesigning the database.

Time Estimates (excluding tasks marked with *)

Expert:	45 minutes
Intermediate:	1.25 hours
Novice:	2 hours

Tutorial for Database Case 2 Using Access 2007

In the previous case, you learned to use Table Design View to change the structure of a table by adding new fields and setting field properties, and how to use Datasheet View for adding and editing records. This case introduces the *memo* data type and *report design*. Start Access and open the FRIENDS table you used for the Case 1 tutorial to practice the skills you will need for this case.

Using Memo Fields

Memo fields are used in tables to store free form text and notes. You use a memo field to store descriptive or narrative information and even large documents. A memo field in Access 2007 can hold up to 65,536 characters of text. Creating, entering, and saving data in an Access memo field is a very simple procedure. Because of their unstructured nature, memo fields cannot be indexed or sorted, but they can be searched. We will look at indexing, sorting, and searching in later cases.

1. Open the SOLVEIT_CH5 database. Double-click on the FRIENDS table to open it in Datasheet View. Click the *Design View* button or click *View* on the Home tab of the Ribbon.

2. Let's add a new field to the end of the existing table. The name for the new field will be COMMENTS and the data type will be *Memo*. (Review the tutorial for Case 1 if you are unsure how to add new fields and select data types.) Notice that the Field Size cell in the Field Properties pane does not appear when you select the memo data type. Save the changes to the table structure by clicking the *Save* button or selecting *Save* on the Office menu.

3. Return to Datasheet View by clicking the *Datasheet View* button or by clicking the *View* button on the Ribbon. Scroll or tab over to the new COMMENTS field and enter text for each record to describe their relationship (e.g. personal or professional friend, family member, or a specific familial relationship). Press the down arrow key on the keyboard to move to each new record. (Remember that as you move to a new record, Access automatically saves the data.)

Printing Memo Fields

Memo fields can be printed like any other field in a table or query. To create a query that will select only certain fields in the table, including the memo field:

1. On the Create tab of the Ribbon, in the Other group, click the *Query Design* button.

2. In the Show Table dialog box, select the FRIENDS table, click *Add,* and then click *Close*.

3. In the FRIENDS field list, select the Last_Name and Comments fields and drag them to the design grid. Release the mouse button when the pointer is over the first Field cell.

4. Click the *Run* button on the Query Tools: Design tab to display the data in the Last_Name and Comments fields (see Figure 5-9).

5. Click the *Print* button on the Office menu to open the Print dialog box, and then click *OK* to print the query. Then click the *Close* button at the top right of the query window and click *No* when a warning dialog box asks if you want to save the changes to the design of Query 1.

Figure 5-9

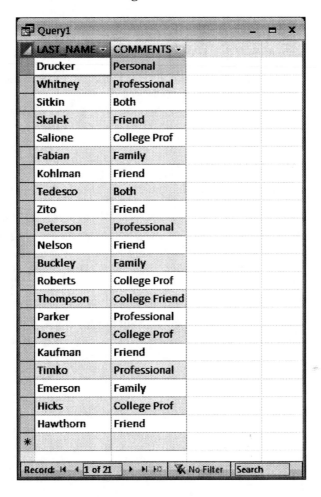

LAST NAME	COMMENTS
Drucker	Personal
Whitney	Professional
Sitkin	Both
Skalek	Friend
Salione	College Prof
Fabian	Family
Kohlman	Friend
Tedesco	Both
Zito	Friend
Peterson	Professional
Nelson	Friend
Buckley	Family
Roberts	College Prof
Thompson	College Friend
Parker	Professional
Jones	College Prof
Kaufman	Friend
Timko	Professional
Emerson	Family
Hicks	College Prof
Hawthorn	Friend

Record: 1 of 21   No Filter   Search

Creating Reports in Access

A more polished look can be achieved by creating an Access report. Reports are the database objects in Access specifically designed for printing. Reports can be based on tables and/or queries. They are used to provide subtotals and grand totals for numeric fields, and to produce summaries of information contained in the database, mailing labels, and presentation quality display of your data. Report Wizards speed up the creation, display, and printout by providing a series of dialog boxes to help you determine the data you want the report to contain, as well as a group of popular style templates from which to choose.

The items on a report that contain the data for display and printing are called *controls*. Different types of controls are used to display data of the various data types. Controls are used to display data from fields, along with the labels that identify this data and the results of calculations for report headers and footers that will print identifying information at the top and bottom of every page of the report, as well as group footers that identify a particular group of related data. Report controls can also be used to include graphs, pictures, and other Access objects.

1. On the Create tab of the Ribbon, in the Reports group, click Report Wizard to open the Report Wizard.

2. The first Report Wizard dialog box opens. Here you can choose the fields that you want to display in the report and decide the order in which you want them to display. Notice that, because Fields is the currently selected table in the Navigation Pane, Access has selected the FIELDS table as the basis for the Available Fields list. Select four fields, Title, First_Name, Last_Name, and City, for inclusion in the report. With the Title field selected in the Available Fields box, click the Add Field button [>] to add it to the Selected Fields box (refer to Figure 5-10). Next, select the First_Name field in the Available Fields box and click [>] again to add it to the list of selected fields. Follow the same procedure to add the remaining two fields. (If you accidentally add the wrong field to the report, select the unwanted field and click the Remove Field button [<] to return it to the Available Fields box.) When you have finished, click *Next*.

3. The second of the six Report Wizard dialog boxes opens. Here you can add grouping levels for the data in your report based on one or more fields. Data can be grouped by City, for example, so that all contacts that live in a particular city will be grouped together in the report. Without adding any grouping levels, click *Next*.

4. In the third dialog box, you can impose a sort order on the data in the report based on one or more fields. Select *City* in the first sort order list box and then click *Next*.

Figure 5-10

5. In the fourth dialog box, you can choose the layout for the report. Option buttons are provided to choose either *Portrait or Landscape* orientation for the report and a *Columnar, Tabular,* or *Justified* layout. Select the *Tabular* layout if necessary, make sure the *Adjust the field width so all fields fit on a page* check box is selected, and click *Next*.

6. In the fifth dialog box, you can select a style for your report. Select *Office* if necessary and click *Next*.

7. In the final dialog box, you can enter a title for your report. By default, Access enters the name of the table or query that serves as the record source for the report as the title name, which in this case is FRIENDS. Type *Report of My Friends*.

8. Make sure the *Preview the report* option button is selected and click the *Finish* button. Access will generate the report and open it in Print Preview, with the Print Preview tab open on the Ribbon. Note that the records are displayed alphabetically by City according to the sort order selected in the Report Wizard. Click the *Print* button on the Print Preview tab or select *Print* on the Office menu to open the Print dialog box, and then click *OK* to print the report. Close the report.

How to Use Reports to Display and Print Selected Fields

You can change the record source for an existing report, which will, in turn, change the
records the report displays. For example, you can change the record source for the Report of
My Friends report to the second query created in the tutorial for Case 1 (e.g. *Tute1Query2*).
This query filters out all records in the FRIENDS table that do not have the title MR.

1. On the Navigation Pane, double-click *Report of My Friends*. (If the Navigation pane
   is not displaying all database objects, then click the down arrow at the top right of the
   Navigation Pane, make sure that *Object Type* is selected as the Category and then
   click *All Access Objects*.)

2. On the Home tab, click the *View* button arrow and then click *Design View* to open the
   Design View for the report (see Figure 5-11). Notice there are three Report Design
   Tools tabs on the Ribbon now: Design, Arrange, and Page Setup.

Figure 5-11

Report Header: Contains controls that print once at the beginning of the report

Page Header: Contains controls that print at the top of every page

Detail: The heart of the report that contains all of the records specified in the record source for the report

Report Footer: Contains controls that print at the end of the report, often calculated controls that display a grand total, grand count, or

Page Footer: Contains controls that print at the bottom of each page

As Figure 5-11 shows, the Report Design View window is divided into sections. The **Report
Header** prints once at the beginning of the report. It generally contains the report's title. The
Page Header prints at the top of every page in the report and contains the labels or column
headings. The **Detail** section contains the records that are being displayed in the report. The
Page Footer prints at the bottom of each page and often contains calculated controls that
display the current system date and time, along with the page number and total number of
pages in the report. The **Report Footer** prints once at the end of the report. It often contains

calculated controls that summarize or total the data contained in the report. Additionally, group headers will be automatically added to a report in which records are grouped based on like values. You can add group footers to include summary information about the group such as *Count*, *Sum*, or *Average*. We will look at report groups in a later tutorial.

3. On the Report Design Tools: Design tab, click the *Property Sheet* button on to open the property sheet for the report. Report properties define the data source for the report, as well as its overall appearance.

4. Click the Data tab on the property sheet if necessary. Click in the *Record Source* property settings box and click the list arrow ⌄ to open a list of the available data sources in the FRIENDS database. Select the second query you created in the Case 1 tutorial (Tute1Query2) to change the record source for the report (see Figure 5-12.)

5. Close the property sheet by clicking the ✕ in the top right corner.

6. On the Report Design Tools: Design tab, in the Views group, click the arrow on the *Views* button and select *Print Preview* to view the new report. A reduced data set displays based upon the criteria set up in the query, but the sort order based on the City field and the report style selected in the Report Wizard remain.

Figure 5-12

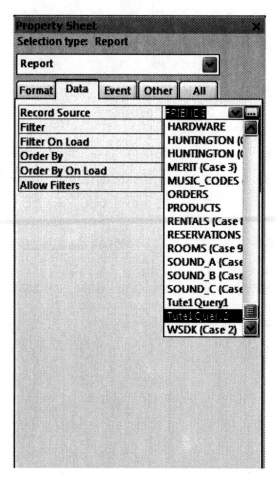

7. On the Print Preview tab of the Ribbon, in the Print group, click the *Print* button to open the Print dialog box. Click *OK* to print the new report.

8. Click the Office button and then click *Save As* to open the Save As dialog box. Type *Tute2Report2* in the top text box and click *OK*. Close the report and the FRIENDS table.

Using Expressions in Reports

Calculated controls are used to display the results of expressions that can be built using Access functions, mathematical operators, raw values, and any values contained in the fields in the report. For example, the expression = **[UnitCost]*[Quantity]** multiplies the contents of the two fields with these names and displays a single value as the result. A *function* is a predefined formula that helps simplify the process of building expressions. For example, the function *Sum* will add all of the values specified. The *Now* function in the Page Footer section, shown in Figure 5-11, returns the current date as stored in your computer's system clock.

You can create calculated controls using expressions in one of three ways:

- By typing an expression directly into a text box control

- By entering an expression into the Control Source property for a control

- By using the Expression Builder to help you to create the expression

To learn and practice the skill of creating calculated controls using expressions, we will use the first method and the sample table HARDWARE provided in the SOLVEIT_CH5 database. First, create a new empty database with the name HARDWARE.ACCDB and then import the HARDWARE table from the SOLVEIT_CH5 database. (If you still have tables or reports open from the FRIENDS database, save and close them, and close the FRIENDS database.)

1. In the opened HARDWARE database, double-click the HARDWARE table to open it in Datasheet View. There are four fields: Invoice, Item, UnitCost, and Quantity. Press [F11] to view the Database window.

2. Open the Create tab on the Ribbon. In the Reports group, click *Report Wizard* and use the Report Wizard to create a new report using the HARDWARE table as the record source. Include the fields Invoice, UnitCost, and Quantity. Sort the records by the Invoice field, use the Tabular layout and the Office style, and give the report the title *Calculating Total Cost*. Click *Finish*. The report is generated and opened in Print Preview.

3. On the Print Preview tab, click the *Close Print Preview* button to switch to Report Design View.

To practice using expressions, we will create a field that calculates the total cost for an ordered hardware item by multiplying UnitCost by Quantity. Since this calculation, or expression, will use the values in two existing fields to calculate a new value, we must create a calculated control. A calculated control contains an expression and displays the result of that expression when the report is opened.

4. Open the Report Design Tools: Design tab on the Ribbon if necessary. Click the *Text Box* button in the Controls group. Click once with the Text Box pointer at the 5-inch mark on the horizontal ruler in the Detail section of the report. An unbound text box control and a label control to identify it are added to the report. The label text (*Text 11*) will vary depending on the number of controls on the report. Click the label control to select it and press the [Delete] key on the keyboard. You will add a label for the calculated control to the page header later.

5. Unbound controls are not linked to any existing field in the record source or sources for the report. They are used to display the results of *calculation*s, text, or graphics. Click inside the unbound text box to get a blinking insertion point (called an *I-beam*).

Type =*UnitCost*Quantity*, making sure to begin the expression with an equals sign, and press the [Enter] key. Access automatically adds the correct syntax for you by enclosing each field in square brackets. Access is not case sensitive, so it does not matter if you enter your field names in upper or lowercase. You must, however, spell them correctly and use the correct spacing!

Note: If the field names contain spaces, you must enclose them in square brackets because Access will not recognize them as field names (e.g. [Time to Market]).

All expressions in Access must begin with an = sign. The asterisk is used to denote multiplication. A listing of other operators and functions used in Access is presented at the end of this tutorial.

6. You have now created a calculated control. The Detail section of your report should resemble Figure 5-13.

7. You will now add a label control to the page header to identify the calculated control. Click the *Label* button on the Ribbon. Click the Label pointer once in the Page Header section of the report at the 5.5-inch mark on the horizontal ruler. Type *TOTAL*.

8. Double-click the new calculated control in the Detail section to open the property sheet for the control. Click the Format tab. Click in the *Format* property settings box. Click the list arrow and select *Currency* on the list. Close the property sheet and switch to Print Preview. Your report should look similar to Figure 5-14. Save the changes and close the report.

Figure 5-13

Figure 5-14

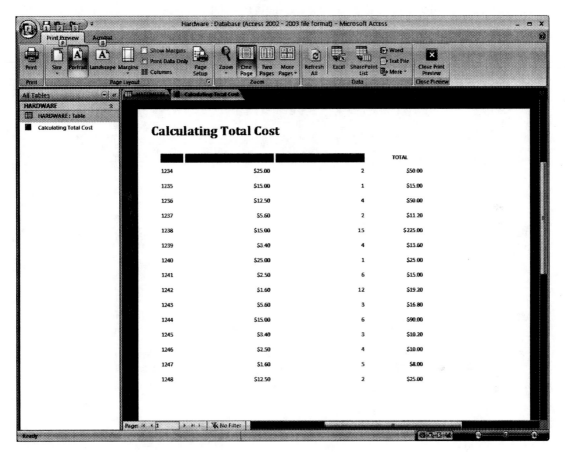

Calculations in Queries

A more rapid way of achieving the same result is to create a query that includes the calculated field you want to display in the report and then to use the query as the record source for the report.

1. In the HARDWARE database window, open the Create tab of the Ribbon and click *Query Design*. Add the field list for the HARDWARE table to the Select Query window and close the Show Table dialog box. Drag three fields—Invoice, UnitCost, and Quantity—to the design grid.

2. In the fourth Field cell, type *TOTAL: [UnitCost]*[Quantity]*. Your query window should look like Figure 5-15.

3. Click the *Properties Sheet* button on the Query Tools: Design tab of the Ribbon to open the properties sheet for the calculated field. On the General tab, click in the

Format property settings box. Click the list arrow and select *Currency*. Close the properties sheet.

4. Click Run on the Query Tools: Design tab (Results group) to run the query. Save the query as *CalculatingTotalCost*.

5. Use the Report Wizard to create a new report called *Calculating Total Cost 2* using the query as the data source for the report

Figure 5-15

Expressions can play many roles in Access, and they can be used in virtually every type of database object. For example, you can use expressions in Table Design View to define default values for fields. In queries, expressions can be used to create calculated fields and criteria. The table below lists only those operators likely to be used in *Solve it!* For a more complete list, search the Access Help facility using the term *operators*.

Operators in Access

An *operator* in an expression describes the type of action that the expression should perform or the way in which a comparison between two values should be carried out. Access has four kinds of operators: Arithmetic and Text, Comparison, Logical, and Miscellaneous. The table below classifies, lists, and explains these operators. For a more complete list of operators, consult the Access Help facility.

Arithmetic and Text	
^	Raise one number to the power of the other (exponentiation)
*	Multiply two numbers
/	Add two numbers
+	Divide two numbers
-	Subtract two numbers
Mod	Divide two numbers and return the remainder
&	Concatenate: join two strings of text
Comparison	
< and <=	Less than; less than or equal to
> and >=	Greater than; greater than or equal to
= and <>	Equal to: not equal to
Logical	
And	Both comparisons are True
Or	One comparison or the other is True
Xor	One comparison or the other is True , but not both
Not	The comparison is not True
Miscellaneous	
Like	Text matches a pattern (Use with wildcard symbols ? and *)
Is	Comparison is True (e.g.: is Null)
Is Not	Comparison is not True (e.g.: not Null)

Functions in Access

A *function* in Access performs a calculation on data and returns the result of that calculation.
There are over 100 functions available in Access in eight different categories. The table
below lists only those likely to be used in *Solve it!* For a complete list, search the Help files
using the keywords *functions* and *reference*.

Date/Time	
Date	Returns current date
Now	Returns current date and time
Logical	
IF	Tests and returns a value based on whether an argument is True or False
Choose	Selects a value from a list based on the content of its argument
Aggregate	
Avg	Average
Count	Count how many
Sum	Sum total

The Access Form and Report Design Tools

The buttons displayed in the table below appear in the Controls group on the Report Design Tools: Design tab. You use them to create labels, text boxes, option buttons, etc. for forms, subforms, and other Access objects.

	Select Objects	Use to select a control, section, or form. Click this tool to unlock a control button that you have locked down.
	Control Wizards	Turns control wizards on or off; Use control wizards to help you create a list box, combo box, option group, command button, chart, subreport, or subform.
	Label	A control that displays descriptive text, such as a title, a caption, or instructions on a form or report; Access automatically attaches labels to the controls you create.
	Text Box	Use to display, enter, or edit data in either a form or report's underlying record source, display the results of a calculation, or accept input from a user.
	Option Group	Use along with check boxes, option buttons, or toggle buttons to display a set of alternative values. For example, you can use an option group to specify whether an order is shipped by air, sea, or land.
	Toggle Button	Use as a stand-alone control bound to a Yes/No field, an unbound control for accepting user input in a custom dialog box, or as part of an option group.
	Option Button	Use as a stand-alone control bound to a Yes/No field, an unbound control for accepting user input in a custom dialog box, or as part of an option group.
	Check Box	Use as a stand-alone control bound to a Yes/No field, an unbound control for accepting user input in a custom dialog box, or as part of an option group.
	Combo Box	Combines the features of a list box and a text box; You can type in the text box or select an entry in the list box to add a value to an underlying field.
	List Box	Displays a scrollable list of values; In Form View, you can select from the list to enter a value into a new record or to change the value in an existing record.
	Command Button	Use to perform actions, such as finding a record, printing a record, or applying a form filter.
	Image	Use for displaying a static picture on a form or report. Because a static picture is not an OLE object, you can't edit the image inside Microsoft Access once you've added it to a form or report.
	Unbound Object	Use to display an unbound OLE object, such as a Microsoft Excel spreadsheet, on a form or report. The object remains constant as you move from record to record.
	Bound Object	Use to display OLE objects, such as a series of pictures, on a form or report. This control is for objects stored in a field in either the form or the report's underlying record source. A different object displays on the form or report as you move from record to record.
	Page Break	Use to insert or remove a new page on a form, printed form, or report.
	Tab Control	Use to create a tabbed form with several pages or tabbed dialog box (such as the Access Options dialog box on the Office menu). You can copy or add other controls onto a tab control. Right-click on the Tab control in the design grid to modify the number of pages, the page order, the selected page's properties, and the selected tab control properties.

	Subform/Subreport	Use to display data from more than one table on a form or report.
	Line	Use on a form or report to emphasize related or especially important information.
	Rectangle	Use for graphic effects, such as grouping a set of related controls on a form, or for emphasizing important data on a report.
	Insert ActiveX Control	Adds an ActiveX control (such as the Calendar control) to a form or report; ActiveX controls are stored as separate files.

Database Case 3

Abraxas Office Furniture

Problem:	Develop an automated Bill of Materials
Management Skill:	Plan Coordinate
Access Skills:	Creating Queries Sorting (tables, queries, reports)
Data Table:	ABRAXAS

Ellis Singh, Production Manager of Abraxas Office Furniture, walked out of the Chief Executive Officer's office muttering to himself. He had just left a meeting between Randall DeMaria, the CEO; Shanda White, the Chief Financial Officer; and Eric Kotani, the Purchasing Officer. They had more or less ordered him to computerize the Bill of Materials (BoM) and purchasing systems. He argued that such an instruction was easier given than implemented. They had finally compromised on automating a section of the factory's assembly facilities as a pilot project. The pilot project would provide an opportunity to improve the design of the new system and measure the benefits before moving to complete implementation in the entire factory.

Abraxas Office Furniture, based in Salt Lake City, Utah, had experienced steady sales for its range of high quality office furniture until 2000 when less expensive imports of similar quality began to capture a significant market share. Costs had to be reduced, and senior management decided that increased production volume was needed before their office furniture products could regain competitiveness in such a capital-intensive industry. These increased volumes would provide economies of scale in materials purchases and enable a new, more efficient plant to be purchased. The increased volume would be obtained by entering the mid-priced home office furniture market. Abraxas Office's quality hardwood tables would be particularly suitable in such a market. In addition, a range of new desks was developed. The strategy proved fruitful. Abraxas Office's home products were acclaimed in shelter magazines across the country. The strategy, along with a continuous improvement program initiated at the same time, reduced production costs, and gains occurred in both the household and business markets.

Management found that the increase in production rapidly outpaced the ability of the old manual, paper-based production control system. The result was poor market intelligence, an inability to implement activity-based costing, and reduced efficiency in production. For instance, supplies were being ordered and put in inventory, but there was no way to link the supplies to specific products. To understand the cost of building a particular desk or table,

Abraxas needs know the cost of all the supplies used in its production, down the smallest screw and even the amount of glue used in construction. The old manual production system could not supply this information.

Ellis considered the best ways to start the process. Even if his budget permitted a full-blown Materials Requirement Planning system, the jump would be too large for Abraxas. He decided that creating an in-house database system using Access would be the most suitable solution since White and Kotani were not specific about what computer platform to use and future requirements were unclear. This approach would provide the necessary flexibility for incremental development and expansion. Because he had a poor understanding of databases, Singh called the School of Business at the University of Utah to seek help. The Placement Office at the university referred him to Camille Dennis, a first-year MBA student seeking a summer internship with a manufacturer. Dennis agreed come on board as a consultant.

Although she had a liberal arts background, Dennis had minored in Information Technology in her undergraduate program and was keen to learn about production systems. Ellis Singh explained what was required in the preliminary stages. Currently, the BoM for each product type was recorded on paper and used exclusively in the production area. Singh was sure that a BoM could be constructed for use by both production and the purchasing department. Currently, the purchasing department used a separate list of components, which often resulted in difficulties in attributing supply costs to particular product lines.

A BoM, Singh explained, was a list of materials, sub-parts, and quantities used in a finished product. Typically, the list would be arranged to represent the sequence of fabrication and assembly, highlighting manufacturing dependencies. For the pilot project, this would not be needed because of the relative simplicity of the production sequence.

Dennis decided to use the company's line of professional tables and desks for the pilot project, and run the new system in parallel with the existing system. In this way, Abraxas Office could refine and cost out the system before committing to a complete implementation. This range had four products: two tables, the Winston and the Charleston; and two desks, the Sterling and the Executive. These four products were made of 15 different components, excluding taper screws.

The design for each product was very similar. The Winston tables were made of six legs supporting four 5.5' beams and five 3.5' beams, which in turn supported two 6'x 4' tabletops that were laid end to end. Eight 3' and four 2' struts were added for additional strength and aesthetic considerations. The other two products in this range, the Sterling and the Executive, are personal desks that have four legs, two 5.5' beams, three 3.75' beams, four 2' and 3' struts, and a single tabletop. The Sterling desks have three drawers, while the Executive desks have six. The Charleston table and the Executive desk also have leather tops—two pieces for the Charleston and one for the Executive.

Abraxas Office's designers decided to use bolts to join the tables for strength and reliability rather than the mixture of bolts, nails, and adhesives used by their competitors. Two 1.5"x 8" bolts are used for each leg, each 5.5' beam and each 3.75' beam. Two 1"x 6" bolts are used in each 2' strut and 3' strut. For each bolt, a matching nut and spacer are used. Each product has differing levels of carved detail and finish.

Abraxas Office manufactures the tops and legs. They purchase the struts from Chapin Milling, the leather from Petaluma Tannery, and the hardware from Shephard Hardware.

Dennis recorded each of the components as a record in an Access database table, with the number used for each product listed in separate fields. She also recorded the number of each component currently in inventory and the unit cost.

This partial Bill of Materials is supplied for you in the table ABRAXAS in the SOLVEIT_CH5 database. Create a new Access database and import this file now.

Tasks

There are seven tasks in this case:

1. (a) Complete the supplied bill of materials by adding fields to represent inventory holdings (UNITS_IN_STOCK) and unit costs (UNIT_COST) of the materials, and by fabricating the appropriate data.
   (b) Add new part codes, quantities used, and the other information for the bolts, nuts, and spacers. Note that the part codes begin with a letter representing the first letter of the supplier's name: A for Abraxas, C for Chapin Milling, P for Petaluma Tannery, and S for Shephard Hardware. The letter is followed by four numbers to complete the part codes.
   (c) Print out the completed table.

2. Managers in a number of functional areas have heard of Dennis's progress and have requested information from the computerized BoM. Sales managers want to know the total dollar amount of the materials costs in each product type so they can more easily set appropriate prices for these products. Accounting managers want to know the total dollar value of each component type in each table or desk. Singh wants an estimate of the investment in dollars in inventory holdings of the component types and a total dollar value of inventory holdings. Dennis is certain that these needs can be furnished within a single report.
   (a) Create a report to satisfy these needs and (b) print this report.

3. Harney Corporation, a regular and valued customer, has ordered tables for their new Provo office. They require 5 Winston and 38 Sterling tables. CEO DeMaria and Kotani from Purchasing want a detailed Materials Requirement report for this order, showing the number of each component required for each of the two products ordered, a total components required field, and the amount held in inventory. Create and print the report.

4. Eric Kotani has heard rumors that Chapin Milling is having financial difficulties. DeMaria is worried by these rumors and the implications this may have for the Harney

contract. Print out a listing of the components supplied by Chapin Milling, sorted by PART_CODE, to facilitate the investigation.

5. Engineering and Design wants a list of the components, sorted by value. (a) Create a query and (b) print the resulting listing.

*6. Suggest any improvements or additions to the Bill of Materials as it currently exists. Could the BoM be extended to encompass other aspects of Production Management or any other associated domains?

Time Estimates (excluding tasks marked with *):

Expert:	1.75 hours
Intermediate:	2.5 hours
Novice:	4 hours

Tutorial for Database Case 3 Using Access 2007

Creating Queries with Multiple Criteria

In the Tutorial for Case 1, we looked at creating queries for viewing and printing certain fields in the FRIENDS table, as well as fields that met simple selection criteria. In this tutorial, we will look at constructing more complex queries using logical operators.

1. Open the SOLVEIT_CH5 database. Double-click on the FRIENDS table in the Navigation Pane to open it. Create a new query following the instructions given in the Tutorial for Case 1. Include the fields Last_Name, Zip, Professional, and Personal in the query.

2. The *Criteria* and *or* cells in the design grid allow for multiple conditions involving the logical operators "AND" and "OR". Conditions entered in the Criteria cell are "AND." Let's say you wanted a listing of all Personal friends with ZIP Codes greater than 35000. In the Criteria cell of the design grid), type *>35000* in the Zip field and enter *True* in the Personal field (see Figure 5-16).

Figure 5-16

3. Click the *Run* button on the Query Tools: Design tab to run the query. Results should show that there are seven records in the FRIENDS table that match the criteria.

4. Click to return to the Query Design View window.

5. Try using the OR operator by deleting *True* from the Criteria cell in the Personal field and entering it in the *or* cell on the next line down (see Figure 5-17). In this instance, we are searching the table for people whose ZIP codes are greater than 35000 *or* people who are personal friends. Run the query again. This is a less stringent condition, and the resulting dynaset should show that there are seventeen records that match the chosen criteria. A "dynaset" is a sub-table in a database that results from a specific query.

6. Print your queries by clicking the Office button and then *Print* to open the Print dialog box. Save your query as *Tute3Query1* and close it.

Sorting Tables in Access

It is often useful to sort a table by one or more fields. For instance, you may find it helpful to sort the records in your table alphabetically by Last Name, in chronological order, or by some numerical order. There are several ways of sorting data in Access. A quick sort on a single field in either ascending or descending order can be achieved in Datasheet View. You can also sort by multiple fields in either the Query Design View or in a Report.

Figure 5-17

Field:	LAST_NAME	ZIP	PROFESSIONAL	PERSONAL		
Table:	FRIENDS	FRIENDS	FRIENDS	FRIENDS		
Sort:						
Show:	☑	☑	☑	☑	☐	☐
Criteria:		> "35000"				
or:				True		

To Sort on a Single Field

1. In the SolveIt_CH5 database, make sure the FRIENDS table is open in Datasheet View. Let's say you would like to sort the records alphabetically by last name. To do this, move the mouse to the Last_Name field selector so that the ↓ arrow appears. Click to select the Last Name column (see Figure 5-18).

2. On the Home tab of the Ribbon, in the Sort & Filter group, click the *Sort Ascending* button 🔼) so Access will sort the records by last name in alphabetical order. Close the table, saving the change to the design when prompted. (Clicking the *Sort Descending* button will sort in reverse order.) **Warning:** *This is a dynamic sort and cannot be saved.*

Sorts within Sorts

You can sort by multiple fields in a query to achieve a sort within a sort. This is analogous to a telephone book, where entries are first alphabetized by last name and then by first name.

1. In the Navigation Pane, double-click *Tute1Query2* to open it in datasheet view. Then click the *View* button on the Home tab to toggle the query to Design View.

2. Let's sort by the Title field, and then, within this, by the Last_Name field in ascending order. Before we do this, first delete *Mr* from the *Criteria* cell in the TITLE field. Then click in the *Sort*: cell in the Title field and select *Ascending order*. Repeat this action for the Last Name field. Your screen should now look like the one shown in Figure 5-19.

Solve it!

Figure 5-18

CONTACT N↓	TITLE	LAST NAME	FIRST_NAME	STREET	CITY	STATE	ZI
1	Dr.	Drucker	Peter H.	345 Warren Road	Hudson	New York	12305
2	Mr.	Whitney	Craig	25 Wood Lake Road	Morris	New Jersey	25059
3	Mr.	Sitkin	Howard W.	17 Morace Street	Springvale	New Hampshire	49492
4	Mr.	Skalek	William F.	8 Yorkshire Place	Teatown	South Dakota	39285
5	Mr.	Salione	Phillip	35 Truesdale Ave	Phoenix	Arizona	35842
6	Mr.	Fabian	James T.	36 Palmer Court	Chicago	Illinois	30928
7	Mr.	Kohlman	Frank	35 Miller Drive	Milwaukee	Wisconsin	49740
8	Mr.	Tedesco	George R.	346 Skytop Drive	Spokane	Washington	35828
9	Ms.	Zito	Helen K.	64 Albany Post Rd.	Dana	Maryland	35080
10	Mr.	Peterson	Jack S.	54 Elmor Ave	Barston	Ohio	39897
11	Mr.	Nelson	Robert M.	1 Franklin Ave.	St. Louis	Missouri	34097
12	Ms.	Buckley	Denise	23 Georgetown Rd.	Chicago	Illinois	30928
13	Mr.	Roberts	James	567 Ridge Rd.	Columbus	Ohio	56778
14	Mr.	Thompson	Howard	799 Tucker Ave.	Blakeley	Wisconsin	35899
15	Mrs.	Parker	Gina	640 Palm Tree Lane	Phoenix	Arizona	35899
16	Mr.	Jones	Timothy	89945 Marydale Lane	Starkey	New Hampshire	49478
17	Mr.	Kaufman	William	7654 Flamton St.	Milwaukee	Wisconsin	49788
18	Ms.	Timko	Rebecca	34 Salem Ave.	Spokane	Washington	35829
19	Mr.	Emerson	Douglas	789 Carmichael Ave.	Boston	Massachusetts	12345
20	Mr.	Hicks	Kevin	3407 Nathrop Dr.	Chicago	Illinois	30987
21	Ms.	Hawthorn	Diane	3034 Jones Alley	New York	New York	10011
(New)							

Record: ◄ ◄ 1 of 21 ► ►I ►≈ No Filter Search

Figure 5-19

Field:	TITLE	LAST_NAME	FIRST_NAME	CITY		
Table:	FRIENDS	FRIENDS	FRIENDS	FRIENDS		
Sort:	Ascending	Ascending				
Show:	✓	✓	✓	✓	□	
Criteria:						
or:						

3. Click the *Run* button on the Query Tools: Design tab to view the results of your query. The records should be sorted first by Title (i.e. Dr. before Mr., Mr. before *Ms.* or *Prof.*), and then within each Title grouping, in ascending Last Name order.

4. Save your query with a new name by selecting *Save As* on the Office menu and typing in *Tute3Query2*. Close the query window when you are done.

Sorting Data in Reports

When you print a report, you usually want to ensure that the records are displayed in a particular order. For example, if you were printing a list of suppliers, you may wish to sort the records alphabetically by company name. When you are setting up the parameters for a new report using the Report Wizard, Access enables you to specify the sort order. If you change your mind after the report has been created, you can use the Group, Sort, & Total tool in Report Design View.

The Group, Sort, & Total tool allows you to sort by multiple and expressions, and you can sort on the same field or expression more than once. For example, in a five-character field, you could apply an ascending sort to the first three characters and a descending sort to the last two characters.

Let's repeat the query sort we have just performed in Report Design View. (We could, of course, simply change the record source for the report to the query we have just created to achieve the same results).

1. With the SolveIt_CH5 database open, double-click *Report of my Friends* in the Navigation Pane to open the report created in the Tutorial for Case 2. Click to open the report in Design View.

2. On the Report Design Tools: Design tab, in the Grouping & Totals group, click the *Group & Sort* button to open the Group, Sort & Total pane.

3. In the first entry in the Group, Sort, & Total pane, click the list arrow beside *City* and change the field from *City* to *Title*.

4. Below the first entry, click *Add a Sort*, which will add a second entry to the pane.

5. Click the list arrow beside *select field* in the second entry and select *Last_Name*. Note that the default sort order is ascending ("with A on top"), which is perfect for our needs. Your screen should now resemble Figure 5-20.

6. On the Ribbon, click *View* and then click *Print Preview* to see the effect that imposing the sort order has had on the report. Print your report.

7. Save the report as *Tute3Report1* by selecting *Save As* from the Office menu. Close the *Tute3Report1* report.

Figure 5-20

Database Case 4

Cascade Pharmacy

Problem:	Summarize and analyze data from a transaction processing system for government reporting requirements
Management Skills:	Organize
	Control
Access Skills:	Queries
	Sorting
	Data Reduction
	Reporting with Subtotals
Data Table:	CASCADE

David Brooks, the owner and pharmacist of Cascade Pharmacy in Augusta, Maine, was going through his daily mail when he came across a letter he had been expecting from the state government. The letter informed him of new regulations and reporting requirements for certain categories of drugs.

The Maine state government had begun an initiative to restrict the growing use of addictive and dangerous drugs. One of the first steps involved is identifying the type and amount of these drugs sold by each pharmacy in the state. The state then intends to analyze this data and identify any regional trends.

The new regulations had been discussed at a recent meeting of Brooks' local chapter of the Pharmacy Guild, the Maine state professional body for pharmacists. Most pharmacists agree that implementing the new controls is a good idea, but the thought of yet another record-keeping chore is not attractive.

Three years ago, each member of the Pharmacy Guild had installed a personal computer with software to manage the pharmacy prescription process. When a customer wanted a prescription filled, the pharmacist entered his or her personal details (for all new customers), along with the drug and dosage requirements prescribed by the doctor. The system produced three outputs: a label to affix to the medication, a renewable prescription if required, and a detailed receipt for the customer for insurance purposes. For regular customers, the software could check whether new medication would interact adversely with any existing medication.

The letter from the government specified that usage information was required for only six classes of drugs: sedatives, analgesics, anti-hypertensives, diuretics, anti-inflammatories, and anti-depressives. At any given time, Cascade Pharmacy stocked approximately 100 drugs in these target groups.

The government required each pharmacy to submit a quarterly summary report indicating the usage of each drug issued in the six target classes during this period. Total usage of these six classes was also required. The government would conduct random crosschecks with drug company delivery records to check the accuracy of the reporting. Severe penalties were specified for non-compliance.

The table below shows a sampling of the codes assigned to drug classes used by Cascade Pharmacy's prescription program. Use this to identify the drug codes of interest to the government.

DRUG_CODE	DRUG_CLASS
Z2	Steroids
Z3	Diuretic
Z4	Anti-hypertensives
Z5	Analgesics
F1	Anti-diarrhea
F2	Birth Control
F3	Sedatives
B3	Anti-inflammatories
B4	Anti-malaria
B5	Antibiotic
B6	Anti-depressives

PharmTek, the firm that had provided the first computerized prescription system, had also attended the Pharmacy Guild's meeting. They said it would take many weeks to change the current system to meet the government's requirements. They quoted a very high fee and advised that a three-month delay would be possible before conversion. They could, however, immediately deliver an add-on program that would convert each quarter's prescriptions into a generic data format, which could be readily used by various Windows-based database packages.

For a low cost, alternative solution, PharmTek recommended that each pharmacist purchase a Windows-based database package and use it with the conversion program to perform the government's usage analysis. The database package could serve other purposes as well. Many of the pharmacies stocked a range of gift lines, vitamins, and fashion accessories, and they used a manual-card system to keep track of their inventory and suppliers in these areas. Using a database to automate this side of the business was another attractive idea.

Brooks felt confident that he could design his own database program to meet state government needs. The job could be performed on the pharmacy's personal computer on weekends when the store was closed. Brooks estimated that he used only two or three of the drugs on the target list on any given day. He also believed that some of the information required by the government would be useful for his business. For example, it would be beneficial to know how much he sold of each company's drugs.

One problem still bothered Brooks. Each drug company supplied medication in different tablet sizes. The strength of each tablet also varied in terms of milligram dosage. The government needed its usage statistics to be reported in milligrams (mgs). Fortunately, the pharmacy prescription system recorded both the number of tablets and their strength (in mgs) used for each prescription. To satisfy the government's requirements, Brooks only needed to multiply the number of tablets by strength to get total milligram usage.

Part of the table produced by the conversion program for a quarter's worth of prescriptions issued by Cascade Pharmacy has been created for you in the CASCADE table in the SOLVEIT_CH5 database. Create a new empty database and import this table now.

Tasks

There are six tasks in this case:

1. Design a query to filter out all of the drugs **not** of interest to the state government. Print the datasheet.

2. Design and print a summary report to present to the state government each quarter. Include only the total drug usage and the sub-total usage for each of the state's targeted Drug Codes. It should be sorted by Drug Code and then by Drug Name.

3. Brooks would like to discover which drug companies produce the drugs he sells under each Drug Code. Design and produce a report that presents all the quarter's transactions sorted by Drug Code. Within each Drug Code, sort alphabetically by Supplier. Include all appropriate fields, including Drug Name and Supplier.

4. Brooks has been frustrated by the slow delivery of supplies by Roche. The Roche sales representative is coming to visit next week and Brooks will raise the subject. Brooks would like to prepare for the visit by finding out how much of Roche's products he actually uses. Create and print out a report of all the prescriptions Cascade Pharmacy dispensed when the drug was provided by Roche. He would like this list sorted by Drug Code with sub-total usages included for each class.

*5. Cascade has extended their pharmacy system. The new system is compatible with several Windows-based database packages, including Access. The system is menu driven, and the pharmacist just selects the operation that is required. Menu options include "Enter a New Customer" and "Fill Prescription." The system has 4 main data files: customer, drug information, inventory, and transaction records.

The customer enters the store and gives the prescription to the pharmacist or shop assistant. The pharmacist goes to the computer and checks whether the customer is on file. If not, customer details are entered; otherwise, the customer's record is located by the system. Prescription details are then entered. A check automatically occurs to ensure that the new drug does not interact with any medication currently used by the customer.

The pharmacist then fills the prescription, the inventory level for that drug is adjusted downwards, a sticky label prints out, and a record is added to the transaction database. The transaction database is just a log of every prescription issued. A repeat script is printed if required, and a detailed customer receipt is printed for insurance purposes.

Draw a data flow diagram (first-level only) describing Cascade's new system. Include the major processes, data files, data flows, system outputs, and people involved in the system. Identify all the fields in each of the data files.

At the end of each week, a number of management reports are produced. Suggest what you think these reports will be and what fields they are likely to contain.

Information on producing data flow diagrams is contained in most information systems texts. Our reference is: *Essentials of Management Information Systems: Managing the Digital Firm*, 7th Edition, K.C. Laudon & J.P. Laudon, 2006, Prentice Hall.

*Time Estimates (excluding tasks marked with an *)*

Expert:	1 hour
Intermediate:	1.5 hours
Novice:	2.5 hours

Tutorial for Database Case 4 Using Access 2007

How to Create Record Groups in Reports

For many reports, sorting the records isn't enough; you may also want to divide them into groups. A *group* is a collection of records that share a common characteristic, such as the same Product Number or the same ZIP Code. In Access, a group consists of a group header, a series of detail records, and a group footer.

Grouping enables you to separate records of groups visually, as well as display introductory and summary data for each group. For example, the report extract shown below groups sales by date and calculates the total amount of sales for each day.

Data Grouped by Date

Delivery Date:	Invoice No.	Company	Sale Amount
11-Nov			
	10423	Hungry Macs	$1,323.34
	10425	Barnacle Jill	$2,457.40
	10426	Blue Rooster	$161.18
	10428	Hot Chipps	$741.88
Total for 11-Nov			$4,683.80
14-Nov			
	10441	Chicken 'n' Chips	$1,074.20

Total summarises the Group   Sales sorted by Invoice No.

Let's produce a report with groups using the FRIENDS database and the *Report of My Friends* report created in the Tutorial for Case 2. We want to group the report by state to produce a listing of friends sorted alphabetically (ascending order) by state. For friends in the same state, we want to sort these alphabetically by Last Name. Before we can do this, we must make some modifications to the existing FRIENDS table.

1. Open the SOLVEIT_CH5 database. Double-click on the FRIENDS table in the Navigation Pane. Add the five new records shown in Figure 5-21 to the table, making sure that some of the state names you enter in the State field duplicate those of existing records (see Figure 5-24). To speed up this procedure, just enter the new records with the TITLE, LAST NAME, FIRST NAME, STREET, CITY, and STATE fields.

Figure 5-21

TITLE	LAST_NAME	FIRST_NAME	STREET	CITY	STATE	
Mr.	Roberts	James	567 Ridge Rd.	Columbus	Ohio	56
Mr.	Thompson	Howard	799 Tucker Ave.	Blakeley	Wisconsin	35
Mrs.	Parker	Gina	640 Palm Tree Lane	Phoenix	Arizona	35
Mr.	Jones	Timothy	89945 Marydale Lane	Starkey	New Hampshire	49
Mr.	Kaufman	William	7654 Flamton St.	Milwaukee	Wisconsin	49
Ms.	Timko	Rebecca	34 Salem Ave.	Spokane	Washington	35
Mr.	Emerson	Douglas	789 Carmichael Ave.	Boston	Massachusetts	12
Mr.	Hicks	Kevin	3407 Nathrop Dr.	Chicago	Illinois	30
Ms.	Hawthorn	Diane	3034 Jones Alley	New York	New York	10
Mr.	Eddy	Steven	12 Hedge St.	New York	New York	
Ms.	Singer	Simone	111 Eagle Ave.	Green Bay	Wisconsin	
Mr.	Sorini	Roberto	4 Capital Ct.	Tucson	Arizona	
Ms.	Nation	Diana	90 Buzzard Rd.	Winslow	Arizona	
Mr.	Henderson	Henry	278 Seaspray Dr.	Manchester	New Hampshire	
*						

Record: 22 of 26 ▶ ▶I ▶⊞ No Filter Search

2. Double-click *Report of My Friends* in the Navigation Pane to open the report. Click *View* on the Ribbon and then click *Design View* to work with the report in Design View.

3. On the Report Design Tools: Design tab of the Ribbon, click *Group & Sort* to open the Group, Sort, & Total pane.

4. Click the list arrow beside *City* in the first entry and change the primary sorting criterion from *City* to *Last_Name*.

5. Click *Add a Group*.

6. In the second entry in the pane, click the list arrow beside *select field* and select *State* as the group criterion.

7. Make sure the Group entry in the pane is selected (it will be highlighted in orange) and on the right of the pane click the up arrow once to move the *Group on State* entry up one level (Figure 5-22).

Figure 5-22

8. Close the Group, Sort, and Total pane by clicking on the X in the top right-hand corner. In the Report Design View, you should notice that a blank *State Header* area has been added to the layout.

9. On the Report Design Tools: Design tab, in the Tools group, click *Add Existing Fields* to open the Field List pane. Select the STATE field in the field list. Drag the STATE field to the State Header area and position it against the left margin. Two boxes—a label box and a text box—are inserted. Click the label to select it and press [Delete] on the keyboard. Drag the State text box to align its left edge with the left edges of the City fields above and below the State Header section.

10. Double-click the State text box to open its property sheet. Click the *Format* tab, if necessary. Scroll down the list of properties and change the *Font Size* property to *14* and the *Font Weight* property to *Bold*. Close the property sheet and resize the text box to suit the changes. Your screen should look similar to Figure 5-23.

11. On the Ribbon, click *View* and then click *Print Preview* to see the effect that the changes have had on the report. Return to Design View and increase the size of the State text box if necessary to accommodate the lengths of the state names. When you have completed the change, return to Print Preview. If your report appears in Landscape orientation, Click *Page Setup* on the Print Preview tab (in the Page Layout group) to open the Page Setup dialog box. On the Page tab, change the orientation to *Portrait*. (You can also click the *Portrait* button on the Print Preview tab.) Print the report.

Your report should display the FRIENDS records grouped alphabetically by state, and within each group, ordered alphabetically by last name.

Figure 5-23

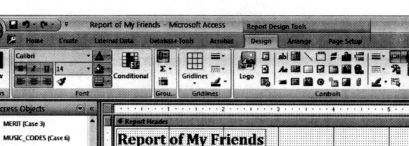

12. Save the report as *Tute4Report1* by selecting *Save As* from the Office menu. Click the *Close Print Preview* button on the Print Preview tab to return to Report Design View.

Calculating Group Summary Statistics

Under certain circumstances, you will want to ask questions about groups of data, such as "How many orders did we receive this month?" or "What's the average price of all the products in our Toothpaste category?" You can perform calculations on groups of records in reports or queries. The following table shows some of the types of *functions* (calculations) you can use with Access (refer also Access Tutorial for Case 2).

Use This Type of Calculation	To Find:
Sum	The total of values in a field
Avg	The average of values in a field
Min	The lowest value in a field
Max	The highest value in a field
Count	The number of values in a field (not including null values)

Let's use the *Count* function to count the number of friends we have in each state and display that number at the end of each group in our report.

1. In Report Design View, on the Report Design Tools: Design tab of the Ribbon, click Group & Sort to reopen the Group, Sort, and Total pane.

2. Select the first Entry, *Group on STATE*, and click the *More* button to display additional settings.

3. Click the list arrow beside *without a footer section* and change this setting to *with a footer section*. A blank *State Footer* section has been added to the report design.

4. Click *Add Existing Fields* on the Ribbon, in the Tools group, to open the scrollable field list. Drag the Last_Name field from the field list into the State Footer section. Delete the Last_Name label box and drag the Last_Name text box to the right so that its left edge is at the 5" mark on the ruler. Double-click the Last_Name text box in the State Footer to open its property sheet. On the Data tab, edit the *Control Source* property to be:

   =CONTROL([LAST_NAME])

Be careful with the syntax here, as well as with the entering of parentheses and square brackets. When you use a function, you must enclose the expression on which it is being performed in parentheses. All field names must be enclosed in square brackets, as learned previously (Figure 5-24). Close the property sheet.

Solve it!

Figure 5-24

5. Click *View/Print Preview* to see the effect of this change on your report. Results should resemble Figure 5-25. Print your report.

6. Save the report as *Tute4Report2* by selecting *Save As* from the Office menu.

Figure 5-25

Report of My Friends

CITY	TITLE	FIRST_NAME	LAST_NAME

Arizona

Wins	Ms.	Diana	Nation
Pho	Mrs.	Gina	Parker
Pho	Mr.	Phillip	Salione
Tucs	Mr.	Roberto	Sorini

4

Illinois

Chic	Ms.	Denise	Buckley
Chic	Mr.	James T.	Fabian
Chic	Mr.	Kevin	Hicks

3

Maryland

Dan	Ms.	Helen K.	Zito

1

Deleting Records in Access

To delete a record in an Access table, highlight the record row intended for deletion, and then either press the [Delete] key or click the *Delete* button on the Home tab of the Ribbon, in the Records group. Access will ask you to confirm your action. Click the *OK* button to delete the record.

Database Case 5

Hollister University

Problem:	Develop an Admissions database
Education skills:	Coordinate Decide
Access Skills:	Queries Finding Records Sorting and Grouping Reporting
Data Table:	HOLLISTER

The prestigious Graduate School of Education (GSE) at Hollister University began operations in the mid-1960s. Since that time, it has grown to become one of the most competitive and well respected schools of education in the United States. Hollister has a particularly strong faculty in the area of Environmental Education.

Eric Biermann has been Dean of Admissions at the GSE for more than ten years, and he feels that it is time for a change in the way the applications are handled. He has promised himself and his boss, Alicia Dabrowski, president of Hollister, that he will build a new admissions system. He could use your help.

The Office of Admissions gathers applications and supporting documentation from various sources. Each student submits a completed application form and an essay. Faculty members who have worked with the students at their undergraduate institution submit references. The undergraduate university also submits transcript verification forms and the College Board submits Graduate Record Exam (GRE) scores. Miscellaneous information regarding student ethnicity, age, and sex is also collected to meet various legal requirements and reporting standards.

The Alumni group has made it very clear that they want Admissions to treat the sons and daughters (but not more distant relatives) of alumni with special care.

All of this information is collected by the Admissions Office staff and summarized on an Admissions Sheet. The Admissions Sheet is the first piece of paper in the bulging folders kept on each student. The essays and outside faculty references are graded on a 1 to 5 scale (with 5 being the highest score) by faculty committees.

This procedure was developed in the mid-1980s when the school had 600 or so applicants for 200 openings. Today the school receives 5,500 applicants for approximately 500 openings. Although the Admissions Office (AO) staff has doubled in size to 8 full-time personnel, the workload is still heavy, and the process is breaking down as older, experienced staff retire and the number of applications increases.

The procedure for processing the Admissions Sheet is one source of the problems. Because the data arrive from different sources at different times, the AO clerks must go back to each student folder numerous times to enter and update the information.

Students, parents, faculty, institutions, and alumni frequently call to see if certain information has been received. Sometimes clerks pull the sheet to answer queries and then the sheet is misplaced. New sheets must be coded up in this case.

A number of data integrity problems have emerged. For instance, more and more students are claiming that their GRE scores are not correctly recorded. Changes from the University Board are submitted with growing frequency, but AO staff is often so pressed for time that sometimes these record changes are not made. Other data quality problems involve the undergraduate grade point average, address errors, and majors. The current system must be able to keep track of these changes.

The existing system does not appear to support the group decision-making process, which is at the heart of admissions. A small group of ten faculty members and three Admissions Officers make all the decisions on the Admissions Committee. Each member of the Admissions Committee takes a look at the data, wants the data organized differently, and feels frustrated when they are told that this is impossible. As a result, committee members spend too much time arguing over the decision criteria and weightings, and too little time searching for appropriate candidates. For instance, some faculty are interested only in GPA and GRE scores, and they want to see the applicant pool sorted first by GPA and then by GRE. Other faculty members are more interested in GPA and references, and do not even want to see the GRE scores.

Administrators want to ensure that within accepted academic criteria, the alumni's children get special hearings. There is little opportunity to find those candidates who score high on all the criteria. All in all, the manual resorting of lists and list compilation is a tedious process characterized by long delays and mistakes.

All of these problems have produced a political dimension: no one is happy with the existing system and everyone blames the Admissions Office. As Dean of Admissions, Biermann is now under attack from many sides. The AO staff is also unsatisfied, even a bit surly at times, because of the long hours they must spend each spring compiling lists, updating files, and meeting last minute deadlines.

Rather than rely on the Administrative Computing Center (which is already extended beyond capacity), Biermann has decided to build a PC-based admissions database using Access.

A sample of the admissions data table has been created for you in the HOLLISTER table in the SOLVEIT_CH5 database. Create a new Access database and import the HOLLISTER table now.

Tasks

There are five tasks in this case:

1. There are two main lists that the faculty requires:

(a) A listing of all the applicants for professors on the Admissions Committee who want to see the applicants listed by decreasing GPA scores; students with the same GPA should be sorted by decreasing GRE scores.

(b) A second listing showing the applicants sorted by decreasing GPA; students with the same GPA should be sorted by decreasing reference scores. Print out the results of both listings.

2. The AO clerks absolutely insist on having rapid access to students' complete records on the basis of Last Name only. That is, they want to type the last name of the student into a PC and have the complete record appear on the screen. Because so many people call in checking on student applicant files, this capability would save an enormous amount of time. Using the HOLLISTER table, identify the Access sequence of commands that would enable the AO staff to do this.

3. Biermann wants a report or listing of just the applicants who are children of alumni. He will use this list as a crib sheet in committee deliberations. Whenever a candidate is settled on, he will check his list of alumni applicants to see if that person is on the list. If not, he will suggest an equally well-qualified alumni applicant. Thus, alumni applicants should be sorted by decreasing GPA. Students with the same GPA should be sorted by decreasing GRE scores.

4. A small group of professors is concerned that the Education school is loading up with Natural Science majors. They would like to ensure that students from Liberal Arts and Social Science backgrounds are considered as well. The non-science students tend to have better GPA scores than GRE scores (because of an alleged quantitative bias in the GRE test). They also tend to have better recommendations.

These faculty members would like a report that plays to the strengths of the non-science majors. Create a report that lists applicants by college major, showing name, GPA, and reference scores. Students of the same major should be sorted by GPA.

5. There is an ongoing dispute among Admissions Committee members about the comparative strengths of the various majors. Calculate the average scores by major on all quantitative variables and display the number of applicants from each major. Then compare the groups in a one-paragraph statement.

*6. There are number of ways this database system could be improved to better meet Hollister's needs. List the ways the system could be improved. Pick one of these improvements and implement it in the database.

Time Estimates (excluding tasks marked with *):

Expert: 1/2 hour

Intermediate: 1 hour

Novice: 1.5 hours

Tutorial for Database Case 5 Using Access 2007

Indexing in Access

If you often search a table or frequently need to sort records by a certain field, you can speed up these operations by assigning indexes to your fields. Access uses indexes in a table in the same way as you would use an index in a book: to find data, it looks up the location of the data in the index.

In Access, you create an index on a single field by setting the Index property. The table below lists the possible settings for Indexed properties.

Index Property Setting	Definition
No	Do not create an index for this field (the default)
Yes (duplicates OK)	Create an index for this field
Yes (no duplicates)	Create a unique index for this field

If you create a unique index, Access will not allow a value that already exists in that field to be entered in the same field for another record. Primary key fields (see the Chapter 4 Tutorial) are automatically indexed by Access to help speed up the execution of queries and other operations. Up to 32 indexes can be assigned to a single table or query, and each index can contain up to 10 fields. Fields with Memo or Counter data types cannot be indexed.

You want an index only if it speeds up the execution of queries, searching, or sorting. A Last Name field is a good candidate for an index since the values stored in it vary greatly and it is often used to find specific records.

1. Open the SOLVEIT_CH5 database. Double-click on the FRIENDS table in the Navigation Pane. Click *View* on the Home tab of the Ribbon to switch to Design View.

2. In the Field Name column, select the Last_Name field. In the Field Properties pane, click in the *Indexed* property settings box. Click the list arrow and select *Yes (Duplicates OK)* to set the index for the Last_Name field. Click the *Save* button or select *Save* from the Office menu. Your Design View window should look like Figure 5-26.

Figure 5-26

3. To view and/or edit existing indexes, open the Indexes window by clicking the Indexes button ![icon] on the Table Tools: Design tab in the Show/Hide group (see Figure 5-27).

4. Change indexes or index properties as needed. To delete an index, select the intended row and press the [Delete] key. This removes only the index, not the field itself.

5. Close the Indexes window by clicking 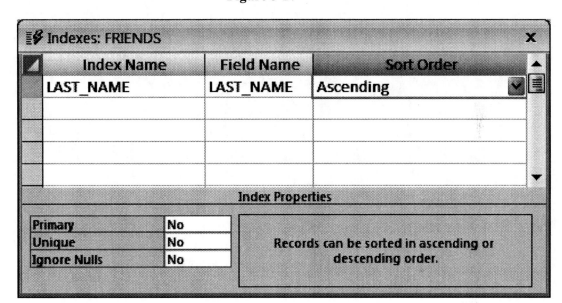 in the top right-hand corner.

Figure 5-27

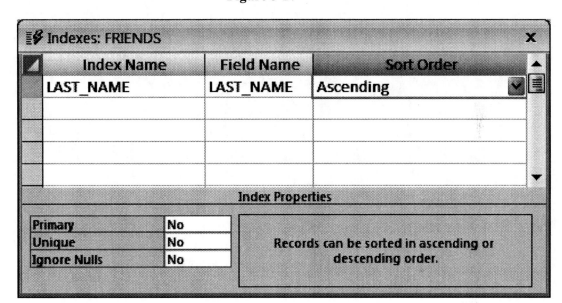

Creating Multiple Field Indexes

If you often search or sort by two or more specific fields at the same time, you may need to create a multiple field index. For instance, if you often set criteria in the same query for Last_Name and First_Name fields, it makes sense to index both fields. When you sort a table by a multiple field index, Access sorts first by the first field listed in the Indexes window. If there are records with duplicate values in this field, Access then sorts by the second field listed.

Multiple field indexes are created in the Indexes Window by including a row for each field in the index, but including the Index Name in the first row only (see Figure 5-28). Access treats all rows as part of the same index until it reaches a different Index Name. To insert a new row between existing indexes, select the row *below* the location of the row to be inserted and then press the *Insert* key.

Figure 5-28

Indexes: FRIENDS			X
Index Name	**Field Name**	**Sort Order**	
LAST_NAME	LAST_NAME	Ascending	
	FIRST_NAME	Ascending	

Index Properties

Records can be sorted in ascending or descending order.

To create a multiple field index in the FRIENDS table:

1. Reopen the Indexes window. Click in the *Field Name* cell directly below the one containing the Last_Name field. Click the list arrow and select First_Name on the list. Ascending is automatically selected as the sort order.

2. Close the Indexes window. Save the changes. Close the FRIENDS table.

The Find Command

When you want to find a specific record or certain values within fields, you can use the *Find* command to go directly to a record. *Find* can be used with most Access objects. To use Find, click the *Find* button on the Home tab to open the Find and Replace dialog box (see Figure 5-29). The Find and Replace dialog box enables you to search and replace text within a field.

Type the text you want to locate into the *Find What* list box. For added flexibility, *Find* enables you to enter word stems and wildcard symbols. A question mark (?) stands for any single character in the same position as the question mark. The asterisk (*) stands for any number of characters in the same position as the asterisk. The pound sign or number sign (#) stands for a single numeric digit in the same position as the sign.

Choose between searching across fields or a single field, and whether to search forward or the whole file. Practice using *Find* with your FRIENDS table.

Figure 5-29

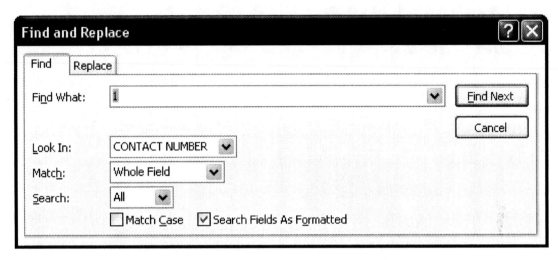

Database Case 6
Uber Audio I

Problem:	Develop a mailing list database
Management skills:	Organize
	Control
Access skills:	Database Design
	Queries
	Reports
	Linking Tables
Data Tables:	UBER_A
	UBER_B

Uber Audio is a medium-sized company based in Ann Arbor, Michigan. The business was established in the early 1990s by Dennis and Tim Uber, and grew out of a hobby the two brothers shared in music and electronic circuitry. The company has two distinct business divisions. The Uber Audio Lab side of the business designs, manufactures, and retails a range of audio equipment at the high end of the market. This business includes custom-built sound systems, the famous Uber Amp valve amplifier, which is eagerly sought by audiophiles around the world, and high performance ribbon speakers. This side of the business, managed by Dennis Uber, is high margin and very successful.

Audio Lab's main customers are audio retailers, as well as music production houses, such as EMI, Warner Music, and Polygram Records. Every six months, Uber Audio Labs distributes a product catalog to its 3,500 customers.

Tim Uber manages Uber Arcanum, the other division in the company. Uber Arcanum is a lucrative mail-order business that locates and purchases rare and hard-to-find sound recordings through contact agents around the world. Many of these items are sourced from the estates of deceased musical performers. Musical genres include classical, opera, jazz, rock, country and western, folk, soul, reggae, and ethnic (Asian and African). The business currently carries approximately 15,000 titles in this area, which are held in audio CD, vinyl record, tape, or video format, and they are sold to audio retailers and music production houses throughout the world. Uber Arcanum currently has approximately 12,000 customers on its mailing list and distributes a catalog of new and current offerings on a biannual basis.

The existing Uber Arcanum' mailing list presents a problem for Tim Uber. While the marketing side of Audio Lab has been handled by a PC-based database package for some years, Tim has been unsure of how to go about integrating the Uber Arcanum' mailing list into this system, although he knows this could make good business sense. Tim suspects that at least 30% of the customers on his mailing list are also customers who regularly purchase from Audio Lab.

The Uber Arcanum's mailing list has been steadily growing since the mid-1980s when this side of the business was formed. The mailing list was originally kept on a series of 3 x 5" cards that recorded customer mailing information and music interest details. This method soon became unwieldy as the list grew. In the late 1990s, Uber Arcanum outsourced the data management of its list to Next Step Computer Services. Next Step provides data entry and maintenance services, and produces mailing label printouts for Uber Arcanum whenever a catalog mailing is required.

Tim Uber has several problems with outsourcing his mailing list. He has recently received an invoice from Next Step requesting its usual quarterly payment of $3,500 for maintenance of his mailing list. Tim has been concerned about the escalating costs of using Next Step for some time, and he no longer believes their services are worthwhile. He also believes that outsourcing does not give him control of his own data.

The current mailing list is not stored in a database. In the 1990s, Next Step created the original list as a long sequential file that is organized alphabetically by customer last name. Tim is not happy with this structure, which he feels is inflexible and does not provide information vital to the management of his business. For example, he cannot easily obtain information about the music interests of his customers for targeted mailings. A simple query like *Print a list of all Australian customers with an interest in Opera* requires a special programming task by Next Step. This entails a lengthy delay before Uber Arcanum receives the information and incurs an additional charge for the company. More complex queries are simply impossible.

The structure of the current mailing list also complicates updating existing data or checking whether a customer is already on the list. Tim knows that a large portion of his mailing list is probably out of date. He has noticed that the number of return-to-sender envelopes Uber Arcanum receives has rapidly increased as customers relocate or contact names change. The present system makes it difficult to incorporate these changes. Meanwhile, Uber Arcanum is incurring a great deal of unnecessary mailing-associated expenses. Tim has also noticed that some of these returns have been sent to the same customer several times. This means that there is a level of data duplication in the mailing list. From current indications, he suspects the duplication may be as high as 20 percent.

Another inherent problem with the current system is that, if there are 45 customers at a large music company like Warner Music, the name and address of the company is repeated 45 times! If the name of the company were to change (as is common in the music business), the new name would have to be re-entered 45 times!

Tim is frustrated by the deficiencies of his current mailing list. Although Uber Arcanum is profitable, he suspects it could be more so if he had the right information when he wanted it and was able to do targeted mailings with ease. He has decided that the only way to get what he wants is to build a new mailing list system from the ground up. After consulting with his brother, Tim has purchased a computer and the same relational database package used by Uber Audio Lab. Once the new mailing system is working satisfactorily, he plans to dispense with Next Step's services. At a later stage, he will consider integrating his system with that of Audio Lab.

The existing mailing system has the right information, but it is not stored efficiently, nor is it not easy to interrogate. The existing system has the customer's name, primary music interest (MusIntA), secondary music interest (MusIntB), organization name, address, city, state, country, and ZIP code. The music interests of customers are coded using an internally developed schema.

To make storage and updating of the mailing list more efficient, Tim wants the data stored in two tables: one containing the names of the customers, and the other containing the name and addressing details of the company for which they work. Whenever a mailing list is required, the two tables could be joined and the results printed. Tim needs your assistance in developing this project.

The Access data tables in your SOLVEIT_CH5 database, UBER_A, and UBER_B, provide the overall design and sample data for the new mailing system. These tables form the basis of this case.

Tasks

There are six tasks in this case:

1. Link the two tables, UBER_A and UBER_B, on the Org field. It may be helpful to print out the structure of these tables first and then print the results of this join.

2. Create a report for marketing purposes that list all customers separated into alphabetical organizational groups. The fields describing the music interests and addresses are not needed. Each group should contain one organization with the records sorted alphabetically by last name within these groups.

3. Design this report as a professional document. Include a title, group headings, and any other useful features that you think would be appropriate. Print the report.

4. Design a custom label with four lines of information that can be used as a mailing label.

5. Uber Arcanum has recently obtained some new Hip Hop and Hard Rock sound recordings. Print a report of all USA customers with one of two music interests (i.e. 39 or 47) in these areas as either their primary or secondary music interest. Be careful with the Boolean logic in this problem.

*6. The current system uses codes (e.g. 39, 47) for data in the music interest fields. The user of the system and recipients of its reports must know what these codes mean. Devise a way to include the meaning for these codes into the database. You will need to make up meanings for each of the music interest codes (e.g. 39 is Hard Rock Music and 47 is Hip Hop Music). You can import the MUSIC_CODES (Case 6) table to make this easier.

Make sure that the method you devise does not include data redundancy. It would be poor database design to have the meanings for these codes repeated (redundantly) throughout the database. With your new table structure, produce a report of customers, their organizations, and their music interests that does not include codes.

Time Estimates (excluding tasks marked with *):

Expert:	45 minutes
Intermediate:	1.5 hours
Novice:	3 hours

Tutorial for Database Case 6 Using Access 2007

In this case, you will learn two important new skills: joining table files (creating relationships), and creating labels in reports.

Joining Tables

In many earlier database applications, the joining of tables is a procedure that would require you to generate a programming code. Access allows you to do this simply via the Relationships feature, and then run the results of the join in a query (or a report). Access will also generate the SQL (Structured Query Language) programming code for the procedure so you can see the effect of your actions.

Before you can join two tables, there must be a related field in both tables. While the field names need not be the same for the join to work, the two fields must contain matching data in the records. For this procedure, we will be using the FRIENDS database and a second practice table BUSDRESS. The latter contains the last names and business addresses of persons in the FRIENDS database.

1. Open the SOLVEIT_CH5 database.

2. In the Navigation Pane, double-click the FRIENDS table to open it in Datasheet View. Resize the table so that only the first three columns including the Last_Name field are showing. Then open the BUSDRESS table and resize it so that you can compare the two tables. Note that both Last_Name fields contain identical data (Figure 5-30). Remember that the field names themselves do not have to be the same. Close the two tables.

3. Open the Database Tools tab on the Ribbon, and in the Show/Hide group, click the *Relationships* button to open the Relationships window. Drag the FRIENDS and BUSDRESS tables from the Navigation Pane to the Relationships window.

4. We will now create a relationship between the two tables. This will speed up the execution of the query we will create in a moment. Table relationships were last discussed in the tutorial for Chapter 4. Drag the Last_Name field in the BUSDRESS table over to the Last_Name field in the FRIENDS table and release the mouse button. The Edit Relationships dialog box opens. Click the *Create* button. Access generates a dynamic link (line) between the two known as an *equi-join*. An equi-join selects all the records from both tables that have the same value in the selected field.

5. Your Relationships window should look similar to Figure 5-31.

6. Save the relationship by clicking the *Save* button on the Quick Access toolbar.

Figure 5-30

Figure 5-31

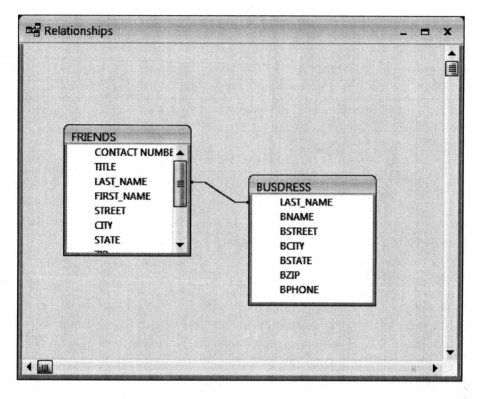

7. Close the Relationships window. You are now ready to create a query to generate the effect of the joining action.

8. Open the Create tab on the Ribbon and click *Query Design*.

9. In the Show Table dialog box, select the BUSDRESS table and click *Add*. Repeat this action for the FRIENDS table. Click *Close*. Notice that Access has remembered the table relationship and has immediately established a join between the two Last_Name fields.

10. Click *View* on the Ribbon and then click *SQL View* to see the equivalent of this action in the Access Basic programming code:

    SELECT
    FROM BUSDRESS INNER JOIN FRIENDS ON
    BUSDRESS.LAST_NAME = FRIENDS.LAST_NAME;

11. Click *View* and then click *Design View* to return to Query Design View.

12. In the query window, select and drag the following fields down into the Field row of the design grid.

From FRIENDS	From BUSDRESS
Title	BStreet
First_Name	BCity
Last_Name	BState
	BZip

13. Finally, click in the *Sort* cell for the Last_Name field and choose *Ascending order*. Your query window's design grid should now look similar to Figure 5-32.

14. Click *View* and then click *SQL View* again to see the effect this action has had on the Access Basic programming code:

SELECT FRIENDS.TITLE, FRIENDS.LAST_NAME, FRIENDS.FIRST_NAME, BUSDRESS.BSTREET, BUSDRESS.BCITY, BUSDRESS.BSTATE, BUSDRESS.BZIP

FROM BUSDRESS INNER JOIN FRIENDS ON BUSDRESS.LAST_NAME = FRIENDS.LAST_NAME

ORDER BY FRIENDS.LAST_NAME;

15. Click the *Run button* and view the resulting dynaset. Access has matched and merged the business address data in the BUSDRESS table with the name data in the FRIENDS table to create a composite display containing non-duplicated data from both (see Figure 5-33).

16. Print the query if you wish to or use as the basis for a new report.

17. Save the query as *Tute6Query1* and then close it.

Figure 5-32

Field:	TITLE	FIRST_NAME	LAST_NAME	BSTREET	BCITY	BSTATE	BZIP	
Table:	FRIENDS	FRIENDS	FRIENDS	BUSDRESS	BUSDRESS	BUSDRESS	BUSDRESS	
Sort:								
Show:	☑	☑	☑	☑	☑	☑	☑	
Criteria:								
or:								

Figure 5-33

TITLE	FIRST_NAME	LAST_NAME	BSTREET	BCITY	BSTATE	BZIP
Ms.	Denise	Buckley	786 Rice Street	Cleveland	Ohio	43203
Dr.	Peter H.	Drucker	345 Ohio St.	Cleveland	Ohio	34203
Mr.	Steven	Eddy	873 Dupont Ave.	St. Paul	Minnesota	55444
Mr.	Douglas	Emerson	67 Thistle Way	Detroit	Michigan	45577
Mr.	James T.	Fabian	98 Kansas Street	Burlington	Vermont	94532
Mr.	Henry	Henderson	8956 Front Street	Springvale	California	75893
Mr.	Kevin	Hicks	458 Southmont Drive	Catonsville	Maryland	21228
Mr.	Timothy	Jones	10050 Baltimore Pike	Baltimore	Maryland	21042
Mr.	William	Kaufman	567 Ridge Road	Baltimore	Maryland	21044
Mr.	Frank	Kohlman	856 Irvine Road	Irvine	California	54323
Ms.	Diana	Nation	1098 Cornridge Drive	Ellicott City	Maryland	21117
Mr.	Robert M.	Nelson	75 Yorktown Circle	Yorktown	New York	58964
Mrs.	Gina	Parker	459 Palm Drive	Springvale	California	75834
Mr.	Jack S.	Peterson	900 Lake Drive	Detroit	Michigan	45563
Mr.	James	Roberts	900 Lake Drive	Detroit	Michigan	45563
Mr.	Phillip	Salione	459 Palm Drive	Springvale	California	75834
Ms.	Simone	Singer	7893 Gregory Avenue	Irvine	California	75945
Mr.	Howard W.	Sitkin	4523 8th Avenue	Hartford	Connecticut	34120
Mr.	William F.	Skalek	57 Morris Drive	Seattle	Washington	45026
Mr.	Roberto	Sorini	56 Georgetown Street	Hartford	Connecticut	22335
Mr.	George R.	Tedesco	98 Lakes Drive	St. Paul	Minnesota	55434
Mr.	Howard	Thompson	10050 Baltimore Pike	Baltimore	Maryland	21044
Ms.	Rebecca	Timko	1098 Cornridge Drive	Ellicott City	Maryland	21117
Mr.	Craig	Whitney	345 Westin	Portland	Oregon	34230
Ms.	Helen K.	Zito	23 Ocean Drive	Cambridge	Mass.	93942

Record: 1 of 25   No Filter   Search

How to Create Labels in Access

A report designed to print names and addresses on labels is a common feature of most database applications. Access includes a Label Wizard that can be used to create mailing labels with sizes to match most common commercial adhesive labels. Let's use the table FRIENDS to create a simple three-line address label.

1. Open the Solveit_CH5 database. Open the Create tab on the Ribbon and click *Labels* in the Reports group to open the Label Wizard.

2. In the first Wizard dialog box, accept the default label type and dimensions. Click the *Next* button.

3. On the second screen, select the font, font size, font weight, and text color you want for the label. Click the *Next* button.

4. Choose fields for your label:

First Line

Select TITLE, and click the Add Field button to enter it onto the prototype label. Press [Space bar] on your keyboard.

Repeat this action with the FIRST_NAME field. Press [Space bar].

Select LAST_NAME and click [>]. Press [Enter].

Second Line

Select STREET and click [>]. Press [Enter].

Third Line

Select CITY and click [>]. Add a comma (,) and press the [Space bar].

Repeat this action with the STATE field. Press the [Space bar].

Select ZIP and click [>]

The Label Wizard screen should now look like the one in Figure 5-34. Click the *Next* button.

5. In the next Label Wizard dialog box, select the LAST_NAME field to sort by. Click the *Next* button.

6. In the last Wizard dialog box, type in *Tute6Report1* as the name for your report. Click the *Finish* button. Access will generate your labels and display them in Print Preview.

7. Send your labels to print, close the report, and exit Access.

Figure 5-34

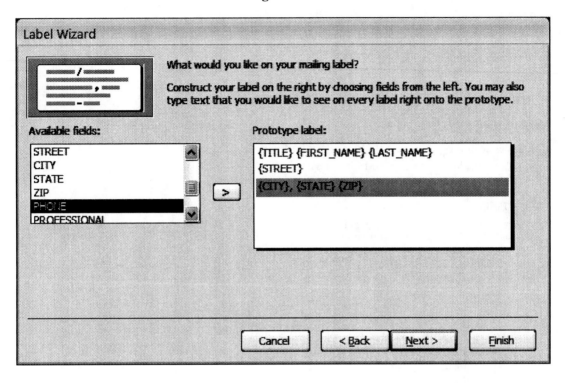

Database Case 7
Henderson Contracting

Problem:	Develop a payroll system
Management Skill:	Control
Access skills:	Select Queries (calculated fields)
	Append Queries
	Reports (wizards)
Data Tables:	HENDERSON
	1_MONTH
	2_MONTH
	3_MONTH

After working for a general contractor for eight years, Malcolm Henderson started his own road construction firm, Henderson Contracting, in 1998. For a start-up firm, Henderson had done extremely well. In 2008, the company showed gross revenues of $22 million and a net profit of $990,000.

Before starting his own company, Carl had gained a sound understanding of the road building and public sector market working as an estimator for a general contractor in Montgomery, Alabama. He developed a network of contacts among local government officials and learned the procedures and pitfalls of responding to government contract solicitations. Fortunately, the local economy grew very rapidly as major corporations, government agencies, and related housing created a boom market for road construction.

The key to Henderson's success has been in keeping permanent employee numbers low, relying on sub-contractors, and keeping his capital costs down by renting or leasing heavy equipment. Automated tools have also played an important role.

About 70% of Henderson's business is in road construction. Henderson responds to government agency solicitations for bids on construction projects. Henderson and other firms prepare competitive proposals and then offer bids. A large part of the bid preparation process (especially the design, cost estimation, and technical specification) is aided by using a proprietary decision support system (DSS) written for the road construction industry. The DSS runs on a PC in Henderson's office.

Payroll and personnel-along with other office administrative tasks-are somewhat more chaotic. There are only 6 full-time employees (Henderson, three engineers, and two office staff). However, about 45 sub-contractors work for the firm during a typical monthly payroll period. More than 400 individuals will work for the firm in a year.

Currently, one of the office staff spends 75% of his time keeping track of the firm's part-time and full-time employees. Originally, Henderson had considered outsourcing his payroll, but this proved far too expensive an option. Carl is convinced the answer lies in building a simple in-house personnel system to handle employee wages and related payroll information.

Last year, the situation became serious when the Internal Revenue Service (IRS) audited the firm's books. The IRS wondered why Henderson had more than 400 employees but showed very low tax withholdings. Carl explained that most of the employees were short-term, part-time workers and/or sub-contractors. In recent times, the IRS has taken a dim view of employees being declared as "contract workers" because federal tax is not withheld for contract workers and the IRS has trouble collecting taxes from them later.

While Henderson's contract workers appeared legitimate, examination of the records found a number of errors in withholding statements for regular employees who were part-time workers. For 21 part-time workers, no withholding was deducted or submitted to the IRS because of clerical errors. The IRS has given Henderson one year to straighten out the records.

Henderson has decided that an Access database system would be ideal for a small payroll. He wants you to design such a system for a sample quarter. Employees are paid monthly.

A sample of the employee database showing the ID number, name, and address can be seen in the HENDERSON table in the SOLVEIT_CH5 database. Create a new Access database and import this table now. A monthly file has been created for each monthly payroll period. Three hand-calculated files for the first quarter have been built for you in Access: 1_MONTH, 2_MONTH, and 3_MONTH.

Tasks

There are five tasks in this case:

1. Combine the three individual monthly reports (i.e.: 1_MONTH, 2_MONTH, 3_MONTH) into a single data table representing the First Quarter.

> **Hint:** Use an append action query to do this. You should end up with 45 records in a single, new data table.

2. Develop a query that will calculate the gross, pay, federal and state withholdings, FICA, and resulting net pay for all employees in the first quarter. Set federal withholdings at 20.4% of gross, FICA at 6.2% of gross, and state withholding at 9% of gross, and then calculate net pay as gross pay minus all deductions.

3. Use this query to create a report that shows the gross pay, all deductions, and net pay for all employees for the quarter, sorted by Employee ID number. Provide subtotals for each employee and a grand total for the firm.

4. Develop a payroll report that shows only the firm's grand totals for the quarter for gross pay, all the deductions, and net pay.

5. Produce a report for the IRS for the first quarter that shows the employees' name, address, all deductions, and net pay.

Time Estimates

Expert:	1.5 hours
Intermediate:	2.5 hours
Novice:	4+ hours

Tutorial for Database Case 7 Using Access 2007

Copying and Pasting Table Structures

Using the Access Copy and Paste commands, you can create an empty copy of an existing table (i.e.: field structure only) as a first step in merging records from a number of different tables to a single table. Let's practice this by creating an empty copy of the FRIENDS table:

1. Open the SOLVEIT_CH5 database. In the Navigation Pane, select the FRIENDS table.

2. Right-click the FRIENDS table, and from the shortcut menu, select *Copy*.

3. Right-click the FRIENDS table again, and select *Paste*.

4. In the Paste Tables As dialog box, give the table the name *Tute7CopyTable*.

5. In the Paste Options section, select the *Structure Only* option button and click *OK*.

Access creates an empty table with an identical field structure to the FRIENDS table.

Action Queries

When you create a new query with the Simple Query Wizard or in Design View, Access generates a Select query by default. *Select queries* retrieve and display data from tables according to specified criteria. We have used Select queries for *Solve it!* Database Cases 1 through 6. In contrast, *Action queries*, which are constructed starting with the Select query window, actually alter data in tables. Action queries can be used to add, delete, or change data and to create new tables from existing records. For example, a Delete action query is used to delete obsolete records from a table. Access uses four types of action queries. A brief description of each type appears in Figure 5-35, and the icons that identify them in the database appear on the Query Tools: Design tab (Query Type group) shown in Figure 5-36. In this tutorial, we will concentrate on *Append queries*. Other Action query types will be covered in later tutorials.

Append Queries

Append queries copy some or all records from one table and add them to the bottom of another existing table. This is especially useful if you use separate tables to manage certain data (e.g.: you keep payroll data on a month-by-month basis and need to merge it every financial quarter).

Figure 5-35

Type of Queries
Access query types include:
- **Select queries**
  Select a group of records from one or more tables.
- **Action Queries**
  The following action queries change the date in your tables:
  Make-table queries Create a new table from all or parts of other tables.
  Delete queries Delete records from one or more tables.
  Append queries Add a group of records to a table.
  Update queries Make changes to data in a group of records

Figure 5-36

Append queries are also handy for storing historical data. For instance, in an Orders table, completed orders could be separated from active, incomplete orders to prevent the Orders table from becoming too large, as well as to provide a backup for future reference.

When data is appended, the tables involved in the query need not have the same structure, but the data types of the appended fields **must** match. (The exception is Counter data types, which may be appended to Long Integer data types). When records are appended to a table, the records in the original table remain intact. Access does not delete the original records.

Note: If two tables involved in an Append query have identical field structures, the * in the table field list can be used instead of the individual field names in the Field row of the design grid.

Let's use the FRIENDS table and the empty copy of the FRIENDS table, (Tute7CopyTable) we created earlier in this tutorial to generate an Append action query.

1. On the Create tab, click *Query Design* to create a new query in Design View. Add the FRIENDS field list using the Show Table dialog box.

2. On the Query Tools: Design tab, click the *Append* button to change the Select query into an Append query. An Append dialog box opens.

3. In the Append dialog box, type *Tute7CopyTable* in the *Table Name* list box and click *OK*. This means we will append records from the FRIENDS table to Tute7CopyTable. An *Append To*: row is added to the design grid below the Sort row.

4. In the Append query design window, select and drag the all fields symbol (*) in the FRIENDS field list down to the first cell in the Field row in the design grid. This tells Access two things: that all FRIENDS fields should be included in the query, and that the field structure of Tute7CopyTable is identical to FRIENDS. Access immediately adds notation to this effect in the *Append to* cell.

5. Test the Append query before committing to its execution. One of the things to note about any Action query is that it **changes** table data in some way. For this reason, it is good practice to test the query before running it. Testing also allows you to check for errors in the query setup.

   To test your Append query, change to Datasheet View to view the dataset the query results in. The dataset should display all the records in the FRIENDS table. Return to Query Design View and run the query. Access should append all FRIENDS table records to Tute7CopyTable. A warning dialog box will advise you that you are about to append the number of rows selected by the query and that the action will be irreversible. Click *Yes* to append the records to Tute7CopyTable.

6. Save your query as *Tute7AppendQuery* and close it. Double-click *Tute7 CopyTable* in the Navigation Pane to open it and check the contents.

Database Case 8
Austin Auto Rentals

Problem:	Develop a transaction and fee checking system
Management skills:	Control
	Decide
Access Skills:	Forms
	Action Queries
	Macros
Data Table:	AUSTINAUTO

Drew Robinson punched the buttons on his hand-held calculator. Three months ago, Austin Auto Rentals had been an independent rental car dealer based in Austin, Texas. Texas Discount Rentals, a medium-sized operator, then offered a sizeable sum for majority ownership of Austin Auto. Texas Discount had recognized that the recent boom in the Austin area was merely the start of sustained growth. Texas Discount had also realized that the three existing rental agencies (two of them franchises of national dealerships) would provide intense competition for any start-up enterprise in the area, so it decided to approach the single independent dealer with a partnership offer.

Robinson was surprised and relieved when the Texas Discount offer arrived. His 20-year-old dealership was straining under the pressure from the newly established national franchises that could offer some cut-price deals, one-way rentals, and arrangements with frequent-flyer schemes that he could not match. Texas Discount had a cooperative deal with one of the key domestic airlines, and Robinson realized that when rental dealers' prices were very similar, customers made decisions based on issues like frequent-flyer points. Texas Discount could also assist during temporary price wars. Faced with deciding between hard times as an independent dealer and receiving cash for losing control, Robinson accepted Texas Discount's offer.

Robinson soon realized that the extra security offered by Texas Discount came with additional obligations, like monthly reporting duties. These reports involved the calculations he was currently performing manually on his calculator. Robinson already had a computerized reservation and charging system, a necessity in the industry; however, his system could not provide the required reports. Although Texas Discounts was willing to supply its own software, Robinson was happy with his system. He knew that it could write the details of transactions to an exportable file. With this knowledge, Robinson asked Texas

Discount to send one of its system programmers. Texas Discount obliged by dispatching Patricia Chavez.

Chavez examined a typical file on Robinson's system and found that it could be readily imported into any common database management system. Although not ideal, this solution would certainly prevent the need for Robinson to calculate his reports manually. Chavez advised him to purchase a Windows-based database package and use it to meet Texas Discount's monthly reporting requirements.

The senior managers at Texas Discount need quarterly information to make informed decisions. They require the total revenue derived from each of the car model sizes over each month. Each transaction record contains certain information: a sequential code generated by the computer, date of transaction, model code (S=Small, M=Medium, L=Large, X=Sports, W=Wagon), car registration, miles traveled, number of rental days, rental fee, and a logical field signifying whether or not the rental was "limited miles." The customer can usually choose unlimited miles or a limit of 100 free miles with a lower base rate. For a limited-mile transaction, each mile above 100 miles would incur a per mile cost.

The AUSTINAUTO table supplied in the SOLVEIT_CH5 database contains a partial list of transactions downloaded from the Austin Auto Rentals reservation system.

Tasks

There are three tasks in this case:

1. Drew Robinson wants Chavez to develop a simple solution for him so he can check the accuracy of the transactions in the sample list against the paper records he has in his office. He wants the solution to include an entry screen where the user may enter the transaction code (e.g. T24155). The procedure will then display the record corresponding to the code if it is valid. If the code is not valid, the user should be informed that the entry is invalid and be required to re-enter the code. The user also should be able to exit the system easily. The entry screen should have ample instructions for the user to use the system.

Hint: Create forms with command buttons to complete this task.

2. To meet his reporting commitments, Robinson must currently manually calculate the revenue from each transaction. Thus, he wants Chavez to develop a procedure to calculate the fee for each transaction and place the result in the RENTALS table. The charges for each model type appear in the following table:

	Small (S)	Medium (M)	Large (L)	Sports (X)	Wagon (W)
Limited Rate ($)	$60.00	$65.00	$70.00	$75.00	$80.00
Additional cost per mile ($)	$0.59	$0.69	$0.79	$0.89	$0.90
Unlimited Rate ($)	$55.00	$60.00	$65.00	$70.00	$75.00
Depreciation Rate (%)	3.5%	2.9%	3.1%	3.6%	4.5%
Purchase Price ($)	$14500	$17175	$24950	$25575	$22775

> *Hint:* First create a table to store the rate information for each car model type from the first three rows in the table above. Then create three update queries to complete this task. The first query will calculate the charge for customers who choose the Unlimited rate. The second query will calculate the charge for customers who choose the Limited rate and do not go over the allotted 100 miles. The third query will calculate the charge for customers who choose the Limited rate and exceed the 100 free miles. The last expression will multiply the limited rate by the number of days and add to that the total miles driven minus the free 100 miles multiplied by the additional cost per mile. Enclose the parts of an expression that must be performed first (i.e. addition and subtraction to override the order of operations) in parentheses. Each calculation will *update to* the CHARGE field in the RENTALS table.

*3. Texas Discounts is becoming more demanding in its reporting requirements, adding to Robinson's workload. The company wants to know the depreciation of any car in Austin Auto's yard. The method for calculating depreciation in the car rental industry is dictated by the Internal Revenue Service. The depreciation amount for each vehicle depends on the total distance traveled (read from the odometer), the rate of depreciation for the model type (i.e. small, medium, large, sports, wagon), and the purchase price of the vehicle. The IRS says the depreciation amount is defined as a fixed percentage (i.e. the depreciation rate) of the purchase price for every 7,500 miles the vehicle has traveled. Develop a procedure to calculate the amount of depreciation for each car based on the depreciation rates and purchase prices appearing in the table above. Enable the user to enter the registration of a particular vehicle and then calculate the depreciation on that car.

Hint: First create a table to store the depreciation and purchase price information for each car model type from the bottom two rows of the table above. Set the *Format* property for the depreciation rate field to Percent and the *Field Size* property to Single. Then create a Parameter query to complete this task. You first must create a calculated field to compute the depreciation. The expression will divide the depreciation rate by 100 and multiply the result by the purchase price multiplied by the odometer reading divided by 7,500. You must enclose parts of an expression that must be performed first (i.e. dividing the depreciation rate by 100) in parentheses. The parameter query will prompt the user to enter the car registration number.

Time Estimates (excluding tasks marked with *):

Expert:	1.5 hour
Intermediate:	2.5 hours
Novice:	4 hours

Tutorial for Database Case 8 Using Access 2007

Creating Forms in Access

Forms are used to view, enter, or edit data into a database and often serve as the most convenient way of performing these operations. Forms can be based on tables or queries, and they can display data on a record-by-record basis. As with reports, forms can be created using a wizard. A series of dialog boxes enables the user to customize the way data will be organized and displayed. With one mouse click, you can switch from Form to Datasheet View, which is a tabular view of the same set of records.

An Access form, just like a report, is constructed from any number of controls: text boxes for entering and editing data; label controls to identify the text boxes; and other controls, list boxes, or combo boxes from which a user can select a value, and toggle buttons, option buttons, or check boxes for *Yes/No* fields. You can modify forms in various ways, including using colors to highlight important data, inserting graphics, and displaying messages to indicate when an incorrect value has been entered. You can also set up your form so that Access automatically inserts data for you, prints data on the click of a command button, and/or displays the results of calculations. Let's use the FRIENDS table to create a simple form.

Forms

1. Open the SOLVEIT_CH5 database and select the FRIENDS table in the Navigation Pane.

2. Open the Create tab on the Ribbon and then click *Form* in the Forms group. Access automatically generates and opens a new form for the selected table that includes all of the table's fields in one or more columns. The form shows the first record in your table (see Figure 5-40). Notice that two Form Layout Tools tabs of commands, Format and Arrange, appear on the Ribbon.

3. Click *Save* in the Quick Access toolbar. Name your form *FRIENDSSHOW* and save it. In a matter of minutes, you have created a simple form that can be used for viewing, editing, adding, and deleting records in the FRIENDS table.

Access offers a number of different types of forms you can create using the commands on the Forms group on the Create tab of the Ribbon:

*   **Simple form** (Form): This form displays one record with fields in one or two columns.

*   **Datasheet forms** (More Forms>Datasheet): Displays fields in datasheet format

*   **Tabular forms** (Multiple Items): Displays each record as a row of fields

*   **PivotTable forms** (More Forms>PivotTable): Creates a form with a Microsoft Excel pivot table, a feature that enables analysis and summarization of data in lists and tables

*   **PivotChart forms** (PivotChart): Creates a form for displaying PivotCharts.

*   **Split forms** (Split form): Displays the current record as a simple form and additional records as a datasheet form.

*   **Modal Dialog** (More Forms>Modal dialog): Based on asking the user a question as part of an automated process; used with VBA scripting.

*   **Blank form** (Blank form or Form design): Creates a blank layout to which you add all form fields and formatting.

You can also use the **Form Wizard** (More Forms>Form Wizard) which will assist you in selecting the table, fields, layout (Columnar, Tabular, Datasheet, Justified), and style for a form.

Figure 5-37

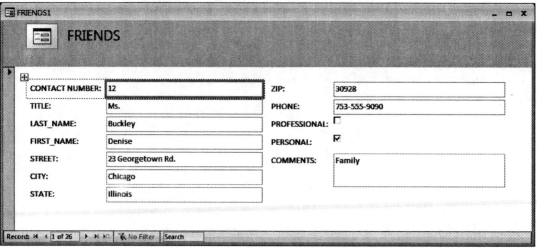

Three Ways of Viewing a Form

Access offers three quick and easy ways to view a form. You will use each of these when designing and using forms. To switch views, simply click on the appropriate toolbar button.

Design View

- Use for customizing the appearance or changing the structure of forms, and for adding and modifying controls

Form View

- Use for viewing, entering, and editing record data

Datasheet View

- Displays the underlying table or query dynaset on which the form is based

You can also use the *Print Preview* button to see how a form will look when printed.

Creating a Form in Design View

As the name suggests, you start with a blank form and use the toolbox to add controls in Form Design View. You use the tools in the toolbox to add all of the text boxes, labels, combo boxes, list boxes, check boxes, and other controls required for your form. For this reason, blank forms often have no initial connection to an underlying query or table.

Hint: You must create a form in Design View by adding unbound controls to a blank form for Task 1 of Case 8.

To create a blank form:

1. On the Create tab of the Ribbon, click *Form Design* to open a blank form in Design View. The initial form will contain only a Detail section. Forms use the same type of sectioning as reports. Review the Access tutorial for Case 2 for an explanation of report sections.

   Let's create a simple customized form using the FRIENDS table. The form is designed to look up and display specific FRIENDS records based on their ID numbers.

Hint: The criteria used could just as easily be product numbers or transaction codes.

2. To add a form header and footer section to your form, right-click on the form and select *Form Header/Footer*. On the Form Design Tools: Design tab, click the *Label* button and use the label pointer to click in the form header section of the form. Type a heading for the form, *Friends Lookup*. Change the label size, font, font size, and font color as you see fit. If necessary, increase the size of the form header by positioning the pointer over the top edge of the Detail section bar and dragging downward with the horizontal split-bar pointer.

3. Click the *Text Box* button and then click in the *Detail* section of the form to create an unbound text box and label for the form. Right-click the label and select *Properties* on the shortcut menu. On the Format tab in the property sheet, change the *Caption* property to *Search for a Friend*. Resize the label (and reposition the text box) so that the label box displays all of the text.

4. Select the unbound text box. On the properties sheet, select the Data tab. Locate the *Validation Rule* property, click in the settings box, and type the following expression (right-click and select *Zoom* if you need more room to type):

> = 1 And <=200

Note: The ID numbers in the FRIENDS table must be greater than or equal to 1 and less than or equal to 200. This will allow you to enter up to 200 names in the table and will catch typing errors that include letters, negative values, or numbers greater than 200. It creates a valid ID number range

5. Press the down arrow key on the keyboard to move to the *Validation Text* property settings box. Enter the following message to display in an error dialog box if a user enters invalid data: *You must enter values between 1 and 200. Click OK and re-enter.*

6. Click the Other tab. Change the *Name* property for the text box to *FriendID*. In the *Status Bar Text* property settings box, type *Enter an ID number*.

7. Save your form as *FRIENDSLOOKUP*.

Next, we will create three *command buttons*: One that links FRIENDSLOOKUP through an event procedure to the FRIENDSSHOW form and displays the relevant record, one that exits FRIENDSSHOW so that FRIENDSLOOKUP displays, and one to exit FRIENDSLOOKUP.

Using Control Wizards in Forms

The Access Control Wizards will help you to create complex controls for your forms by taking you step-by-step through the creation process. Control Wizards are available for creating option groups, list boxes, combo boxes, and command buttons. Command buttons can be created to start many different types of actions or sets of actions. These are referred to by programmers as *event procedures*. An *event* is a particular action that triggers a procedure, such as clicking a command button in a form or report. A *procedure* is a unit of programming code designed to accomplish a specific task.

You will not be directly required to do any programming because the Command Button Wizard will write the Microsoft Jscript or Visual Basic Scripting Edition code for you. You can create command buttons that will automate many frequently-used activities associated with forms and reports, such as opening and closing objects, linking fields between objects, printing individual records, going to specific records, or updating data.

1. Let's create the first of our command buttons. First, make sure that the FRIENDSLOOKUP form is open in Design View. Select the *Control Wizard* button

   on the Form Design Tools: Design tab so that it is highlighted, if necessary.

2. Click the *Button* button on the Ribbon and then click in an empty section of the *Detail* section in the FRIENDSLOOKUP form.

3. The first of several Command Button Wizard dialog boxes opens. Make these choices as you proceed through the dialog boxes:

   a. In the Categories box, select *Form Operations*. In the Actions box, select *Open Form*. Click *Next*.

   b. Select *FRIENDSSHOW* as the form to open. Click *Next*.

   c. Choose to *Open the form and find specific data to display*. Click *Next*.

   d. In the *FRIENDSLOOKUP* box, select *FriendID*. In the *FRIENDSSHOW* box, select *CONTACT NUMBER*. Click *Next*.

   e. Select the *Text* option button and type *Show Record* as the text to display on the button. Click *Next*.

   f. Type *ShowRecord* to name the button. Click *Finish* to generate the command button.

HINT: If you have any problems creating this button, you can follow the steps in Step 5 to open the Code window for the button and type the appropriate code for the button as seen in Figure 5-38.

4.   Save the changes to the FRIENDSLOOKUP form.

5.   Right-click the *Show Record* button and select *Properties*. Click the Event tab. Scroll down the list to the *On Click* property. Notice that Access has added an Event Procedure for this property. Click in the *On Click* property settings box and then click the ... (*Build*) button. The Code window in the Visual Basic Editor opens, displaying the code for the event procedure for the Show Record button (see Figure 5-38). Click the *Close* button at the top right of the Visual Basic Editor window (**not** the Close button for the Code window) to close the Visual Basic Editor and return to Design View.

6.   **Time to Test:** Close the property sheet and switch to Form view. Notice that the text you entered for the *Status Bar Text* property displays in the Status bar. Enter an ID number between 1 and 26 (or whatever the last record number is at present in your FRIENDS table), and click the *Show Record* button. The sequence works, but there is no easy or immediate way to run the procedure again or to exit from FRIENDSSHOW. You must add an *Exit* button to both the FRIENDSLOOKUP form and the FRIENDS SHOW form. Use the *Close* button to close FRIENDSSHOW.

7.   Return to Design View in the FRIENDSLOOKUP form. Use the Command Button Wizard to create another command button in the *Detail* section to exit the form. Select the *Form Operations* category and the *Close Form* action. Use the Exit picture on the button, and name the button *Close Form*. Reposition the command button as necessary, save the changes, and close the form.

Figure 5-38

```
SOLVEIT_5 - Form_FRIENDSLOOKUP (Code)

OpenFriendsShow                          Click

    Option Compare Database

    Private Sub ShowRecord_Click()
    On Error GoTo Err_ShowRecord_Click

        Dim stDocName As String
        Dim stLinkCriteria As String

        stDocName = "FRIENDSHOW"

        stLinkCriteria = "[CONTACT NUMBER]=" & Me![FriendID]
        DoCmd.OpenForm stDocName, , , stLinkCriteria

    Exit_ShowRecord_Click:
        Exit Sub

    Err_ShowRecord_Click:
        MsgBox Err.Description
        Resume Exit_ShowRecord_Click

    End Sub
```

8. Open the FRIENDSSHOW form in Design View. Add a command button under the Comments field to close the form. Use the text *Close Form* on the button and name the button *Close Friends Show*. Reposition the command button as necessary, save the changes, and close the form.

9. Open the FRIENDSLOOKUP form in Form view. Enter *10* in the *Search for a Friend* text box. Click *Show Record*. Click the *Close Form* button to close FRIENDSSHOW. Click the *Exit* button to close FRIENDSLOOKUP.

10. Reopen FRIENDSLOOKUP in Form view and test the procedure several times. Also, enter an ID not in the valid range to make sure the validation procedure is working. With two simple forms and three easy-to-generate command buttons, we have created a robust, easy-to-use FRIENDS lookup program.

Macros in Access

A *macro* in Access is a set of actions that automate common tasks, such as opening a table or printing a report. Macros help you to work smarter and save time without having to learn programming. Macros are simple to create, and Access offers a choice of approximately 50 different macro actions that include:

- Opening and closing tables, forms, and reports

- Opening a form and finding records related to another form

- Automatically printing reports upon opening a particular database

- Checking or improving data validity

The great thing about macros is that they can handle tasks that would often require extensive programming skills in other database packages, and the more you use them, the more you learn about the underlying principles of programming. Macro actions often involve *arguments*. These are simply parameters that govern how an action is executed. If you have problems choosing macro actions or specifying arguments, press the [F1] key to open the Help file.

Let's create a simple macro that will open the FRIENDS table and display only records that contain Zip codes greater than 35000. It will also filter out all records where the State is not Arizona before returning to the full FRIENDS table record set.

1. Open SOLVEIT_CH5 and double-click the FRIENDS table in the Navigation Pane. Switch to Design View and change the ZIP field to the Number data type. Save the change and close the FRIENDS table.

2. Open the Create tab on the Ribbon and click the *Macros* button in the Other group. The Macro Builder window opens. Click in the first blank cell in the *Action* column.

   Click the list arrow ⌄ to display a list of all available Macro actions. Scroll down this list and select *OpenTable*. (Read the information box at bottom right of the window for an explanation of what this action does). In the *Comments* column, type a short description of the action: *Opens the FRIENDS table*.

Figure 5-39

You can press a command
button on a form ...

| Print Monthly Sales |

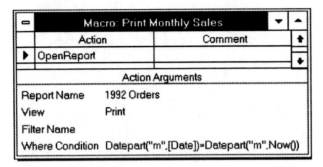

... to run a macro that opens a report. The macro then ...

... finds and prints
sales data for the
current month.

3. In the *Action Arguments* panel at the bottom of the window, click in the *Table Name*
    box. Click the list arrow [image] and select the FRIENDS table.

4. Click in the empty Action cell in the second row and select *ApplyFilter* on the list. In
    the *Comment* column, type a short description of the action: *Only display records
    where the Zip code is greater than 35000.*

5. In the Action Arguments section, click in the *Where Condition* box and type the
    following:
    [FRIENDS]![ZIP] >35000

6. Click in the next empty Action cell and select *ApplyFilter* on the list. In the
    Comments column, type a short description of the action: *Within this reduced record
    set, show records only from Arizona.*

7. In the Action Arguments section, click in the *Where Condition* box (see Figure 5-40)
    and type the following:
    [FRIENDS]![STATE]= "Arizona"

Note: Additional records were added to the FRIENDS table in the Tutorial for Case
4. If you did not do this tutorial, you must add the 5 new records to the FRIENDS
table shown in Figure 5-21.

---

8. Save your macro by clicking the *Save* button or by selecting *Save* on the Office
    menu. In the *Save As* dialog box, name your macro *Tute8Macro1* and click *OK*.

Figure 5-40

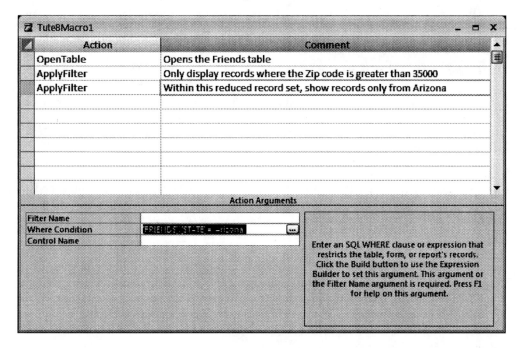

9. Execute the macro by clicking the *Run* button on the Macro Tools: Design tab on the Ribbon, in the Tools group). As the macro runs, it first opens and displays all of the records in the FRIENDS table. The first filter is then applied, and only records where the Zip code is greater than 35000 are shown. The second filter is then applied, and the record set is further reduced to records where the Zip code is greater than 35000 AND the State is Arizona.

10. Close the dynaset and the Macro Design window.

Use Macros When: You are performing tasks, such as opening and closing tables or forms, or running reports. Your application involves custom menus and submenus for forms. Your application is basically simple and uncomplicated, and does not require debugging procedures.

Update Queries in Access

Update queries are action queries that modify data according to specific criteria, such as increasing **all** car rental rates or **certain** product prices by 15%. Update queries are created in much the same way as other queries, except that a new value is specified for a particular field. Like all other types of action queries, update queries save time and effort, but they must be used carefully because they actually change the data in the underlying table. Let's use the sample data table HARDWARE to create a simple update query.

1. Open the HARDWARE database you created in the Tutorial for Case 2. If you did not create this database, create a new empty database and import the HARDWARE table provided in the SOLVEIT_CH5 database. Open the HARDWARE table and browse the records of the table, specifically noting the data in the UnitCost field (see Figure 5-41).

2. Create a new query in Design View using the Item and UnitCost fields from the HARDWARE table. Select *Update* on the Query Tools: Design tab to turn the Select query into an Update query and add an *Update To:* line to the design grid.

3. In the *Update To* cell for the UnitCost field, enter the expression *[Unitcost]*1.15.* This expression will multiply the current value in the UnitCost field by 115%, thereby increasing the prices of all items in the HARDWARE table by 15%.

4. In the *Criteria* cell for the Item field, type *Rake*. This tells Access to limit the update of the UnitCost field to only those records that contain the word *Rake* in the Item field. Click the *Datasheet View* button to make sure that only invoices for rakes are being selected for updating.

5. Return to Design View and save the query as *Tute8Query1*. Run the query. Click *Yes* to update the three rows containing the unit cost for rakes. Close the query. Open the HARDWARE table and notice the changes made to the UnitCost field (see Figure 5-42). All invoices for rakes have been increased by 15%.

Figure 5-41 (before update)

INVOICE	ITEM	UNITCOST	QUANTITY
1239	Screws	$3.40	4
1240	Shovel	$25.00	1
1241	Hinges	$2.50	6
1242	Widgets	$1.60	12
1243	Nails	$5.60	3
1244	Rake	$15.00	6
1245	Screws	$3.40	3
1246	Hinges	$2.50	4
1247	Widgets	$1.60	5
1248	Rack	$12.50	2
1234	Shovel	$25.00	2
1235	Rake	$15.00	1
1236	Rack	$12.50	4
1237	Nails	$5.60	2
1238	Rake	$15.00	15

Figure 5-42 (after update)

HARDWARE			
INVOICE ▾	ITEM ▾	UNITCOST ▾	QUANTITY ▾
1239	Screws	$3.40	4
1240	Shovel	$25.00	1
1241	Hinges	$2.50	6
1242	Widgets	$1.60	12
1243	Nails	$5.60	3
1244	Rake	$17.25	6
1245	Screws	$3.40	3
1246	Hinges	$2.50	4
1247	Widgets	$1.60	5
1248	Rack	$12.50	2
1234	Shovel	$25.00	2
1235	Rake	$17.25	1
1236	Rack	$12.50	4
1237	Nails	$5.60	2
1238	Rake	$17.25	15
*			

Parameter Queries

You can also create a parameter query that will prompt the user to enter criteria each time the query is run. For example, instead of entering *Rake* as the criterion in the Item field, you could enter *[Enter an Item]*. When the query is run, the Enter Parameter Value dialog box will open prompting the user to "Enter an Item" (see Figure 5-43). The text that will serve as the prompt is enclosed in square brackets in the criterion expression. This way, the query can be saved and rerun each time a price increase occurs. As is, the query will increase the price of any product entered by the user by 15%, but the expression can be modified to accommodate larger or smaller percentage increases. Parameter statements can be used with all types of queries-select and action.

Figure 5-43

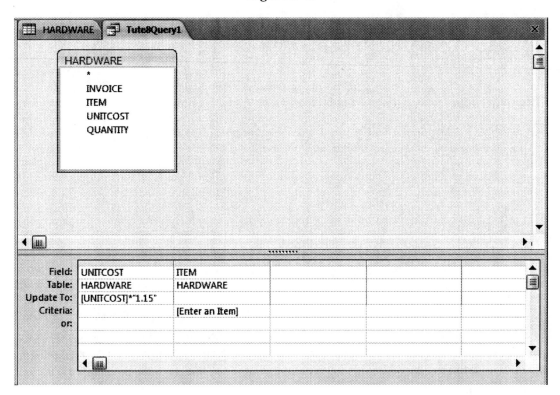

Database Case 9

Pelican Inn

Problem:	Design a hotel reservation system
Management skill:	Control
Access Skills:	Forms Screen Design Macros Queries Functions
Data Tables:	PELICAN ROOMS PELICAN GUESTS PELICAN RESERVATIONS

Mimi Schroeder settled down at her office desk with the accounts and reservation book and started the chore of calculating the month's takings at the hotel she jointly owns and operates with her husband, Vern. When the Pelican Inn in Flagler Beach, Florida was bequeathed to Mimi by her grandparents, Mimi and Vern faced the decision of whether to sell the hotel or manage it themselves. As recent MBA graduates of the Florida State University, the couple prepared a complete business plan as if they were deciding to purchase the business.

Mimi found that while the 23-room hotel was profitable, it was experiencing steadily declining rentals. After talking with owners of nearby hotels, Mimi discovered that up to 65% of hotel patronage in the area came from repeat business. Despite this, the Pelican had no list of past customers, either regular or otherwise, and records of past capacity utilization were patchy. In addition, the current booking and reservation system was manually-based. Even so, Mimi and Vern thought the business had great potential, given a more modern management approach. They believed that, after a few years of successful operation, there would be enough funds to expand the hotel, so they decided to go ahead with running it.

Mimi contacted one of her Operations professors from Florida State, who suggested that the reservation and booking system was amenable to computerization. The professor recommended a PC-based database management system for tracking the rental of rooms, thus automatically establishing a history of customers and recording a transaction list whereby revenues could be easily calculated. The list of past guests could then be used for mail-outs to remind potential repeat customers of the attractions of Flagler Beach, most notably, the Pelican Inn.

Mimi and Vern were excited at the prospect of owning and managing a business at such an early age. However, managing the hotel and its staff was a full-time responsibility, and they did not believe they could develop the required database system themselves. They contacted the Career Placement Office at Florida State, which directed them to Boris Novotny, a first-year MBA student and an IS major proficient in PC database systems. Novotny agreed that he could develop a simple menu-driven program to record guests booking in and out of the hotel.

Mimi and Vern hired Novotny to develop the management system. Novotny decided that several data tables would be necessary for the hotel's reservation system. These would be:

1. A list of rooms and their features (ROOMS)

2. A list of past guests and their details (GUESTS)

3. A list of transactions of each guest's stay (RESERVATIONS)

In addition, a lookup table, ROOMS LOOKUP, would be generated from the ROOMS data table to provide a list of currently available rooms. Jose believed appropriate options on a menu would be:

1. Registering a guest

2. Checking out

3. Listing vacant rooms

4. Exit the program

Novotny explained that he intended to use these different options to operate the three data tables, using customer name as the common field. For example, when a guest arrived, the hotel receptionist would select Option 1 from the menu. The vacant rooms would then be displayed from the ROOMS LOOKUP table. The receptionist would enter the guest's name and offer a room choice to the guest. Once the choice was made, the ROOMS table would be amended to show the details of the new guest, his/her room number, and the room rate. The program would then check to see whether the guest had visited before by consulting the GUESTS table. If the guest was a newcomer, further details, such as mailing address, would be entered and added to the GUESTS table. This new data would eventually build a significant guest list and serve as a valuable marketing tool.

The second option would be used at the end of a guest's stay. The relevant room in the ROOMS LOOKUP table would be changed to vacant status. Also, entries in the GUESTS, ROOMS and RESERVATIONS tables would be amended or updated to reflect details of the current visit. At the same time, a charge would be calculated by subtracting the current date from the date of arrival and multiplying the number of days the guest had stayed by the room rate.

The third option would enable the user to examine a list of vacant rooms at any time using the ROOMS LOOKUP table. The fourth option would simply exit the hotel reservation system.

You have been supplied with three of the four data tables needed to complete this case: PELICAN ROOMS, PELICAN GUESTS, and PELICAN RESERVATIONS in the SOLVEIT_CH5 database. The fourth table, ROOMS LOOKUP, will need to be created. Import the existing three tables to a new database. Open the tables and examine their structure.

Tasks

There are five tasks in this case:

1. Create a form, appropriate command buttons, and macros to register a guest at the Pelican Inn. This will require the use of the ROOMS and GUESTS tables supplied to you in the SOLVEIT_CH5 database. Include on your form all appropriate formatting, header information, and instructional text.

2. Create a new table (ROOMS LOOKUP) that hotel clerks can use to look up a list of all vacant rooms, along with their rates and features. This table will be based on some of the fields in the ROOMS table. Create a command button on the form you created in Task 1 that will allow access to this new table.

3. Create a procedure to check a guest out. This will involve appending a record to the RESERVATIONS table from the ROOMS table, before deleting the relevant record from the ROOMS table. The RESERVATIONS table should then be updated to calculate total charges due. Be sure to use parameters for isolating specific records in this procedure.

4. Create a Main Menu form and appropriate command buttons to enable the user to choose from and use any of the four options described in the case. The 4 menu options should be displayed using forms, which all include an Exit procedure back to the main menu.

*5. Suggest and implement how the Schroeders can incorporate the following improvements:

    - A mechanism to distinguish between guests of the same name
    - A future booking system whereby guests may reserve rooms ahead of time for peak periods
    - A checking system so other guests cannot stay in reserved rooms

Time Estimates (excluding tasks marked with *):

Expert:	2 hour
Intermediate:	3 hours
Novice:	5 hours

Tutorial for Database Case 9 Using Access 2007

More about Forms: Main/Subform

A *subform* is a form embedded inside another form (known as the main form). Main forms or subforms are used to generate and display data from any two tables or queries that have a one-to-many relationship. The main form will be based on the table that's on the "one" side of the relationship, and the subform on the "many" side of the relationship (e.g.: in Case 9, one guest can have many RESERVATIONS).

The relationship between the two tables **must exist before** attempting to create the subform. In addition, the main form (the table on the "one side") should have a primary key, while the subform (the table on the "many side") must contain a field with the same name and data type as that primary key. Primary keys are usually unique identifiers. You must create primary key fields for some of the tables used in Case 9. Review the section *Creating Relationships Between Tables* at the end of Chapter 4 if you are unsure how to do this.

To create a Main/Subform:

1. Create a new empty database named VICTORSFURNITURE and import the CUSTOMERS, PRODUCTS, and ORDERS tables from the SOLVEIT_CH5 database into it.

2. Open the Relationships window and add the 3 tables to the window. Select the CustomerID field in the field list for the CUSTOMERS table and drag it to the CustomerID field in the ORDERS table. Click the *Enforce Referential Integrity* check box and then the *Create* button to create the one-to-many relationship between the two tables.

3. Select the ProductID field in the field list for the PRODUCTS table and drag it to the ProductID field in the ORDERS table. Click the *Enforce Referential Integrity* check box and then the *Create* button to create the one-to-many relationship between the two tables. The Relationships window is shown in Figure 5-44. Close the Relationships window, saving the changes to the layout of the window when prompted.

4. Open the Create tab on the Ribbon. Click *More Forms* and then click *Form Wizard*.

5. In the first Wizard screen, select the CUSTOMERS table and click [>>] to add all of the fields in the table to the form.

6. Click the list arrow on the Tables/Queries box again and now select the ORDERS table. Click [>>] to add all of the fields in the table to the form.

7. Select ORDERS.CustomerID in the Selected Fields list box. Click [<] to remove this field from the form. (This field is a duplicate. The CustomerID field has already been added to the form from the CUSTOMERS table). Click *Next*.

8. You want to view the data by CUSTOMERS with the customer data in the main form and the order data in the subform. Click *Next*.

Figure 5-44

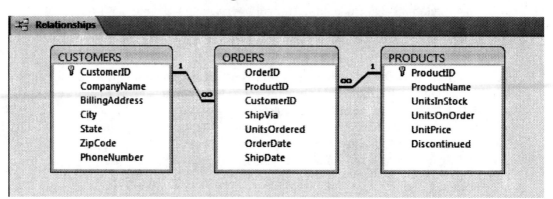

9. Select the *Datasheet* layout. Click *Next*.

10. Select the *Median* style. Click *Next*.

11. The default name for the subform is *Orders subform*. Modify the label for the Orders subform, removing the word *subform*. Keep the default names for the form, CUSTOMERS, and subform, ORDERS. Click *Finish*.

12. Switch to Layout view. Adjust the overall width, column width, and font size of the ORDERS subform, so that all of the fields are visible on the form. Adjust the height of the ORDERS subform to fill the screen. Save the changes and return to Form view. You can now view all orders placed by a particular customer in the subform. New orders can be entered in the subform.

13. Return to the Design and Layout views and make any other changes as you see fit to the sizes or positions of the controls on the form, save them, and close the form. The form/subform is shown in Figure 5-45.

Delete Queries

Delete queries are action queries that remove records from a table according to some specified search criteria. Delete queries are created in the same way as other action queries. Begin by creating a select query, which contains field criteria, such as parameter statements for isolating the records targeted for deletion. ***Warning:*** *A delete query always deletes **entire** records, not just the contents of specific fields.*

Figure 5-45

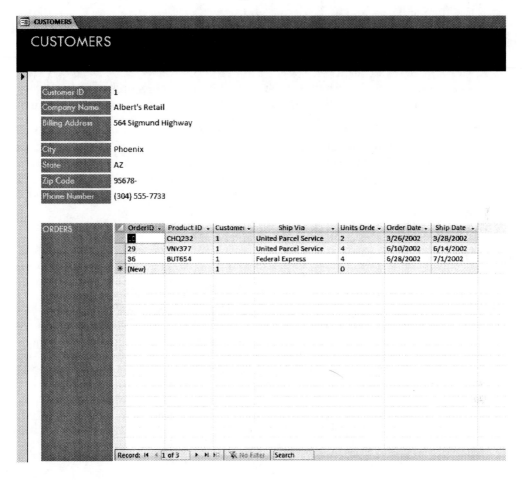

On the Query Tools: Design tab, in the Query Type group, click *Delete* to turn the select query to a delete query. This action adds a *Delete*: row in the design grid. Test the query without committing to execution by using the Datasheet View button to preview the targeted records. Execute the query by clicking the *Run* button on the Ribbon. **Warning**: *Delete queries cannot be undone, so test thoroughly before committing to Run.*

1. In the VictorsFurniture database, open the Create tab and click *Query Design*. Add the ORDERS table to the Query Design window and close the Show Table dialog box.

2. Drag the * (all fields) symbol to the design grid. Drag the CustomerID field to the second column in the design grid. Clear the check box in the *Show* cell for the CustomerID field. (You must clear the check box so that the CustomerID field is not included in the query results set twice.)

3. Type *28* in the *Criteria* cell for the CustomerID field. This is the ID for a customer that has gone out of business.

4. Drag the ShipDate field to the design grid. Type *Is Null* in the *Criteria* cell for the Ship Date field. This command will delete all unshipped orders (those with a blank ship date). Clear the *Show* checkbox to prevent the ShipDate field from appearing twice in the query result set.

5. Click the *Datasheet View* button to check that the correct records will be deleted. There is only one order for CustomerID 28 that has not yet shipped (see Figure 5-49).

6. Return to Design View and select *Delete* in the Query Type group on the Ribbon. The Sort and Show rows are replaced by the Delete row. Orders will be deleted **from** the ORDERS table **where** the CustomerID is 28 AND **where** the ShipDate field contains a null value, as shown in Figure 5-47 Run the query. A warning message box asks you to confirm the deletion of the row. Click *Yes*. Close the query without saving it. Close the database.

Functions in Access

A *function* in Access performs some sort of calculation on data and returns the result of that calculation. There are over 130 different functions available in Access. Functions can be used in Macros or Modules, in Query expressions, or as calculated controls in Form or Report objects. Case 9 involves using two different types of functions:

Type of Function	Name of Function	Calculation Performed
Date/Time	DateDiff	Number of time intervals between dates
Domain Aggregate	DLookup	Finds/Looks Up and displays a Value

Figure 5-46

OrderID ⏷	Product ID ⏷	Customer ⏷	Ship Via ⏷	Units Ordere ⏷	Order Dat ⏷	Ship Date ⏷
101	CCC921	28	Airborne Express	6	6/24/2002	
* (New)				0		

Figure 5-47

DateDiff

The *DateDiff* function is used to determine how many time intervals (e.g.: days, weeks, years) exist between two dates. In the following example, the DateDiff function is used to calculate the number of days between an Entry and Exit date at a parking garage. The result of this calculation is then multiplied by the Daily Parking Rate to give a total amount owed by the driver. Required syntax is exactly as shown.

In Case 9, the DateDiff function is used in an Update action query, first to determine the number of days a guest has stayed at the hotel and then to calculate the appropriate charge.

DLookup

DLookup returns a field value from a domain (a specific set of records as defined by a table or query). The following example first looks up the Tax Rate in a table called *Personnel* where data in the *Skill* field of a table called *Staff* matches data in the Skill field of the Personnel table. The appropriate *Tax Rate* is then added to the Tax Rate field in the Personnel table. Required syntax is exactly as shown.

In Case 9, the DLookup function is used in a Set Value macro sequence to look up a room rate in the ROOMS LOOKUP table and add it to the Rate field in the ROOMS table as part of the registration procedure.

More about Macros

The following macro actions may help in completing the tasks associated with Case 9.

MACRO ACTION	WHAT IT DOES
Close	Closes the current active window
Echo	Hides or shows the result of a macro while it runs
MsgBox	Displays a message box with informational or warning text
Open Form	Opens a specified Form object
Open Query	Opens a select query and/or runs an action query
Set Value	Sets the value for a control field or property on a form or report
Set Warnings	Turns off all system messages such as warnings while a macro is running.

Database Case 10

Uber Audio II

Problem:	Create a complete system
Management skill:	Control
	Organize
Access Skills:	Forms
	Macros
	Advanced Queries (Union)
Data Tables:	UBER_A
	UBER_B
	UBER_C

This case is a continuation of Solve it! Database Case 6. Refer to this case for background information. We recommend that you make a copy of the Case 6 files and save them as Case 10 before starting this case.

Tim Uber was feeling very pleased with himself as he gazed out of his office window at the busy Hoboken street. He had just finished his perusal of Audio Arcanum' financial performance figures for the 2008-2009 year. His mail order music company had performed stunningly last year, with sales improving by nearly 25%. Tim had also noticed that the costs associated with postage and packaging of his mail order catalogs, as well as the maintenance of his mailing list, had dropped significantly.

Tim believed that these results were largely due to the ability of the PC-based database mailing system his company had developed to provide carefully targeted mail-outs for his various customer segments. Previously, Tim had relied on blanket mail-outs to all of the customers on his mailing list whenever he wanted to advertise new product offerings. Thanks to his new mailing system, his company is now able to tailor its mail-outs so that catalogs are sent out only to customers with interests in the music areas relevant to his new products.

Tim now wants to complete the development of his new system by adding some enhancements and new features. He has jotted down his main requirements.

a) A system that is easy to use

The new system has worked well, but it requires a thorough understanding of the database package in which it had been created to operate effectively. Tim is the only one who knows how the system works and what it does, and he currently maintains the system himself. He does not regard this as a productive way to spend his time, and now he wants to pass over the operation and day-to-day maintenance of the system to his clerical staff.

As it stands, Tim must remember which query did what and which report gave him the result formats he wanted. The system is efficient, but it is not the kind of product he wants in the hands of untrained people. What he needs is a more robust and user-friendly version of the system.

Tim's objective is to produce a self-contained mailing system that can be operated by someone with little or no database knowledge. The system must be menu-driven and modular in design. The menu should also execute automatically when the user opens the database that contains the system (i.e.: the .ACCDB or .MDB file). When a task option is selected from the menu, the menu will open the required object and then execute that option. Each option should contain a facility to exit back to the menu.

b) Integrate the Audio Arcanum mailing list with that of Audio Lab

Tim suspects that at least 25% of the customers on his mailing list are also customers who regularly purchase from Audio Lab, his brother's side of the business (refer back to Case 6). While the marketing side of Audio Lab has been handled by a PC-based database package for some time, the system is not menu-driven and requires someone with a good understanding of databases to operate it. Tim and his brother Dennis would like to combine their mailing lists under one menu-based system. They have agreed that while information unique to each of the businesses will be maintained separately, the names and addresses will be shared. Although the two divisions do business with many of the same organizations, Audio Arcanum' customer contact names may often be different than the ones used by Audio Lab.

Tim Uber would like to test how well this procedure will work. Dennis has provided him with a sample listing of Audio Lab' customer names. This is provided on the *Solve It!* data table UBER_C. Tim wants to combine this file with his own listing (UBER_A). The result of this procedure should show no duplicate records. The combined listings will then be incorporated into a menu option on the new system.

Tim needs your help. He does not have the time or expertise needed to create the menu-driven mailing system required, and he would like you to develop a prototype. Part of the job was completed in *Solve It!* database Case 6, and you will need to use the database used in that previous case to complete Case 10.

Tasks

There are six tasks in this case.

1.   Create a Main Menu form (that you will call MAIN MENU) and appropriate command buttons, which allow the user the following executable options:

1.   Add a new customer

2. Add a new company

3. Produce a complete mailing list

4. Exit the system

> **Hint:** *Insert command buttons without the Control Wizards activated on the Main Menu form for the first three options. These options will not initially be active. Use the Command Button Wizard to set up an active Exit procedure for option four.*

2. Create data entry forms for command buttons 1 and 2. Include Exit and Add New Record command buttons, and then test them thoroughly. Call these forms ADD CUSTOMER and ADD COMPANY.

3. Devise a procedure that will automatically execute the Main Menu whenever the database is opened.

4. Create a procedure that will combine the customer name tables of Audio Arcanum (UBER_A) and Audio Lab (UBER_C). There are a number of names that appear in both tables. Your goal is to produce a listing that contains no duplicate records.

> **Hint:** *Use a Union query to complete this task.*

The combined file should then be joined to the UBER_B table to give a full listing of the customers and their organizational details. This task can be accomplished with a Select query.

5. Create a report to display results for Task 4. The report should be sorted first by organization, and then by last name. Incorporate this report as Option 3 on the Main Menu form.

> **Hint:** *Use the existing report created for Tasks 2 and 3 of Case 6 (Marketing Report), and simply change the record source for the report to the TASK4B query. Also, change the title and the name for the report to Full Mailing List (both the Caption property for the report and the Caption property for the title label.) Save the report with the new name: Full Mailing List.*

*6. Extend the system even further to include the sales and number of sound recordings sold to each customer. Add the necessary fields and some sample data to the appropriate table. Then add a new option to the menu that will calculate and display the total sales for Audio Arcanum and the average price per recording.

Time Estimates (excluding tasks marked with *):

Expert:	2 hours
Intermediate:	3 hours
Novice:	5 hours

Tutorial for Database Case 10 Using Access 2007

Advanced Queries: The SQL-Specific Query

SQL (Structured Query Language) is a simple programming language used for querying, updating, and managing relational databases. When you create a select query or action query, Access automatically generates the equivalent SQL statement in the background. You can view or edit the SQL statement by choosing SQL View on the View menu in either the Datasheet View or Query Design View, or by clicking the list arrow on the *View* button and selecting *SQL View*.

Some Access query types, however, can only be created by writing an SQL statement. These queries are known as SQL-Specific queries. This group includes:

- **Union** Queries that combine fields from two or more tables or queries
- **Pass-through** Queries that send commands directly to a database server
- **Data-definition** Queries used to create or alter database tables in the current database
- **Subqueries** An SQL SELECT statement inside another select or action query

SQL statements refer to expressions that define SQL commands, such as SELECT, UPDATE, or DELETE, and include clauses, such as WHERE, GROUP BY, and ORDER BY. SQL statements are typically used in the construct of queries and aggregate functions.

The Union Query ▣

You must use the Union SQL-Specific query type as part of the requirement for completing Task 4 of Case 10. You can use Union queries to combine the result sets of two or more Select queries into a single result set. You can also create Union queries that combine rows in two tables.

Using simple *SELECT ... FROM* SQL statements, *Union queries* enable you to combine fields from two or more tables into one listing. In contrast, *Select queries*, which are based on a join, create a dynaset only from those records whose related fields meet a specified condition. Commands and clauses commonly used in the creation of Union queries include:

- **SELECT** fieldlist

- **FROM** tablenames **IN** database name

- **WHERE** search conditions

- **GROUP** BY fieldlist

- **HAVING** search conditions

- **ORDER** BY fieldlist

Creating a Union Query

1. Open the *COLBY'SCUSTOMCAMPING* database. Open the Create tab and click *Query Design* to open the Query Design View window, but do not add any field lists to the design grid. Union queries do not use the Query Window/QBE Grid for their construction. Close the Show Table dialog box.

2. Click *Union* on the Query Tools: Design tab in the Query Type group. Access displays the Union Query window, into which you type the appropriate SQL SELECT *statements* needed for your Union query.

   For this query, you will create a simple Union query that will combine rows from two tables. The SQL statement will select the records of all customers and suppliers who live in the state of Connecticut. Type the following (See Figure 5-48):

   SELECT CustomerName, BillingAddress, City, State, ZipCode, PhoneNumber, CustomerID
   FROM Customers
   WHERE State = "CT"

   UNION SELECT CompanyName, BillingAddress, City, State, ZipCode, PhoneNumber, SupplierID
   FROM Suppliers
   WHERE State = "CT"

3. Click the *Run* button. The query result set is shown in Figure 5-49. Save the query as *Tute10UnionQuery* and close it. Close the database.

The number of fields in the field list of each Select and Union Select query must be the same. You will receive an error message if the number of fields differs.

The sequence of the field names in each field list must also correspond to the similar entity in the other field list. You will not receive an error message, but the result set may be incoherent.

Commas are used to separate members of lists of parameters, such as multiple field names as in the example.

Figure 5-48

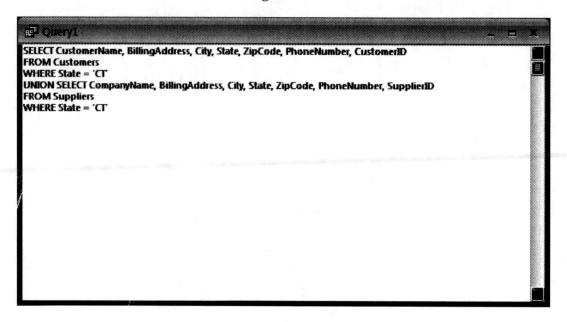

Figure 5-49

CustomerNa ▾	BillingAddre ▾	City ▾	State ▾	ZipCode ▾	PhoneNumt ▾	Cu
Burke and Me	622 Lindale Rd.	Keedysville	CT	00675	6075553444	
Carol Thompso	294 Bradford R	Turner	CT	66844	5785552233	
David Johnson	722 Blanchard I	Greenfield	CT	10784	2045554378	
Georgette Star	34786 Richards	Michaelton	CT	10647	2045551093	
Jim Smith	6887 Grant Ave	Lawrence	CT	35509	7455557532	
Peters Campin	74 Delaponte A	Lawrence	CT	37856	5665559054	
Steven O'Patri	213 Singleton I	Morristown	CT	11988	2045553355	

Record: I◀ ◀ 1 of 7 ▶ ▶I ▶ ☒ No Filter | Search

Square brackets are required only around field names that include a space or other symbols, including punctuation. If fields from more than one table are included in a query, a period must separate the table name and the field name (e.g. Suppliers.[Company Name]).

Be sure to include a semi-colon at the end of each statement (refer to examples below) to complete the required Access syntax. Note also the use of square brackets to enclose field names. This punctuation is necessary if you are using field names composed of two or more words separated by spaces or punctuation.

Here are some other examples of SQL statements:

To retrieve the names and cities of suppliers and customers from the Suppliers and Customers tables:

> **SELECT [Supplier Name], [City]**
> **FROM Suppliers**
> **UNION SELECT [Customer Name], [City]**
> **FROM Customers;**

To retrieve the names and cities of suppliers and customers located in Brazil, sorted by the City field:

> **SELECT [Supplier Name], [City]**
> **FROM Suppliers**
> **WHERE [Country] = "Brazil"**
> **UNION SELECT [Customer Name], [City]**
> **FROM Customers**
> **WHERE [Country] = "Brazil"**
> **ORDER BY [City]**

Note: *Unless you specify otherwise, a Union query automatically removes duplicate records from the resulting listing. If you want to show all records, including duplicates, add the word ALL after the word UNION in your statement. For example:*

To retrieve the names and cities of suppliers and customers from the Suppliers and Customers tables, and show all records including duplicates:

> **SELECT [Supplier Name], [City]**
> **FROM Suppliers**
> **UNION ALL SELECT [Customer Name], [City]**
> **FROM Customers**

Task 1 of Case 10 requires you to create a merged file of the customer records of Audio Arcanum and True Tones Contrast the difference between omitting and including ALL in the Union query you need to create to complete this task.

Warning: Do **not** convert an SQL-specific query to another type of query, such as a Select query. If you do, you'll lose the SQL statement that you entered. *You can, however, use an SQL-specific query as part of a Select query.*

Creating an AutoExec Macro

You can create a special macro that automatically runs whenever you open a Microsoft Access database. For example, you may wish to open certain tables and forms every time you open a database.

To create a macro that runs whenever you open a database:

1. Create a macro.

2. Add the actions that you want this macro to perform.

3. Save the macro. **Its name must be AutoExec**.

AutoExec macros can be used to create a custom workspace, import data from other databases, or execute tasks that you want to perform every time the database is opened. To prevent the AutoExec macro from running, hold down the *Shift* key while opening the database.

Setting Startup Options

You can easily control many aspects of how an Access database looks and behaves when it opens without writing a macro or any Visual Basic code. You can set startup options to give your database a title and/or to program Access to open a particular form first when a user opens the database. Click the Office button and then click *Access Options* to open the Access Options window. Select *Current Database* in the left pane to open the options for the current database. Type the name you want for your application in the *Application Title* text box. Click the list arrow on the Display Form list box and select the form you want to open first.

Other startup options include using a custom application icon and choosing whether or not to display the Status bar. You can also decide if you want full menus to display in the database and whether or not you want users to be able to make changes to the menus or toolbars.

Database Case 11

Jackson Hole Trading Co I

Problem:	Develop a comprehensive database for use with an e-commerce website
Management Skill:	Plan Coordinate Control Organize
Access Skills:	Creating a Database Creating tables Creating relationships Creating and running queries
Data Source:	JACKSONHOLE.xlsx

Dylan Jennings was facing one of the biggest decisions in company history: whether to take her successful mail order catalog business, Jackson Hole Trading Co., online. Jennings knew from others in the mail order business that success in mail order did not automatically mean success online. In fact, a few of her competitors had lost significant amounts of money in their online ventures and had to declare bankruptcy. Jennings wants to explore the issue fully before committing significant resources.

Jackson Hole Trading Co. was founded in 1970 by Dylan's father, Wesley Jennings, in Jackson Hole, Wyoming. The company started by supplying cross-country and downhill skiers with high quality, affordable outerwear. It has since grown to offering a wide range of outdoor gear, covering not only skiing, but hiking, camping, climbing, and mountain biking. The company takes pride in the fact that it still offers high quality outdoor gear at affordable prices and has established a loyal customer base that produces more than 1 million orders annually. Dylan Jennings has recently taken over the company after her father's retirement and is reviewing the company's operations and financial position.

Jackson Hole Trading sends out catalogs to customers quarterly and occasionally mails out a special sale catalog when higher-than-normal levels of inventory warrant it. The time between selecting items for the catalog, producing the publication, and printing it, and the time when customers actually receive it is four to six months; this requires significant planning throughout the entire company to ensure that proper inventory levels are maintained during the period in which the catalog is active.

Jennings has been considering an online e-commerce presence for the company for more than a year. She decided to start with an informational site to assess the level of interest a Jackson Hole Trading site would generate. To date, the site has received a great deal of positive feedback, but site visitors are becoming increasingly frustrated that it does not support online ordering.

A well-designed and executed e-commerce site could save the company money in the long run through the automated processes (ordering, inventory control, and shipping) that would be embedded in the site. However, there would be a substantial initial investment for the site: hardware and software to host and maintain it, design and maintenance of the site itself, training for staff on the new processes, and advertising to draw traffic to the site. Jennings wants to know if this investment will pay off and how it will impact the company.

Jennings has met with the heads of the marketing, sales, customer service, product development, inventory control, human resources, and shipping departments to discuss how they currently process information. She has discovered that the data entry process in each department is mostly manual in nature. Employees enter information into Excel spreadsheets designed specifically for that department. There is significant redundancy in the data entry process across the company. For example, the product development department establishes the product ID number and product description for an item when they finalize it for the catalog. They create a spreadsheet with all this information. The customer service department must enter all of the product ID numbers and descriptions into their spreadsheet to correspond to orders they have taken. Jennings wants to eliminate this redundancy.

Last week, Jennings met with Ben Nguyen, a web developer who runs his own company, Grand Teton Tech. Nguyen's specialty is e-commerce sites with database back ends, which means he designs websites that allow the information gathered on the site to be merged into a database. Nguyen also designs the databases that support his sites. This is an extremely efficient way to process information from a website because the data only has to be entered through a form on the site once by the customer, and then it can be accessed and queried in a variety of different ways by the company. Nguyen has designed a prototype website for Jackson Hole Trading that includes an online catalog and shopping basket so that users of the site can purchase items online. Users will submit their orders through a form on the site and the information from those orders will be merged into an Access database Nguyen will design for the company.

Nguyen has asked Jennings to provide him with representative data from each of the departments involved so he can design the database. Jennings's assistant, Brad Bernstein, has compiled this information into one Excel spreadsheet and has given it to Jennings for this meeting. Jennings would like to see the following before she decides how extensive the shopping cart portion of the site will be:

- How the database will be divided into tables

- How the database will reduce or eliminate redundancy of order entry

Tasks

There are three tasks in this case:

1. The data that Bernstein has gathered is provided for you in JACKSONHOLE.xlsx. Determine how the data should be divided into tables to create the least amount of redundancy possible. Create a database named JACKSONHOLE and the appropriate tables (name the tables after the function represented (orders, employees, sales, customers, for example). Save this database.

2. Establish the relationships between the tables so that you can easily create queries from the tables.

3. Jennings wants to do a test query to see how the data can be manipulated. She wants to know how often the men's full-length down parka (product ID # 20010) is ordered. Create a query that determines this information. Save this query as Case11Query1.

Time Estimates:

Expert:	1.5 hours
Intermediate:	2 hour
Novice:	2.5 hours

Tutorial for Case 11 Using Access 2007

There is no tutorial for Case 11. It draws upon the knowledge and skills you have acquired in previous cases and tutorials. The following lists what skills are required for this case and the tutorials in which they were covered:

Creating Databases	Chapter 4
Creating Tables	Chapter 4, Chapter 5 (Case 1)
Joining Tables/Relationships	Chapter 5 (Case 6)
Creating and Running a Query	Chapter 5 (Case 1, Case 3)

Database Case 12

Jackson Hole Trading Co. II

Problem:	Obtain information from the completed database created in Database Case 11.
Management Skill:	Plan Coordinate Control
Access Skills:	Creating and printing reports Creating and utilizing forms Creating and running macros
Database:	JACKSONHOLE.accdb

This case is a continuation of Solve it! Database Case 11. Refer to this case for background information relating to Case 12. You will be using the database you created in Case 11 for this case.

Nine months ago, Dylan Jennings made the decision to create an online e-commerce presence for his company, Jackson Hole Trading Co. The new website has received positive reviews from users and seems to be attracting new customers. Jennings decided to spend extra money on the database back end for the site so that data entry would be more efficient. She feels it is working, but knows that it can be more efficient and provide more information than the original design is supplying.

Jennings initially met with the heads of the departments that would be affected by the implementation of the website: Hector Moreno from Sales, Ryan Buckley from Product Development, Olivia Robbins from Customer Service, Susan McBride from Order Fulfillment, and Noah Solomon from Human Resources. They each gave Jennings an outline of the data they collect and the ways in which they use it. Ben Nguyen then designed the website and database to solicit the information from customers when they ordered.

The transition from the manual system Jackson Hole Trading had been using to the new automated system was not easy. It took hours of work to create the database that holds all of the information. Employees had to be trained in the new processes and systems. There were numerous test orders entered into the website to make sure all pertinent data was collected, and then queries, forms, and reports were created to make sure all departments' data needs were met.

Jennings is now ready to test the new website with a system-wide evaluation. The following tasks will help her do so:

Tasks

There are six tasks in this case:

1. Design and create a report that details the total amount of orders taken by each employee.

2. Noah Solomon from Human Resources wants to evaluate how employees hired after 2003 are doing in terms of productivity. Produce and print a report for him that details orders taken by employees hired after the year 2003.

3. Ryan Buckley would like a form his employees can use to enter new products into the system. Design and create a form that will allow Product Development employees to enter Product ID, Product Name, Product Description, Cost, and Selling Price easily and efficiently. Name the form PRODUCTS.

4. Buckley would also like anyone in the company to be able to quickly locate information about products. Design and create a form using command buttons that allows employees to look up products by Product ID number. Label the button *Find Product*.

5. Hector Moreno would like to target customers who have bought specific products when sales of the same or related products are offered. Create a form with a subform that lists Product ID number, Product Name, and Product Description as the main form and Customer ID, Last Name, and First Name as the subform. Name this form PRODUCTS AND CUSTOMERS.

6. Dylan Jennings has requested that she receive an annual report that details orders by zip code. Susan McBride would like to automate this report by using a macro so that she can run it very quickly each month. Design and create a macro that will open a report that lists orders by zip code for each month.

Tutorial for Case 12 Using Access 2007

There is no tutorial for Case 12. It draws upon the knowledge and skills you have acquired in previous cases and tutorials. The following lists what skills are required for this case and which tutorial they were covered:

Creating and Printing Reports	Chapter 5 (Case 2, Case 4)
Creating Forms	Chapter 5 (Case 8, Case 9)
Creating and Running Macros	Chapter 5 (Case 8)

6

Internet Cases

Web Case 1

Casseopia.com Web Portal

Problem:	Prepare a report on Web portal technology
	Calculate the return on investment for a portal project.
Management skills:	Planning
	Deciding
Web skills:	Business research
File:	CASSEOPIA_Q.xlsx

Casseopia.com started as a simple search engine in 1996. Today it provides a wide range of travel, entertainment, and financial services, as well as in-depth content on sports, medical issues, and news in an effort to find a wider audience and keep visitors at its site for longer periods of time. The longer visitors can be induced to stay at the site, the greater the revenue potential for Casseopia. Companies and individuals now use Casseopia to find low-cost airline fares, discounted hotel rates, rental car deals, and related travel information. Individuals often use the site to research entertainment packages at popular tourist destinations and find financial information about companies for stock picks. Using Casseopia's unique reservation system, registered site users can make airline reservations and purchase tickets, rent hotel rooms, reserve cars, buy entertainment packages, and make other travel arrangements all in one Web site visit.

Since Casseopia has grown from fifteen employees providing a simple search service to a Web portal with 450 employees providing many services, the management team has become overwhelmed with information. The small management team must keep track of various Web activities at its site, including the number of visitors, sales for each of its services, and results of promotional campaigns, as well as weekly and monthly cost reports. Although they are a Web services company, managers are overloaded with paper-based reports. Different managers need different types of reports, and each report requires data that the IT Department must provide on a routine basis. With so many employees, there is a growing demand for information on training, pensions, and benefits. As the customer base has expanded, it has become increasingly difficult to respond to customers seeking help with Casseopia's various service offerings or deal with customer complaints.

As a result, the costs of managing the firm have skyrocketed despite a long-term effort to keep the management head-count down.

CEO Amber Burke wants to move the firm toward a more uniform information management environment, one that would be more efficient, provide better service to customers, impart employees with more information on company activities and programs, and offer managers a coherent online information environment. She is considering the development of an internal Web portal as a tool for organizing and accessing the company's critical management information.

A corporate portal is an internal Web site running on a corporate intranet that organizes and distributes important management information for decision-makers, as well as general corporate information required by all employees. Portals provide a single point of access and a delivery vehicle for important corporate information. Users can customize and personalize the content they see to focus on just those pieces of information they require to do their jobs. Portals can also be configured to call information from a variety of back-office legacy systems and present it to users in an easy-to-use Web environment.

Although the Casseopia technical development team could build such a corporate portal, this is not one of their core competencies, and Hensley does not want to pull the technical team off more valuable Web site development work. Therefore Hensley is planning to purchase an off-the-shelf Web portal service from a firm that specializes in this technology.

CEO Burke has given the job of designing and developing a successful corporate portal project to CIO Michael Chambers. Chambers supports the idea of purchasing a corporate portal from an outside firm that has experience with this technology rather than building it in-house. He needs some help identifying vendors in this area and acquiring background information on costs and benefits. As Chambers' executive assistant, your first assignment is to use the Web to research corporate portal vendors and develop a report for the portal project.

Tasks

There are three tasks in this case.

1. Use a search engine such as Google.com or Yahoo.com to find three Web sites of companies that sell corporate portal technology. Prepare a short report (3-5 pages) or PowerPoint presentation (5-7 slides) describing the features of corporate portals, their benefits, and costs. Many sites will include case studies of "success" stories. Be sure to include at least one successful case in your report. Include a section in your report or presentation that describes some of the potential risks and pitfalls of using this technology.

2. Chambers has provided you with some initial estimates of the costs and benefits of the new portal for the next three years. These estimates are provided in the accompanying spreadsheet Casseopia_q.xlsx. He would like your help in analyzing the results.

Calculate the following:

    a. Total projected costs for each year, and the total costs for all years

    b. Total projected benefits for each year, and the total benefits for all years

    c. Depreciation: Assume a straight line depreciation over three years.

    d. Annual net benefits (nominal) for each year (benefits-costs for each year)

    e. Cumulative payback (nominal)

    f. The accounting rate of return for the next three years; The accounting rate of return is defined as:

$$\frac{\textbf{(total benefits—total costs—depreciation)/useful life}}{\textbf{total costs}}$$

We will assume in this problem that the useful life of the portal is three years, the depreciation is equal for each year, and at the end of the period, the portal has no salvage value (the value is zero after three years).

    g. Prepare a brief statement arguing for or against this investment by the firm.

*3. Calculate the net present value of the investment in the portal technology. Assume a prime interest rate of 5%. You must calculate the present value of the annual net benefits.

Hint: Use Excel's NPV function to do this. The net present value is defined as the present value of annual net benefits minus the total investment cost.

On the basis of your results, do you recommend this investment? Write a paragraph describing the benefit of this investment for the firm.

Tutorial for Web Case 1

Search Engines on the Web

Search engines are software programs that help people find information stored in computer systems, including the Web. Users enter a word or phrase or other argument (such as a telephone number or zip code) into the search engine, and it returns to the user a list of references to the location of content which meets the search criteria. The list is typically sorted by relevance and/or popularity, which can be determined by the use of software algorithms or human editors, or some combination of these. From the list of references users can navigate to the actual content which is typically in the form of documents. The most common search engines are those which are used to search the public Web, but the same software can be used to search your own computer, or a corporation's library of documents stored on a private intranet. Though there are hundreds of search engines available for use on the Web, most of them free, the search sites listed below account for more than 98% of U.S. search activity (source: Nielsen Online, 2009).

Top Three Search Sites

- Google www.google.com
- Yahoo yahoo.com
- MSN Search www.msn.com/

Other Popular Search Sites

- Ask.com www.ask.com
- Altavista www.altavista.com
- Bing www.bing.com

Multi-Site Search Engines

- Excite www.excite.com
- Web Crawler www.webcrawler.com
- DogPile dogpile.com

Continuing search technology improvements as well as industry consolidation and shared indexing technologies among the search sites make it difficult to predict which the "best" or "most comprehensive" search site is at any particular time. Different search engines produce some differences in results, especially for very specialized search topics. Researchers have found, for instance, that there is about a 60% overlap among search engines. Nevertheless, this also suggests that 40% of the pages found on one search engine will not be found on another search engine even when using the same search argument. Repeating a search on multiple sites is not only a good technique, but will also provide ideas for refining your search.

Search engines typically produce very large lists of search results. Therefore, be careful to narrow your search arguments. For instance, if searching for information on "security alarms," narrow your search by specifying "home," "business," "boat," or "automobile." What type of security alarm are you really looking for? If you are really looking for a wireless car alarm that will sound an audible alarm and then send a radio signal to your beeper, your search argument on a keyword search engine should be something like "security alarm and automobile and wireless." A good search approach is to enter the minimum number of words which uniquely refer to information you want, then—if necessary—add additional words to further limit the search.

The most widely used search engine is Google which at one point claimed to index over 6 billion Web pages. Google uses a combination of techniques, including Web crawlers and proprietary relevancy algorithms. As of late 2006, Google stopped publishing a claimed number of pages indexed, stating that freshness and relevance were of more importance to searchers. In any case, pages-indexed claims must be viewed skeptically because of the impact of duplicate pages, link-only pages, and other Web anomalies.

Understanding the Financial Value of Information Systems

Businesses invest in information technology applications for a variety of reasons. In some cases, the investment is undertaken to achieve growth in market share, in other cases, it is simply as a requirement for staying in business, and in still other cases, it is undertaken to achieve a return on invested capital. Sometimes all three motivations are important. Whatever the reason for investment, most businesses will perform a financial returns analysis. The two most common financial return calculations are the accounting rate of return (ROI) and net present value analysis.

Accounting Rate of Return

The accounting rate of return is defined as:

$$\frac{\textbf{(total benefits—total costs—depreciation)/useful life}}{\textbf{total costs}}$$

For instance, in the example below, the total benefits of an investment over four years are $450,000, total costs are $100,000, and depreciation of the investment is $50,000. The useful life is four years in this example. Using the formula above, the accounting rate of return is 75% over the life of the project.

Total benefits	$ 450,000
Total costs	$ 100,000
Depreciation	$ 50,000
Useful life	4 years
ROI=	75%

Net Present Value Analysis

The accounting rate of return does not take into account the time value of money, and the fact that the benefits you receive in future years will be worth less than their nominal or face value because of the opportunity cost of money and inflation. For instance, if I promise to pay you back $15 one year from now in return for a $10 loan from you to me today, you would have to take into account at least two facts: 1) you will lose the $10 you loan me for one year and give up the interest you could have earned in a bank, and 2) inflation will erode the value of money, so the $15 I pay you next year will be worth less because of inflation.

In net present value analysis, you must first understand the value in today's dollars of a future set of payments (this value is called "the present value"). In net present value analysis, both the opportunity cost of an investment and the inflation factor are summed up and taken into account by the use of a "prime rate" or other bank rate to deflate the value of future payments.

The net present value is defined as:

Present value of total annual benefits—total investment cost

In Excel, you use the net present value function (NPV) to calculate the present value of total future annual benefits. Unfortunately, the Excel NPV function is misnamed and does not give you a true net present value, but in fact returns the present value of a set of payments in the future. To calculate the net present value, take the present value of future payments and subtract the total initial investment (usually made in today's dollars).

In the spreadsheet below, there are future benefits of $100, $150, and $300 in the next three years. The initial investment is $300 made in the first year, and the interest rate is 6%. Is the investment worth it?

Benefits		
Year 1	**Year 2**	**Year 3**
$100	$150	$300
Cost	$300	
Interest rate	6.00%	
Present value	$480	
Net present value	$180	

This investment is "worth it" because in today's dollars it has a net present value of greater than $0 and will return, in fact, $180 today's dollars in the future.

You can use the Function Wizard to calculate the Excel NPV function. Follow these steps:

1. Click on the cell in the spreadsheet where you want the NPV calculation to appear.

2. On the Formulas tab on the Ribbon, click the *Insert Function* button in the Function Library group or click the *Fx* button on the formula bar to open the Insert Function dialog box.

3. Select *Financial functions*.

4. Select the NPV function.

5. Fill in the wizard information for the interest rate and the values of the annual payments. You can also enter cell references for these values if you think they might change.

6. Click *OK*.

Web Case 2

Gainful.com

Problem:	Analyze the online job posting industry
Management skills:	Planning
	Deciding
Web skills:	Competitive intelligence
File:	GAINFUL_Q.xlsx

Gainful.com is a start-up venture founded by a group of human resources professionals who have decided they would rather be entrepreneurs than employees. CEO Dan Mullins and CFO Abigail Rose—the two main founders—have approached an East Coast venture-capital firm, GLP Ventures, to provide start-up capital for the Web site. GLP Ventures believes Gainful.com could be profitable if the financials worked out. Venture is worried about the potential number of visitors, the competition from well-funded and established competitors, and potential operational costs.

The human resources officers who started Gainful.com have great track records in matching job candidates to open positions. Together the founding team of eight training instructors has a combined experience of more than 80 years in professional human resources. They feel confident they can leverage this knowledge into a successful online service business, and can differentiate it from its larger competitors by providing a cleaner and more targeted site and a more limited menu of service options than offered by the larger job posting sites. Despite this experienced management team, GLP is cautious about investing in start-ups given the recent failures of so many dotcoms.

Venture has requested that CEO Mullins and CFO Rose do additional research on the financials of the online job posting business. Specifically, the investors want a better idea of the overall size of the online job posting market, and the principal competitors; the levels of traffic at the competing Web sites; and a better idea of what Gainful.com's budget would look like based on the experience of a similar firm. The management team at Gainful.com has asked you to develop the information requested by the investors.

Tasks

There are three tasks in this case.

1. Using a Web search engine, identify Web sites that have information about the leading firms in the online job posting industry. Build a spreadsheet of the top five most frequently visited Web sites. A sample spreadsheet has been started for you in GAINFUL_Q.xlsx. Sort the sites in terms of their unique visitors. In addition to visitors, find out how much revenue each of the top ten sites

generates. Identify the major sources of revenue for online job posting sites, such as resume posting fees, advertising fees, and additional services. You may not be able to find this detailed information for all top five sites. Write a short report on your findings.

2. To understand the potential revenue and profit picture for the new company, the investors want you to look at a competitor's financial statements and calculate a series of standard financial ratios. Use Monster.com (Monster Worldwide, Inc.) as the competitor. As a public company, Monster is required by the 1934 Securities Act to report its financial results and all other material developments at the company to the Securities and Exchange Commission (SEC).

   Calculate the following ratios for Monster Worldwide Inc.:

   - Gross Margin (Gross profit /Total revenues)
   - Cost of revenues/Total revenues
   - Net Margin (Net income (or Net loss) /Total Revenues)
   - Sales and Marketing Expense/Total revenues
   - General and Administrative Expense/Total revenues

   Express all ratios as percentages, and copy the formulas to previous years so that you end up with ratios for three years' worth of experience.

3. Wagner also wants you to create a pro forma profit and loss statement for the start-up company. A pro forma profit and loss statement is used to project the amount of money the business should allocate to various activities. Assume the new company will have first year revenues of $17 million. Using the five ratios you calculated in Task 2, calculate how much Gainful.com must spend for product development, for sales and marketing, and for general and administrative costs, assuming total revenues of $17 million.

Tutorial for Web Case 2

This case assumes the reader has already mastered the use of search engines.

Using the EDGAR Database

EDGAR is major research tool for business and stock analysts as well as ordinary investors. EDGAR provides a treasure trove of information that companies are required to reveal to the public to ensure efficient and honest capital markets. Only companies that sell stock to the public report to EDGAR. There are many different types of annual, quarterly, and event-driven filings.

To look up a public company, go to www.sec.gov and click the *Search for Company Filings* link. Then click the *Company or Fund Name...* link. Enter the company name *Monster Worldwide* into the *Company name* text entry box. Then click the *Find Companies* button. Scroll down the list of search results and click the *Documents* button beside the most recent 10-K listing. On the list of documents that is displayed, click the FORM 10-K link.

Once you have the html version of the 10-K filing on screen, read the Introduction and Strategy sections of the report. Then locate the table labeled *CONSOLIDATED STATEMENTS OF OPERATIONS*. This summary is also called the Income Statement.

Select with your mouse the entire table, from the heading *Monster Worldwide, Inc.* to the last line, *See accompanying notes*. Copy the data to the Clipboard (or use CTRL+C). Open Excel and paste the data into an Excel spreadsheet.

You will notice that the data you pasted spreads haphazardly across the worksheet and must be formatted for readability. In the worksheet, delete extra columns and rows as needed to format your categories and data in related groupings and create an attractive format. Delete extraneous formatting symbols and unneeded text. Delete columns containing previous years of data—you are interested only in the latest year's data. You may need to widen the columns, change font sizes and styling, to display all the information properly and legibly.

Select just the financial data and format it with the *Currency Style* button on the Ribbon (Home tab, Number group). Also in the Number group, use the Decrease Decimal button to delete the two decimal places. Resave the workbook.

Display all financial ratios as percentages. In this case, you are only interested in the most recent year's data, so you can eliminate the information from earlier years.

Pro Forma Profit/Loss Statements (Income Statements)

A profit and loss statement (P&L) describes the total revenue and operating expenses of a firm. These statements are also called "Income statements." A "pro forma" P&L is a forecast based on best management judgment either for a new business or for a future year. Generally, a profit and loss statement has the following categories of revenue and expenditures (the starred items are calculated by the user and are not usually a part of the 10-K statement). Companies may present these categories using different terminology, and may combine or split out some categories; interpretation may be required to place the data into appropriate categories, especially when you are comparing the performance of multiple companies.

Revenue:

Net sales...Gross sales revenue minus any returns

Cost of sales ....The cost of physical products or services

Gross profit ....Sales revenue minus cost of goods

Gross Profit Margin........................**Gross profit divided by net sales (%)**

Operating expenses

Marketing and fulfillment......................Marketing and advertising costs

Technology and content.........................Research and development costs

General and administrative ....Administrative costs, mostly labor

Stock-based compensation......................Options programs for employees

Amortization of goodwill and other intangibles ....Costs associated with purchases of other companies for prices higher than their book value

Total operating expenses.........................Total operating costs

Gain/Loss from operations......................Gross profit minus cost of operations

Net Margin...................................**Gain/loss from operations divided by gross profit**

Other Income/Expenses

Interest income......................................Income from interest bearing accounts

Interest expense.....................................Expenses for short term loans

Other income (expense), net ....Miscellaneous income

Net Gain/Loss ....**Gross profit minus operating expenses and other incomes/losses**

Web Case 3

Managed Benefits Corporation

Problem:	Research Internet security and privacy
Management skills:	Research analysis
	Decision-making
Web skills:	Business research

Managed Benefits Corporation (MBC) is a regional firm in Dayton, Ohio, that administers health insurance and retirement plans for the employees of small to midsize businesses. MBC does not provide the services, but acts as an agent between businesses and healthcare providers and investment services.

MBC has achieved moderate success in its twenty-year history. The founders of the company believed that many businesses would prefer to outsource the legwork of researching and maintaining health and retirement plans rather than devote human resources personnel to this work. Their theory was correct. However, the growth of the Internet has allowed MBC to re-examine its services with an eye toward making the company even more successful.

Caitlin Myers, Director of Customer Service for MBC, has worked with the IT Department for several years to make the company's Web site as helpful to customers as it can be. However, until now, that is all the Web site has been: a source of information. In the near future, MBC will launch a new Web site that will allow customers to interact with their accounts online. Some of the new services will include enabling health insurance customers to submit requests for changing their primary care physician or for obtaining referrals. Retirement plan customers will be able to submit requests for changing their contribution amount or for adjusting the allocation of their investment to different funds.

Caitlin realizes that this new venture carries a great deal of responsibility for the company. To make such transactions possible, customers will have to submit personal information, such as name, address, phone number, policy or account number, and Social Security number. For the new services to be successful, customers must feel secure in MBC's ability to protect their personal information. They also must trust that their personal information will not be used for undesirable purposes. Furthermore, MBC must consider their legal obligations regarding privacy as they pertain to the Internet.

Caitlin has determined that she can use the Web to investigate the current state of federal legislation concerning Internet privacy. She will compile details about relevant active legislation in an Access database so that the company can use it as a guideline for designing the new site and setting policy. She will also expand her research on privacy, and prepare a report for the company's CIO that summarizes the advantages and disadvantages of existing and pending legislation to both the company and the consumer. The report will include legal proposals and the main trends in Internet privacy. Ultimately,

Caitlin will make a recommendation regarding the company's official response to the issue of Internet privacy.

Tasks

There are five tasks in this case:

1. Visit www.house.gov (The United States House of Representatives) and http://epic.org (Electronic Privacy Information Center) to find active bills on Internet privacy. The House site contains a link to the Library of Congress's THOMAS search facility, which will allow you to search for bills by topic. The EPIC site features Bill-Track, which tracks pending legislation on privacy and Cyber-Liberties in the current session of Congress.

2. Use Microsoft Access to create a database of existing and pending legislation that is relevant to Internet privacy. The database fields you should use are law (or bill) number, law (or bill) name, proposing legislator (sponsor), and a brief summary of the law or bill. The summary field should use the Memo data type. Save the table.

3. Enter the relevant legislation data you have found on the Web in the database table.

> *Note: If you prefer, you may skip ahead to Task 4 and create the form first so you can use it to enter the data.*

4. Once you have created the initial database table that organizes the data, create a form to facilitate entering additional data and a report for printing the data. Use all of the fields from the table in the form and in the report.

5. Prepare a report or presentation for the Chief Information Officer that summarizes the advantages and disadvantages of various privacy laws to both the company and the consumer. Also, include recent trends in privacy legislation and its application. Present the views of a pro-privacy organization that you find on the Web. Finally, conclude your report or presentation by making a recommendation about how the company should approach the issue of privacy in creating its new Web site. Tutorial for Web Case 3

This case requires you to use the Web to conduct business research. The table below lists URLs that will help you complete the research tasks.

URL	Description
www.house.gov	United States House of Representatives
www.senate.gov	United States Senate
epic.org	Electronic Privacy Information Center
epic.org/privacy	EPIC Privacy page

www.cdt.org/privacy	Center for Democracy & Technology
thomas.loc.gov/home/c107query.html#keyword	Library of Congress bill search

Previous tutorials you may find useful for this case:

- Database Case 1
- Database Case 2
- Database Case 8

In this case, you are required to place data found on Web pages in an Access database table. You can transfer data by manually keying it into the table or using copy and paste techniques. To copy and paste data from a Web page into a database table, use the mouse to drag over the piece of data, such as a bill number or description, on the Web page. Once the piece of data is selected (highlighted in blue), use the Copy command on the Edit menu in the browser to copy the selection to the Clipboard. You can also use [Ctrl]+[C] to execute the copy command. Then switch to Access, click in the appropriate field, and use the Paste command on the Home tab of the Ribbon in Access, or [Ctrl]+[V] to paste the copied data.

Web Case 4

Red River Investment Group

Problem:	Prepare a financial analysis of two publicly held companies based on data from Web sources
Management skills:	Planning Deciding
Web skills:	Financial analysis

Red River Investment Group is a financial advising firm in Flagstaff, Arizona. Red River encourages clients to invest for long-term capital gains. Clients may call, visit, or use Red River's Web site to get advice about stocks they want to buy. Paul Osborne, who owns Osborne Consulting, a firm that provides consulting services to restaurants, wants to invest in a specialty beverage company that provides exotic coffees and teas to specialty restaurants and coffee houses. Sam believes that the long-term market for restaurants that offer brand name specialty drinks such as coffee and tea is increasing, and that patrons will come to expect such items on the menus of restaurants around the nation.

But Osborne knows very little about how to analyze potential specialty drink investments. He has retained Red River to do some financial research for him on two of the leading specialty drink companies in the United States: Starbucks Corporation and Green Mountain Coffee, Inc. Osborne would like to invest in one of these companies, but he does not know which one is the better investment.

- **Green Mountain Coffee, Inc**. is a major player in the specialty coffee industry. The Company offers more than 100 coffee products such as single-origins, estates, certified organics, FairTrade, proprietary blends, and flavored coffees that it sells under the Green Mountain Coffee Roasters® brand. Green Mountain's major revenue source is their wholesale operation serving supermarkets, convenience stores, offices, and other retail locations. They also sell via direct mail and online. The Company went public in September, 1993, and is listed on the NASDAQ (stock symbol GMCR).

- **Starbucks Corporation** is the world's #1 specialty coffee retailer. It operates, licenses, and franchises more than 7,000 coffee shops in more than 40 countries. The shops offer a variety of coffee drinks, along with food items and other beverages. The outlets also sell whole bean coffee and branded coffee accessories. In addition to its shops, the company sells beans through grocery stores and licenses its brand for other food and beverage products. It also trades on the NASDAQ.

To make sound recommendations to Osborne, Red River's analysts will examine two key financial documents of the two companies: the income statement and the balance sheet, which were first introduced in Spreadsheet Case 2. From that case, recall the following types of financial statements:

- Income statements (also called operating statements) summarize the income, expenses, and profits (or losses) of businesses for a period, usually a year, quarter, or month.

- Balance sheets identify the assets, liabilities, and shareholders' equity of a firm at a particular point in time. The difference between assets and liabilities is net worth or equity (literally what the organization is worth net of all other factors).

As you did in Spreadsheet Case 2, you must calculate a number of financial ratios based on the financial statements of these two companies. Before doing this case, review the descriptions and formulas that appear in Spreadsheet Case 2 for the following ratios:

- Current Ratio

- Quick Ratio (or "Acid Test")

- Total Assets Utilization

- Debt Ratio

- Return on Total Assets (ROA)

- Return on Equity (ROE)

- Profit Margin

- Price/Earnings Ratio

Tasks

There are two tasks in this case:

1. Obtain the financial statements of the two companies, Green Mountain Coffee and Starbucks, and import the statements to an Excel spreadsheet. Go to the Security and Exchange Commission's Web site (www.sec.gov) and obtain the data from each company's latest 10-K filing. Follow the directions for capturing the data at EDGAR and pasting into an Excel spreadsheet given in the Tasks section for Web Case 2.

    Copy and paste the income statement and balance sheet, one at a time, for the first company— Green Mountain Coffee, Inc.—onto a blank Excel worksheet. Copy the income statement first, and the consolidated balance sheet second. Place the balance sheet below the income statement in your spreadsheet. Immediately save the worksheet with an appropriate file name (e.g., WebCase4 Green Mountain.xlsx).

    Repeat these steps for Starbucks. Create a new spreadsheet file WebCase4 Starbucks.xlsx.

2. Below the bottom of the financial statements, calculate the first seven financial ratios outlined above for each company. Look up the most current price/earnings ratio on the Web for both companies and manually enter it into the spreadsheet.

    In a few paragraphs, write an analysis of both companies. Based on the information provided in this case, which firm has the strongest set of ratios? Which would make the better investment? Review the financial statements of both companies for any items that might help explain their financial condition. Include a table of your financial ratios for both companies as supporting evidence.

You may also use financial content Web sites such as Finance.Yahoo.com, Bigcharts.com, Hoovers.com, Smartmoney.com, etc. to find additional information on these companies. The 10-K statement also contains very insightful sections on firm strategy, operations, and future prospects.

Tutorial for Web Case 4

Web Case 4 requires skills for obtaining financial data from the SEC EDGAR database that are covered in the Tutorial for Web Case 2. The new skill in this case is learning how to read a typical consolidated balance sheet that is a part of the 10-K statement.

Consolidated Balance Sheets

A balance sheet describes the assets and liabilities (debts) of a firm. Because the assets must equal the liabilities, the statement is called a "balance" sheet. Generally, an SEC 10-K balance sheet contains the following types of information:

Summary Balance Sheet Data	
Assets	
Cash and cash equivalents	Cash or immediately available funds
Marketable securities	Usually stock in other companies
Other assets	Real estate and office equipment
Total assets	
Liabilities	
Current liabilities (short term debt)	Payments required in the current year
Long-term debt	Usually long term bonds
Stockholders' equity	Shares issued to stock holders

Along with information on the SEC 10-K income statement, you can calculate the ratios required in this case.

Web Case 5

Chattanooga Telecom

Problem:	Analyze the communications market
Management skills:	Data analysis
	Developing strategy
Web skills:	Market research

Chattanooga Telecom is a regional communications company serving eight states. Chattanooga provides a number of communications services, the main ones being local and long distance telephone service, cellular phone service, and cable television. The company has known for some time that it has the infrastructure in place to add Internet service to its stable of services. Until now, it has resisted this move due to a saturated market. However, a number of local and regional Internet service providers have gone out of business in the last two years, leaving a gap in the marketplace.

Chattanooga's CEO, Jack Burgess, wants to cautiously approach an entrance into the Internet service market. Chattanooga' Marketing Director, Isobel Peters, knows she must consult hard statistics to make the proper recommendations to the CEO.

Peters' first goal is to determine whether Chattanooga should even consider expanding its services in the first place. For this, she intends to research the growth of Internet usage since it became a common tool for both business and home users. She wants to know if Internet usage will continue to increase or if it will plateau in the near future.

Next, Peters must devise a marketing strategy, assuming that Chattanooga will choose to introduce an Internet service brand. She has already given the task some thought, and she has determined that Chattanooga should begin by targeting its existing customers. Since Chattanooga phone service users and cable subscribers are already familiar with the company, they would likely trust Chattanooga as their first Internet service provider or as an alternative to their current provider. Targeting existing customers would initially allow Chattanooga to quickly build a customer base for its Internet brand at a lower cost than if the company tried to target the general public. Including all of its services, Chattanooga already has a database of 5 million customers. Acquiring a database of new prospect names that large is an expense the company would prefer to avoid at the stage of the venture.

Going further, Peters would like to determine which segment of Chattanooga's existing customer base should be most aggressively targeted with promotional material for a new Internet service. She has already narrowed down the choices to cellular customers and cable subscribers, who are more technically savvy. She has found no data indicating a significant growth in landline telephone use, and people who have only landline telephone service are far less likely than cell phone users to want Internet service. Peters' approach will be to target the segments of Chattanooga's customer base which are showing the most growth in recent years. She believes that if people are already embracing technology products or services, they are more likely to continue spending money on technology.

The result of Peters' research will be a full-scale report to CEO Burgess that includes an outline, statement of goal, presentation of the facts, and concluding statements. Hard statistics will be introduced in written arguments and illustrated with spreadsheets and charts.

Tasks

There are seven tasks in this case:

1. Go to relevant government Web sites to find statistics on Internet usage. Be certain you can answer these questions: Has the number of Internet users increased consistently over the past few years? Has the number of people using the Internet at work increased during that time? Has the number of people using the Internet at home also increased? What are the statistics regarding "intensity of use" or hours using the Internet?

2. Transfer the statistical data you have found into a spreadsheet file either by copying and pasting it from a Web page or by manually keying it in. Some online resources will also allow you to download data tables directly into an Excel file. If you wish to cut and paste data from online sources into an Excel spreadsheet, consult the instructions in Web Case 2 first.

3. Display the Internet growth data you have found in the form of a chart in the spreadsheet file.

4. Go to relevant government Web sites to find statistics that track the number of cellular phone subscribers and the number of cable television subscribers over the last several years. Be certain you can determine which is the more promising market based on Pat's criteria.

5. Transfer the subscriber comparison data you have found into a separate worksheet in the same spreadsheet file you used for the Internet growth data. Display the subscriber data in the form of a chart.

6. Search the Web for companies or services that sell mailing lists. Determine what the approximate cost would be to acquire a list of potential customer names equal to the number of customers Chattanooga already has (5 million). Decide whether you can use this figure to fortify the position of targeting existing customers first.

7. Write a report for the CEO as described above (include an outline, statement of goal, presentation of facts, including your spreadsheets and charts, and concluding statements). Do not forget to cite your statistical sources.

Tutorial for Web Case 5

A great source for statistics such as those required for this case is the U.S. Census. The Census web site is located at www.census.gov. From the Census home page, you can access the Statistical Abstract of the United States www.census.gov/compendia/statab/). From the Statistical Abstract home page, pay particular attention to the USA Statistics in Brief link in the section titled *Summary Statistics* and the *Browse Sections* section, which provides tables of statistics for major market sectors." Also, the Pew Foundation Internet and American Life Project conduct regular surveys on Internet usage (www.pewinternet.org).

Use of the suggested sources is not mandatory, but they are stable sources that provide accurate, user-friendly data. As a whole, U.S. government sites are very useful for this type of research. Another source you may want to consider is the U.S. Department of Commerce's National Telecommunications & Information Administration report entitled "Falling Through the Net: Defining the Digital Divide." The document and accompanying charts are located at www.ntia.doc.gov/ntiahome/fttn99/contents.html.

Previous tutorials you may find useful for this case:

- Spreadsheet Case 1
- Spreadsheet Case 5

Web Case 6

Uber Audio Lab

Problem:	Research competing patents
Management skills:	Data analysis
Web skills:	Research

You were introduced to Uber Audio Lab in Database Cases 6 and 10

Dennis Uber wants to expand Uber Audio Lab to include soundproofing material for music studios. Many of his customers who purchase the custom-built sound systems, the famous Uber Amp valve amplifier, and high performance ribbon speakers want to incorporate this technology into their recording studios, and they need soundproofing material to ensure high quality recorded sound. Soundproofing is integral to a recording studio as it eliminates noise from outside of the studio and makes sounds within the area more true. Dennis has been developing acoustical foam for his own home-based studio and feels he has a product that would work better than similar products currently offered on the market. The soundproof acoustic foam material that Dennis has developed reduces echo and is made of a molded polymer material. Current products on the market are flat or egg-crate-shaped, but Ryan's foam is wavy, looking much like a piece of foam with rounded ridges in it.

Dennis would like to patent his acoustical foam invention, but he needs to make sure that a similar product is not already holding a patent. He must research all of the issued patents for acoustical foam material to assess whether his is unique. Dennis has asked you to develop a database of all the relevant patents so he can easily review them and determine which, if any, compete with his invention.

Tasks

There are 3 tasks in this case:

1. Determine all patents that appear to be relevant to Dennis's search. Go to www.uspto.gov and perform a patent search for acoustical foam or soundproofing foam or similar terms. Search the Abstract portion of the document to determine the patent's relevancy.

2. Once you have determined the relevant patents, create a database that details the patent number, the title of the patent, the inventor(s) name, the date the patent was filed, and a brief description of the patent.

3. Create a lookup form with command buttons so Ryan can easily look up patents by the patent number.

Tutorial for Web Case 6

The United States Patent and Trademark Office (USPTO) has a website that allows visitors to search for issued patents and trademarks. Patents dating back to 1976 can be searched online using the database at the site. Searching the database is relatively easy and uses the skills you learned for performing BOOLEAN searches on search engines. Patent and Trademark searching is found at patft.uspto.gov.

The USPTO site has two methods for searching its database: Quick and Advanced. The Quick search allows you to input two terms and choose which field of the patent to search. The Advanced search allows you to make a query of the US Patent Full Text Database using command line search syntax. You are not limited in the number of terms when using the Advanced search, but you must write your query using specific language. The Help link on the Advanced search page assists you in writing your query using the correct syntax.

Previous tutorials you may find useful for this case:

- Database Case 1
- Database Case 8

Web Case 7

Finnegan Consulting

Problem:	Evaluate export markets
Management skills:	Data analysis
	Developing strategies
Web skills:	Market research

Finnegan Consulting, located in Seattle, Washington, was founded by Gabriel Finnegan in 1976. Prior to starting the company, Finnegan worked in the fish products industry for many years in locations up and down the Pacific seaboard, including Alaska. He accumulated significant knowledge about the fish products industry, including import and export patterns, and has leveraged this knowledge into a successful consulting business. Finnegan Consulting advises clients inside and outside the fish products industry about the consumption patterns of countries around the globe and their import/export regulations.

Finnegan has recently acquired a client that is interested in exporting its flash frozen salmon to countries outside the United States. They are unsure which countries they should target for their export activities. Likely targets are those countries that already are major importers of salmon, or those whose market has yet to be developed. The client has requested that Finnegan provide a detailed analysis of the export volume of the United States of all types of salmon—Atlantic, Chum, Coho, Chinook, Sockeye, and any other variety available in the data. Finnegan must analyze the value, and destination of these exports before making his recommendation.

Tasks

There are five tasks in this case:

1. Obtain the data regarding the export of salmon from the USDA's Foreign Agricultural Service at www.fas.usda.gov/ustrade/. Use the following criteria to perform your search:

    *   Under *EXPORTS* select *HS-10*. (This commodity code level is the most granular. You will learn more about these commodity codes in Web Case 8.)

    *   In the *COUNTRIES* list box, select *SELECT ALL COUNTRIES*.

    *   In the *HS 10-DIGIT CODES* list box, select all the codes for all varieties of salmon. Select all types—frozen, fresh, etc. You can make multiple selections by holding down the CTRL key as you click on each selection.

- In the *Order* drop-down list, select *Cmdty/Cntry*.

- For now, accept the default values for all other choices on the search screen.

- Click the *Submit* button.

2. Once you have performed the search and obtained the results, copy the entire report (including column headings) and then paste this data into an Excel spreadsheet.

3. After creating the Excel spreadsheet, open Access and create a new database named *FINNEGAN*. Import the data from the various sections of the Excel spreadsheets you created into new tables in this database. Delete all the records that pertain to category totals.

4. Finnegan would like a report that details the export dollar value of each type of salmon. Create a report that outlines the export dollar value of each type of salmon sorted by country with the results in ascending order.

5. Write a report that advises Finnegan which countries his client should target for the export activities. Should they target those countries with a healthy export trade or those whose trade is still developing and why?

Tutorial for Web Case 7

This case requires you to import data from an Excel spreadsheet to an Access database. Once you have created the Excel spreadsheet, you can import data into your Access database.

1. Open the External Data tab on the Ribbon and in the Import group, click the *Excel* button.

2. Locate your Excel spreadsheet using the *Browse* button and select *Import the source data into a new table* in the current database. Click *OK*.

4. The Import Spreadsheet wizard will appear, asking you which worksheets or ranges you would like to import. Choose the worksheet or range you would like to import as a table. Click *Next*.

4. If your spreadsheet has header columns, make sure the *First Row Contains Column Headings* checkbox is checked. If not, uncheck this box. Click *Next*.

5. To create a new table with this data, make sure the *In a New Table* option button is activated and then click *Next*.

6. The next part of the wizard allows you to specify the field names and data types of the fields. Select appropriate names and types for your fields. Make sure *No* is selected for *Indexing the fields* and click *Next*.

7. The wizard now allows you to choose a primary key for your data. You can allow the wizard to select one, you can select it, or you can pick *No Primary Key* and select one later in Design View. Click *Next*.

8. The last part of the wizard asks you the name of your table. If you do not change the default name, it will import with the name you have given the worksheet in Excel. Click *Finish*.

Previous tutorials you may find useful for this case:

- Database Case 1
- Database Case 2
- Database Case 3
- Database Case 6

Web Case 8
Begum Worldwide

Problem:	Analyze the historical valuations of currency
Management skills:	Data analysis
	Developing strategy
Web skills:	Financial research

Begum Worldwide is one of the top import/export firms in the Northeast. Run by Oliver Begum, its founder, it imports goods from around the world for sale in the United States, and exports products to countries throughout Asia, Central and South America, Europe, and Africa. Begum's success is built on the good relationships it has with its vendors and suppliers as well as the competitive prices it offers in the marketplace. Begum is able to offer such competitive prices because he tirelessly monitors currency rates throughout the world, waiting for the most advantageous time to buy or sell goods.

Grace Ferguson, Henderson's Director of Import, has been approached by Jamie Young of Young's Wines, a vintner in Sydney, Australia, to review a flight of Australian wines for possible inclusion in Begum's sales in the United States. Ferguson is intrigued by the possibility of adding wines to their list of goods because Begum does not have a strong presence in the wine arena and Australian wines are becoming very popular in the United States.

Ferguson must determine the stability of the Australian dollar to the U.S. dollar to evaluate whether Begum can purchase Young's product at a profitable price. If there are large variations in the rate the currency trades, Begum can either make or lose a great deal of money on its transactions with Young. On the other hand, if the currency proves to be relatively stable, Begum can feel fairly confident that their profit margin will remain constant.

Tasks

There are six tasks in this case:

1. Determine the historical exchange rates for the U.S. dollar and the Australian dollar for the two most recent full calendar years.

2. Transfer the statistical data you have found into a spreadsheet file by either copying and pasting it from a Web page, or keying it in manually. Some online resources will also allow you to download data tables directly into an Excel file. If you wish to cut and paste data from online sources into an Excel spreadsheet, consult the instructions in Web Case 2 first.

3. Display the exchange rate data you have found in the form of a chart in the spreadsheet file.

4. Go to relevant government Web sites to find statistics that track the volume of Australian wine exports to the United States. Ferguson wants to know how much Australian wine has come into the United States over the past two years.

5. Transfer the import data you have found into a separate worksheet in the same spreadsheet file you used for the currency rate data. Display the import data in the form of a chart.

6. Ferguson also wants to evaluate the volume of Australian wine exports to the United States to determine the level of competition Henderson would face. Write a report for Ferguson outlining your recommendation regarding importing Young's wine. Your conclusion should factor in the historical stability of the currency and the amount of Australian wine imported into the United States. Do not forget to cite your statistical sources.

Tutorial for Web Case 8

Use of the suggested sources is not mandatory, but they are stable sources that provide accurate user-friendly data. As a whole, U.S. government sites are very useful for this type of research. The tutorial in Web Case 5 introduced you to a great source for statistics: the Census web site located at www.census.gov.

For statistics on import or export activity by commodity (for example, "wine"), go to www.fas.usda.gov/ustrade. You will be able to search imports or exports, by FAS groups or 2-, 4-, 6-, or 10-digit "Harmonized Codes" (more digits = more precision). Harmonized Codes are simply commodity codes used mainly in import and export documents, and are used to aggregate trade statistics. FATUS (FAS) Codes are 211 trade codes which aggregate the Harmonized Codes into more general categories.

To find the figures on Australian wine imports into the United States:

- Go to www.fas.usda.gov/ustrade/
- Under *IMPORTS* select *FATUS*.
- In the *COUNTRIES* list box, select *AUSTRALIA*.
- In the *FATUS COMMODITY GROUPINGS* list box, select *WINE*.
- Select the most recent full year in the *From* drop-down list, and accept the default format.
- Click the *Submit* button.

The report you receive onscreen will show five years of data, with your selected year as the later of a two-year comparison included in the report.

Numerous format options are available, and can best be understood by reading the site information and running test reports.

A comprehensive site for determining exchange rates is www.x-rates.com. There you can find current and historical exchange rates for a wide range of currencies.

Previous tutorials you may find useful for this case:

- Spreadsheet Case 1
- Spreadsheet Case 5

Web Case 9

Torrington Plastics

Problem:	Analyze the wages in a geographic region
Management skills:	Data analysis
Web skills:	Business research
File:	TORRINGTON_Q.xlsx

Bill Sampson is the Human Resources Director at Torrington Plastics, a plastics casting company located in Torrington, Connecticut. Torrington Plastics makes a wide range of molded plastic parts, from computer tower cases to interior parts for automobiles, and employs more than 500 people in a wide range of positions. The turnover rate among employees is rather low for the industry, as Torrington prides itself on providing a working environment that values its employees and emphasizes longevity. The salary structure starts employees at the mid-range for their position, and then offers wage and salary increases on an annual basis based on job performance.

Each year, Sampson is responsible for presenting his recommendations for wage and salary increases to the CEO and CFO. He starts by reviewing the U.S. Department of Labor's Bureau of Labor Statistics report on the National Compensation Survey for his geographic region. This report details the hourly and salaried earnings of over 800 occupations based on the reporting of public and private companies (non-farm positions excluding the Federal government). This report, along with information about the competitors in Torrington's market, was used to establish the wage and salary structure for the company. Sampson wants to ensure that the company stays within these guidelines when administering its compensation program so that it can continue to remain competitive in the industry and attract qualified applicants.

Managers and supervisors are given a range (in the past three years, it has typically been six to eight percent) that they use to give wage and salary increases to their employees. This range is based on the Consumer Price Index (CPI), the financial health of the company, and information about other companies in their industry regarding their practices in terms of giving annual increases. This range coordinates with the performance review system and ensures that monetary increases are in line with the rating employees receive and are not subjective.

Sampson has asked you to assist him in analyzing the annual performance review, and the wage and salary increase period this year. He needs data to support his recommendations to senior management, which you will provide to him by performing the following tasks:

Tasks

There are five tasks in this case:

1. Open TORRINGTON_Q.xlsx. Column two of the spreadsheet shows the average salary for selected occupations in the New York metropolitan area. The third column shows the actual salary paid by Torrington Plastics for that position. Calculate the difference between the average metro salary and Torrington's compensation for each position. Express this as a percentage (either above or below the metro region average).

2. Find the mean hourly wage data for the following positions and include them with those already provided:

3. Sampson has decided that the range for increases will be 5% to 7%. He needs to obtain an estimate of the total cost of increases for this evaluation period. Use 6% to estimate what the new hourly wages will be, and then determine the total amount that will be paid in increases. Print these results.

4. Sampson would like to see what the total dollar figure would be if increases averaged 7%. Recalculate the increase percentage at 7% and print the results.

5. Find other sources for wage and salary data on the Internet and provide Sampson with a report listing those sources.

POSITION	CURRENT WAGE
Shipping/Receiving Clerk	13.90
Assembler	9.05
Order Clerk	19.85

Tutorial for Web Case 9

A great source for data like that required for this case is the U.S. Department of Labor: Bureau of Labor Statistics website (www.bls.gov). This site provides a wide range of information, from the Consumer Price Index to wage and salary data broken down by geographic regions to unemployment data. This data is used by companies to establish wage and salary guidelines, monitor the Consumer Price Index (CPI), and check unemployment rates. The CPI is important because it gives an indication of inflation, which contributes to the Cost of Living Adjustment (COLA) that many companies factor into the raises they give to employees.

Previous tutorials you may find useful for this case:

*   Spreadsheet Case 1
*   Spreadsheet Case 2